To Debbie Harvie,

Hope you enjoy the book, especially the sections on parking.

— Sheldon Goldfarb

March 29, 2018

THE HUNDRED-YEAR TREK

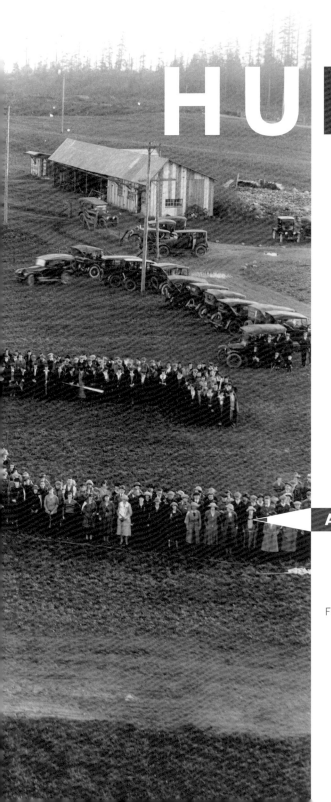

THE HUNDRED-YEAR TREK

A HISTORY OF STUDENT LIFE AT UBC

Sheldon Goldfarb

FOREWORD BY The Right Honourable Kim Campbell

VICTORIA • VANCOUVER • CALGARY

Over the years the students of UBC have

often generously contributed money, time,

and effort to projects that would only see

fruition after they left campus. From Brock

Hall to the War Memorial Gym to the Old SUB

and the AMS Student Nest, students have all

willingly contributed (well, maybe not all

willingly), with the attitude that what

they were doing was a gift or legacy to

generations of students to come.

With this book, the students of today, through

their AMS, salute all those students who

went before and did so much for their Alma

Mater. It is our gift in return.

Heritage House Publishing Company Ltd.
heritagehouse.ca

CATALOGUING INFORMATION AVAILABLE
FROM LIBRARY AND ARCHIVES CANADA

978-1-77203-223-9 (pbk)
978-1-77203-224-6 (epub)
978-1-77203-225-3 (epdf)

Proofread by Lenore Hietkamp
Cover and interior book design by Jacqui Thomas
Cover photo credits provided on p. 294

Every effort has been made to trace the
copyright holders and obtain permission
to reproduce the material in this book.
Please contact the author with any enquiries
or any information relating to images or the
rights holders.

The interior of this book was produced on
FSC®-certified, acid-free paper, processed chlo-
rine free and printed with vegetable-based inks.

Generous financial support of this project by
Alumni UBC and the UBC Centennial Fund is
gratefully acknowledged.

We acknowledge the financial support of the
Government of Canada through the Canada
Book Fund (CBF) and the Canada Council for
the Arts, and the Province of British Columbia
through the British Columbia Arts Council and
the Book Publishing Tax Credit.

Canada Council   Conseil des arts
for the Arts   du Canada

BRITISH COLUMBIA
ARTS COUNCIL
An agency of the Province of British Columbia

21 20 19 18 17   1 2 3 4 5

Printed in Canada

CONTENTS

FOREWORD

In 2013, while being honoured by the UBC Alma Mater Society with its Great Trekker Award, I had an experience that was both delightful and disturbing. As I stood before the audience of student leaders to deliver my acceptance speech, I could see myself as a young student leader in the mid-1960s at the Great Trekker dinners we held then. In those days, there were actually a few participants from the original Great Trek who were still alive and continued to be devoted to their Alma Mater—still imbued with the spirit that took them out to Point Grey to add their stones to the cairn on Main Mall that memorialized their famous march. These original Great Trekkers all seemed extremely ancient to me. Now, in 2013, I was sure that I, who had been a seventeen-year-old freshman in 1964, seemed just as ancient to these students!

In my undergraduate days, Brock Hall was our student centre, and the law students still studied in the "temporary" Second World War army huts alongside it. I returned to UBC in January 1974 to teach in the Political Science department, also on a temporary basis. By this time, the Student Union Building was open and a new building was in the works for the Law School. In the fall of 1980, at the same time as I ran for and was elected to my first public office on the Vancouver School Board, I started my own studies in the Faculty of Law in the new building. So my experience at UBC spanned two decades as a student and teacher.

This history of the Alma Mater Society captures much of the change in culture that has characterized the growth of UBC since my days as a freshman. For me, it is also interesting to learn about the campus in earlier times, including the days when my father (BA'49, LLB'53) joined his fellow Second World War veterans in a burst of growth for the student body that would be repeated with the arrival of my generation, the Baby Boomers, in the mid-1960s.

I am struck, on reading this history, how my brief involvement with the life of the Alma Mater Society stayed with me throughout my life. The post of Frosh President to which I was elected in the fall of 1964 would eventually be abolished—"the blind leading the blind," one wag called it. I also served as AMS Second Vice-President in 1967–68, after two years on the executive of the Booster Club. From that first year on AMS Council I retained a friendship with the president of the Engineering Undergraduate Society, whom I dated that year, and the Med Students president with whom I would collaborate in a variety of issues in my political life as a school trustee and later as minister of justice. People I met in those days continue to pop up in my life and it is fun to read this testament to how young we were then and how much I, at least, had still to learn!

The mid-1960s was a tumultuous time for universities everywhere and this history illustrates how each generation has grappled with the challenges of a changing University in a changing world. UBC is a great school now. I continue to do what I can to support the Law School (in yet another new building) and am pleased when I hear of the achievements of UBC professors and students. I was honoured to be the Great Trekker in 2013 and that occasion allowed me to see how students still devote time to the AMS, making the lives of their fellow students better and serving as a link between all the parts of the UBC community. In living UBC's motto, *Tuum est* ("It is yours," or "It is up to you"), they keep the spirit of the Great Trek alive! This book is a history of that spirit and Sheldon Goldfarb's skillful and lively storytelling makes it a valuable contribution to social history and a memoir to be enjoyed and treasured by all who lived it.

KIM CAMPBELL was the AMS frosh president in 1964-65 and the AMS second vice-president in 1967-68. She served as prime minister of Canada in 1993.

INTRODUCTION

There's a famous line that says the past is a foreign country (they do things differently there). But really it would be more true to say that the past is several different countries, and not always so foreign either.

Two things leap out from this survey of UBC's student history: first that things have always been the same, and second that they have radically changed. Sometimes you look back at what happened and shake your head: They did that? They zapped first years with electricity? They rampaged through the downtown streets? Or, more wincingly, they talked that way about the First Nations?

Other times, when they protest fee increases or ask for discounted bus fares, or try to deal with a budget deficit, you nod and think, *So it's always been like that.*

And then there's the realization that though all this is past, it's not all one thing. The students of 1945 are not the same as those of 1925; they may even have lost touch with what it was like to be a student in 1925, for instance getting the date of the Great Trek wrong. They may even have lost touch with 1935 and 1940, thinking that Brock Hall went up in 1936. Or the students of 1951 will have forgotten that there was a female AMS president in 1917 and state that Nonie Donaldson in their year was the first.

I hope this history of the first hundred years of the students at UBC will not make basic errors like that. And I hope it will do more—that it will capture the essence, or essences, of student life over the various decades, from the wartime beginnings at Fairview through the Great Trek campaign and on to the Depression and the Second World War, the radicalism of the sixties, and the modern era.

One constant throughout the years has been students' willingness to raise extra money to pay for University buildings, a generosity that seems quite remarkable. From gyms and aquatic centres to three different student union buildings, it is the students who have led the way in initiating projects and finding the money to complete them.

In recounting the students' story, the focus here has necessarily been on the larger issues connected with the student society (the AMS, or Alma Mater Society) and Student Council. Hundreds of thousands of students have passed through UBC, and this book cannot pretend to report on all of them, though there has been an attempt to mention those who went on to fame after their university days and also an attempt to discuss the social and cultural atmosphere on campus, to give more of a sense of what the ordinary student might have been experiencing. Still, the focus is on the leadership, as reflected in the pages of the *Ubyssey* student newspaper and other sources, which gives a specific slant to things, a slant that sometimes includes the leadership telling the general membership to shape up and take part in AMS activities, to which the general membership sometimes says, Go away.

This book aims to capture the larger trends and movements, the important stories that affected students generally, and also the quirky little stories, like the saga of poor Louis Chodat (see 1931–32) or the rise and fall of the Jokers Club (see the late forties). Not to mention the stars of later decades, like Stan Persky and Kurt Preinsperg. And what emerges in the telling of all these large trends and little quirks is the huge divide at exactly the halfway point in the students' story, in 1965, when the sixties overwhelmed the campus and changed everything.

Eric Nicol, the Canadian humourist who got his start on the *Ubyssey*, once wrote in one of his Jabez columns about jazzing up the UBC Calendar to turn it into a presentable wedding or Christmas gift. Without too much jazzing up (well, maybe a bit) the aim here has been to tell an entertaining and yet informative story about a century of student life at UBC Vancouver from the beginnings in the Fairview Shacks, when mere hundreds of students showed up at the fledgling institution, to the opening of the AMS Student Nest a hundred years later when the student population had grown past fifty thousand.

The AMS Student Nest opened in June 2015, not quite a hundred years after UBC's students gathered on the Fairview campus to create their Alma Mater Society.

THE FAIRVIEW YEARS

A float in the Great Trek.

The UBC everyone knows today is a sprawling campus in West Point Grey, on the peninsula stretching west from Vancouver, amidst the waters of the Pacific Ocean, with the Coastal Mountains in the distance. But for the first ten years of its existence, UBC was far from the mountainous coast, nestled into buildings in the heart of Vancouver, next to and part of the Vancouver General Hospital, in the Fairview neighbourhood of the city.

These were temporary quarters, the plan always being to move to West Point Grey. But the First World War intervened, and there were other delays, so for a full decade the students had to make do with what were not so affectionately referred to as the "Fairview Shacks." Eventually, they tired of the delays and made their displeasure known, urging the provincial government to "build the university," by which was meant building the Point Grey campus.

In the meantime, though, they built their student society, the Alma Mater Society (AMS). They created publications and a system of student governance, held dances, took part in debating competitions, and, especially in the early years, devoted themselves to the war effort. In the last few years at Fairview, the focus became the need to move to the promised campus in the west, the highlight being the 1922 march that later became known as the Great Trek.

Through it all there was a strong push to build "college spirit," as it was called then. The AMS, through its publications (notably the *Ubyssey*, from 1918 on), urged the students to take part in sports and other activities, to root for the home team (the yet unnamed Varsity), learn the college yells, attend general meetings, wear the appropriate garb during freshman initiation, and so on. From a hundred years on, it looks like a concerted effort to mould an identity, create a unity, reflecting an almost tribal attitude: perhaps it was not for nothing that the yells they were urged to chant were derived from Indigenous or pseudo-Indigenous sources.

There was also a push to defend autonomy, or what was called at the time "student self-government," and not allow the University administration to interfere in what the students and their Alma Mater Society were up to. This was not always successful, but for the most part the students, even in these early years, seemed to be running their own show and trying to mould themselves into a unified group ready to take on projects even as large as the Great Trek to Build the University.

1915 TO 1916

A class in the Arts building at UBC's first campus.

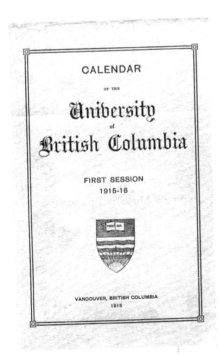

Year One at UBC.

Year One: UBC opened. Classes began on Thursday, September 30, 1915. Just over two weeks later, on Friday, October 15, the students gathered in the Arts building on the original Fairview campus to create an association with the unusual name of Alma Mater Society. In the early years the Society was sometimes referred to as the Alma Mater, but later it became better known by its acronym (AMS), perhaps because Alma Mater made too many people think of the alumni, and perhaps as well because no one was sure how to pronounce Mater. For a guide to pronunciation, see the poem on page 15.

First President (and First Lady): A week after the inaugural meeting of the new student association, Sherwood Lett was elected AMS president. However, he served only a short time before heading off to serve in the First World War and was replaced by John Mulhern. Sherwood Lett, John Mulhern, and Evelyn Story, a member of the first Student Council, had earlier drafted the first AMS constitution, with the assistance of Professor Harry Logan.

Sherwood Lett and Evelyn Story later married, providing an early example of how the AMS, according to a later joke, really stood for "Alma Mating Society." Both the Letts maintained close ties with UBC in subsequent years, and Evelyn Lett in particular became associated with the Society: an AMS childcare bursary was named after her, along with an AMS elections award. Sherwood Lett became the AMS lawyer in the 1920s and later went on to become chief justice of British Columbia and chancellor of the University. The Letts each won the AMS's Great Trekker Award in later years, and Evelyn Lett even showed up to give a speech at an AMS Annual General Meeting in 1996, at the age of ninety-nine.

The first *Annual* and the last.

Evelyn and Sherwood Lett in 1958.

First Publication: The AMS marked the close of the first year of the new University by publishing what was then called the *Annual*, but which later became known as the *Totem* (published almost every year until 1966). It declared itself to be "the official record of student activities" and generally hailed the first year as a harbinger of glorious things to come. However, it did strike a sombre note by reminding readers of "the catastrophic events which have disturbed Christendom," i.e., the war, and went on to lament the fact that after helping inaugurate the new University and its student society the editors would inevitably be pushed aside to be replaced by "younger blood."

The War: The first *Annual* referred to the war jokingly at times, saying that the new AMS president, John Mulhern, would follow in the footsteps of Sherwood Lett by going off to Flanders "for his health." It also talked about how the welcoming home of the first returned soldier was an occasion for a "unique social event." It also felt obliged to justify the holding of parties, saying that "surely the least that we can do is to put on a cheerful countenance and strive to give some little pleasure to those of our boys who are departing from our midst, having cast aside their books to answer the call of duty."

But at other times the *Annual* struck a more serious note, talking of "the great crisis of the war," and noting that athletic activities had been seriously handicapped because so many of the athletes had gone off to fight.

McGill BC: UBC did not come out of nowhere. For several years, there had been a college in Vancouver affiliated with Montreal's McGill University, known officially as the McGill University College of British Columbia, or McGill BC. Students could take the first two years of a university program there, then transfer to a university to complete their degrees. When

Students training at Fairview campus, 1916.

"We'll paddle our own canoe now."

With the closing of McGill BC apparently imminent, the cartoonist for the 1912 McGill BC Annual depicted the student body cutting ties with McGill and setting off on its own as part of the new "B.C. University."

Drama: One of the first student clubs at the new University was the Players' Club, created under the guidance of Professor Frederic ("Freddy") Wood, after whom the University's theatre was later named. In its first year the club put on two plays: *Cinders* by Lily Tinsley and *Fanny and the Servant Problem* by Jerome K. Jerome.

AMS EXECUTIVE
1915–1916

PRESIDENT *Sherwood Lett/ John E. Mulhern*
VICE-PRESIDENT *Isabel MacMillan*
SECRETARY *J.S. Johannson*
ASSISTANT SECRETARY *Evelyn S. Story*
TREASURER *Thomas S.B. Shearman*

UBC opened, McGill BC shut down, and many of its students and faculty moved over to the new University.

Debates: Continuing a tradition begun at McGill BC, the students at the new University created two debating clubs, one for women and one for men: the Men's Literary Society and the Women's Literary Society. The men's first debate was about prohibition and liquor regulation. The women debated whether movies were harmful. The students even ventured beyond the University, going as far as Seattle for a debate with the students there on the subject of whether China would be better off being a monarchy or a republic.

TOP RIGHT The Ladies Literary and Debating Society at McGill BC.

BOTTOM RIGHT The Players' Club in 1921. Freddy Wood at the right.

1916 TO 1917

The War Hits Home: No more jokes this year. The *Annual* reported that nine UBC students had died overseas, and another forty had been wounded. Three were being held prisoner, and five had been decorated. Altogether, 132 men were on active service. "We have indeed reason to be proud of our men at the front," said the *Annual*, while also praising the women on campus for their contribution to the war effort through the campus Red Cross Society.

COTC: One by-product of the war was the establishment of a branch of the Canadian Officers Training Corps (COTC) on campus. The *Annual* waxed lyrical about the possibility of UBC turning into a full-scale military school along the lines of West Point, but in later years the very existence of a COTC branch on campus became controversial.

AMS Constitution: In what proved to be the beginning of a long tradition, the AMS began tinkering with its constitution. The *Annual* noted that a new one was introduced in the fall term, but added that it had caused some difficulties. "Ever new efforts are being made to amend the constitution," it commented, "particularly in regard to the control of the Alma Mater funds."

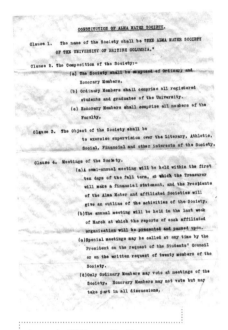

An early AMS constitution.

New Publication: In addition to the *Annual*, the AMS in Year Two launched a monthly publication, mostly literary. It first appeared in December 1916 under the name *Anonymous* because no one could think of a fitting name for it. This later was shortened to *Anon*. In the first issue, the editors said that in desperation over the lack of a name, they nearly resorted to using the initials UBC, and they did eventually come up with a name based on those initials: *Ubicee*.

Yells: An editorial in the *Ubicee* in February 1917 complained of student apathy and urged students to learn the UBC "yells." These yells, or cheers, often consisted of Indigenous or pseudo-Indigenous terms, some of which would now be considered offensive. The most common one began, "Kitsilano, Capilano . . ." In later years, the yells were led by yell leaders and sometimes a Yell King. The leaders were almost invariably male.

Hazing: "Last year being the first term of the University of B.C.," said an editorial in *Anonymous*, "every student was in one sense of the word a Freshman. So it was only natural that no initiation for the Freshman was suggested. But this year the same objection would not hold good, so the three other years decided to initiate the fine new batch of Freshmen on November 3rd."

Part of the initiation ceremony took place at something called the "House of Torture." Presumably, this was just a joke, but in later years there was increasing controversy over initiation ceremonies (called hazing by those who disapproved of them).

AMS EXECUTIVE
1916-1917

PRESIDENT *Charles A. Wright*
VICE-PRESIDENT *Evelyn S. Story*
SECRETARY *W.J. Allardyce*
ASSISTANT SECRETARY
G.K. Henderson

1917 TO 1918

was said to be "the highest jinks on record," with women dressed as strong men, wild beasts, and a hula girl. There was even one in blackface, not something seen as offensive in those days.

But the War: However, it was not all fun and games. The war remained a constant presence. The *Annual* noted that thirty UBC men had now died, and over two hundred were serving overseas. The absence of so many men caused what the *Ubicee* called a "crisis" in student activities, and one observer derided the University for turning into a "ladies' college."

High Jinks: Perhaps as a relief from the war, 1917–18 saw the inauguration of a high-spirited annual party for women only. They dressed up in outlandish costumes, from sheiks to wild men. The 1922 edition even included an early appearance of Lady Godiva (more on her later). The 1921 version, with a vast array of "weird and wonderful costumes,"

The 1921 High Jinks extravaganza.

AMS Constitution Again: This year there was even more fuss about the AMS constitution, because the University authorities vetoed an amendment to it, causing much hand-wringing in the *Annual* about the lack of communication in the matter. The *Annual* also commented on the lack of co-operation between Student Council and the general student body, and somewhat surprisingly blamed the student body, calling on the students at large to

shake off their apathy. "Take an interest in the college," the *Annual* exhorted, and if you can't take an interest, "GET OUT!"

Student Self-Government: Rather than focusing on student apathy as the *Annual* did, the *Ubicee* focused on threats to AMS autonomy. It published letters warning that "the principle of self-government . . . has been violated by the action of the Faculty, who have authorized the Registrar to interfere with student activities." The registrar had suspended some students from AMS activities and required that others resign from AMS positions.

Vandalism: The *Ubicee* criticized the student body for vandalism, which it saw as another threat to self-government: "We have for some time deplored the misdirected energy which resulted in the destruction of magazines in the Common Rooms . . . [and the] wanton vandalism which causes destruction of furniture, breakage of windows and general untidiness about the building. The perpetrators of these outrages should be severely censured if our system of student self-government is not to become anarchy."

First Female President: Norah Coy won election as the AMS president, the first woman to hold that post—and the last until the 1950s. The AMS was notable in granting the vote to its female members from the beginning, before women could vote in provincial or federal elections.

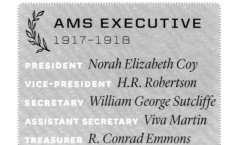

AMS EXECUTIVE
1917-1918

PRESIDENT *Norah Elizabeth Coy*
VICE-PRESIDENT *H.R. Robertson*
SECRETARY *William George Sutcliffe*
ASSISTANT SECRETARY *Viva Martin*
TREASURER *R. Conrad Emmons*

Norah Coy, the first female president of the AMS.

1918 TO 1919

Cramped quarters in Fairview.

War Is Over: But at a cost. Another eleven UBC students died, bringing the total to seventy-eight. And while the fighting wound down overseas, the worldwide influenza epidemic struck Vancouver: three more students died, and the University closed for five weeks. One final blow landed in October 1918: UBC President Wesbrook died after being ill for several months. Still, the *Annual* struck a celebratory note about the war, speaking of the pride that students could feel in having taken part in "the greatest crusade ever entered upon by men in the history of the world."

Space: The influenza epidemic led Vancouver General Hospital to ask for some of its space back

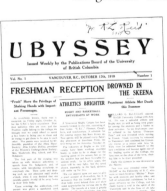

The very first *Ubyssey*.

from the University. This, coupled with the continuing lack of athletic facilities and general overcrowding on the Fairview campus, led to calls for construction of the Point Grey campus to resume.

Ubyssey: A new publication was born this year, a newspaper, the *Ubyssey*, a respelling and a re-imagination of the old literary monthly, the *Ubicee*. Skits and poems are all very well, the new paper commented, but what is needed is news while it is still "hot," by which the editors meant no more than a week old.

Freshman Reception: One of the top stories in the first issue of the *Ubyssey* was about the annual Freshman Reception, a tradition begun in the very first year of the University. Not as raucous as the Welcome Back Barbecues of later decades, these were sedate gatherings at which a professor gave a brief talk, musical selections were played, and the first-year students were encouraged to get to know each other over card games and dancing.

Naughty Oscar: The Players' Club provoked controversy by staging a production of Oscar Wilde's *The Importance of Being Earnest*. The *Ubyssey* expressed "disgust" at this "trash," and said it would prefer something with "a healthy moral tone."

Oscar Wilde: not healthy enough?

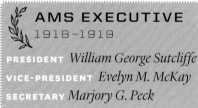

AMS EXECUTIVE
1918–1919

PRESIDENT *William George Sutcliffe*
VICE-PRESIDENT *Evelyn M. McKay*
SECRETARY *Marjory G. Peck*

UBYSSEY EDITOR *Ian A. Shaw*

1919 TO 1920

Some to Des Moines: A mass meeting of UBC students sent a delegation to Des Moines, Iowa, to attend an international convention of the Student Volunteer Movement for Foreign Missions, a Christian organization. Students from around North America gathered in Des Moines during the Christmas break to hear talks about the post-war world, the rights of nations, social justice, and the new economic order.

When the UBC delegates returned, they reported to another mass meeting of students, which was also addressed by the new UBC president, Leonard Klinck. The *Annual* reported that the conference organizer had said the purpose of the meeting was to receive "a new spiritual vision" and "an accession of supernatural power," with a view to bringing about "The Evangelization of the World in This Generation," but the focus seemed as much on socio-economic issues as on religious ones, anticipating the appearance at UBC in later years of a branch of the Student Christian Movement, an organization devoted to liberal and progressive causes.

And Some to Victoria: Continuing a tradition begun in the days of McGill BC, UBC students headed over to Victoria just before Christmas for a series of athletic competitions and dances. Later known as the Victoria Invasion, this event continued into the 1930s. In some years, it included debating competitions as well as sports.

The 1919 trip to Victoria.

Others Come Home: Almost two hundred veterans returned to UBC, swelling the ranks of students. Many of them struggled financially, a problem encountered across the country and leading to the creation of Returned Soldier Students' Clubs. Requests to the federal government for assistance did not meet with success.

Returned soldiers and others in a vocational "short course" in 1919.

And Some Get "Electrocuted": Hazing of the freshmen became so severe this year (the *Ubyssey* called it a "barbaric ordeal" and it included what the paper described as "electrocution" as well as blindfolding, "branding," and hair cutting) that a Special General Meeting of the students was called to discuss it. However, to the surprise of some,

the meeting voted in favour of continuing current practices, even voting down a proposal for a milder form of initiation.

While Others Go for a Run: The Arts students of the Class of 1920 initiated a relay run this year between the proposed new campus in Point Grey and the old Fairview campus.

Or Just Watch:

BELOW LEFT A runner arriving at Fairview during the Arts '20 relay race in 1921.

BELOW RIGHT Crowds looking on at the relay race.

AMS EXECUTIVE
1919–1920

PRESIDENT *Donald Morrison/ William H. Coates (after Morrison resigned)*

VICE-PRESIDENT *Katherine H. Pillsbury*

TREASURER *C.P. Leckie*

SECRETARY *Elizabeth B. Abernethy*

UBYSSEY EDITOR *A. A. Webster*

1920 TO 1921

The AMS in Business: In what seems to have been its first business venture, the AMS opened a cafeteria at the beginning of the second term in 1920–21, offering hot lunches for 25 cents. Afternoon tea was also available, with toasted crumpets, cakes, and jam, and there was a convenience store selling stationery, candy, cigarettes, and something called glacier bars.

The students' cafeteria.

AMS Staff: This year also saw talk of appointing a manager, a non-student staff person to take some of the burden off the student treasurer and secretary. Nothing came of it then, but the "manager system" became a reality by the end of the decade, and eventually the AMS came to employ dozens of permanent staff under a general manager. But that was later.

Marshal: The AMS created the position of marshal this year. Despite the

The cabin on Grouse Mountain, 1923.

name, the position seems mostly to have been intended to serve as a coordinator of activities rather than a law enforcement officer. Within a few years there was a whole system of marshals and sub-marshals.

Building Cabins: The Outdoor Club, later to be known as the Varsity Outdoors Club, built a cabin on Grouse Mountain, only to see it burn down soon after completion. However, the club quickly rebuilt it and in subsequent years put up several other cabins in the mountains, the most notable being the one that became known as the AMS Whistler Lodge.

Picnicking: For those less inclined to climb mountains, there was the annual AMS picnic at the Wigwam

PHOTO
REGAN & McMILLAN

23

TOP Students on the boat to Indian Arm.
MIDDLE Chem lab at Fairview.
BOTTOM Preparing the bonfire for initiation.

Inn at Indian Arm, also arranged by the Outdoors Club.

Studying: Of course, the more serious types just stayed in their labs.

Frolicking: And the wilder ones built a bonfire (for frosh initiation).

AMS EXECUTIVE
1920–1921

PRESIDENT *Arthur E. Lord*
SECRETARY *Isobel Miller*
TREASURER *W.O. Banfield*

UBYSSEY EDITOR *Paul N. Whitley*

1921 TO 1922

Fraternities: Debate about the merits of fraternities began in the spring of 1921, culminating in a general meeting that appointed a committee to look into the issue. Supporters said the fraternities encouraged friendship, college spirit, loyalty, and scholarship. Their opponents called them "aristocratic" and the source of undesirable rivalries. In the end, the AMS approved an amendment to its constitution to allow fraternities to function under the umbrella of an Inter-Fraternity Council, which survives to this day. Sororities were similarly placed under an Inter-Sorority Council.

Student Parliament: The issue of fraternities was one of the subjects debated at a new institution created by the students in 1921: a Student Parliament, intended "to keep the Students' Council in touch with college opinion on matters of university interest." Set up like a real legislative body, with a premier and a leader of the Opposition, the parliament in the early days focused on student issues, such as club finances, athletics, and the honour system. Later, under the name Mock Parliament, it debated real issues in federal politics.

Medical Insurance: Another idea raised at the Student Parliament was that of an Injuries Trust Fund for athletes injured while competing for UBC. This went to Student Council and the University Senate, and by 1923 the fund was in place and athletes could have their medical expenses covered.

Dean of Women: The *Ubyssey* ran a front page editorial in February 1921 suggesting that it might be a good idea if the University appointed a Dean of Women to advise the many female students on campus, and the next year the University did this very thing, naming Mary Bollert to the position, which she held for twenty years. Mary Bollert Hall is named after her.

Dean Bollert.

Stop Thief! The *Ubyssey* sternly editorialized about students stealing books and periodicals from the library. Over one hundred books had gone missing the year before. The editorial shook its head over "the sad lack of common honesty" and the "predatory instincts" of some students.

Moose or Hot Dog: UBC still had no nickname or symbol. Other schools had their lions or their cougars or their bears, the *Ubyssey* reported, as if inviting suggestions—and indeed a week later someone wrote in to suggest the bull moose, "imperious and majestic." To which another correspondent responded with the suggestion of A Hot Dog Rampant on a Field of Bread. "It's good to be hot and exuberant," said the letter writer. "Dogs are loyal; and bread is the staff of life." This inspired the *Ubyssey* to publish the following cartoon:

But nothing came of it, and UBC would have to wait another decade for a symbol.

Pep? The students organized a Varsity Week in February, full of games and shows, but the *Ubyssey* complained that they were just going through the motions, perhaps because they did not really feel at home on the Fairview campus. "We have no shrines on which to focus our emotions," the paper said, a hint of the campaign to come for a real campus in Point Grey.

PHOTO
REGAN & McMILLAN

ABOVE Ready to move to Point Grey. Fairview campus before the move.

TOP RIGHT Eating ice cream.

MIDDLE RIGHT Smoking cigars (that's future UBC chancellor J.V. Clyne at the far left).

BOTTOM RIGHT Clowning around outside the AMS Literary and Scientific Department offices.

PAGE 27, CLOCKWISE FROM TOP LEFT
The women form a sort of train.

More clowning around, or at least sitting around and laughing.

The men build a pyramid.

But Wait: People Still Had Fun. They ate ice cream, smoked cigars, or just clowned around. They even built human pyramids and formed human trains.

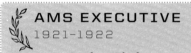

1922 TO 1923

The YEAR of the TREK

One story dominated the 1922-23 session: the Great Trek of October 28, 1922. Tired of waiting for their new campus to be built, the students acted. They gathered signatures on a petition to present to the government in Victoria: more than fifty thousand in the end. They sought support from the public and found it in the newspapers of Vancouver, the Kiwanis Club, various businesses, the trade union movement, and the streetcar company.

Finally, at midday on the 28th the students set out on their march, their "Pilgrimage" to the "Promised Land" in Point Grey. "Build the University," read their banners, and they shouted and cheered and yelled—and marched from the Georgia Viaduct through downtown Vancouver and then rode streetcars out to Alma or Sasamat,

then marched again along rough paths through the wilderness that had not yet been transformed into their campus.

Into the cleared areas they went, clambering up onto the skeleton of the unfinished science building, swaying back and forth perilously as the yell leader below led them in chants. Well-wishers parked their cars nearby. Floats representing the various faculties arrived. Then the students clambered down and formed a giant U-B-C for the cameras. There was even film, a two and a half minute production, silent of course but full of energy.

And after that the student leaders of the Campaign, as it was known, set off for the legislature in Victoria and met the premier and other politicians, who acceded to their demands and pledged $1.5 million to resume work on the Point Grey campus so that, less than three years later, the students could abandon their shacks in Fairview and embark on a new life on the vast acres that had been promised to them.

The students march downtown along Georgia Street.

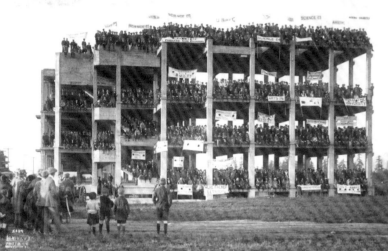

TOP Then march again in Point Grey.

MIDDLE Then clamber up into the shell of the half-finished science building and arrange themselves to spell out the letters U-B-C.

BOTTOM And in the end the government "saw the point" and promised the money to build the campus.

The Ubyssey

Issued Weekly by the Publications Board of the University of British Columbia

Volume V.   VANCOUVER, B. C., NOV. 9, 1922.   No. 6

Government Sees the Point!

VARSITY WINS FROM EDMONTON

College Ruggers Surpass Score Registered By Vancouver Two Days Before

Over three thousand spectators witnessed Varsity's first fifteen in their victory last Monday over the Edmonton "Rep" Team. British Columbia weather has been kind to the visitors from Alberta and the game was played under ideal conditions. The score was 16-0.

Brilliant Play by Tarzan

CAMPAIGN DELEGATION BACK FROM VICTORIA

Last Minute Interview with Student Representatives Elicits Interesting Details Concerning their Reception and Activities

The Government has voted $1,500,000 for the immediate construction of permanent buildings on the Point Grey site.

This news is too momentous to have missed a single member of the Student Body when it spread through these halls yesterday. The return of the Campaign Delegation from Victoria, and the confirmation they brought of rumors which many had hesitated to believe, was, in actuality, "the best

The Petition was brought in to Capt. Ian McKenzie, who piled it up on the desk in front of him until he was almost hidden by the rolls of signatures. It created a decided stir in the House when six boxes were called, loaded with forms, nearby members assisting in the process, and sent to lay the fifty thousand—odd names—before the Speaker's Chair. The Speaker was nonplussed for the moment and there was a pause

FAST PACE IN GAME WITH ELKS

North Vancouver Players Are Unfortunate Enough to Score Against Selves.

Con Jones' Park was the scene of another win for the Varsity soccer team Saturday afternoon, when they took the north shore "Brother Hills" into camp to the tune of three goals to two.

Play opened and the Elks pressed the ball going down the field, putting Varsity's goal in danger. Baker, driving beautifully, relieved a strained

AMS EXECUTIVE
1922–1923

PRESIDENT Albert E. ("Ab") Richards
TREASURER Percy M. Barr
SECRETARY Marjorie Agnew/ Dorothy Walsh

UBYSSEY EDITOR H.M. Cassidy

1923 TO 1924

Building the University (more): The students did not stop after convincing the government to allocate funds for the new campus. Concerned that there would be no athletic facilities, they started fundraising for playing fields, and some even went out to the campus site to do some preliminary work. Let us show our willingness to "roll up our sleeves and dig in—literally and figuratively," said the *Ubyssey*, and the students did.

This was the beginning of a long tradition of UBC students taking the initiative in building projects, from playing fields to gymnasiums to student union buildings—all of which led a later UBC president (Norman MacKenzie) to comment: "No university in the world I know owes as much to its students as does the University of British Columbia."

In fact, even before this, at the time of the Great Trek, the students had put up a memorial cairn to mark the event, despite the objections of the *Ubyssey*, which thought it a waste of money.

But Before They Left: Though they were looking ahead to Point Grey, the students still took time out to read the newspaper, assemble in the Fairview auditorium, or just pose for a photograph. Agriculture students took time out to "judge" a make-believe bull, and students from all faculties eventually graduated and took part in congregation ceremonies.

CLOCKWISE FROM TOP Students planting trees on campus in the 1930s.

The memorial to the Great Trek, photographed decades later.

UBC president Norman MacKenzie praised the students for their contributions.

PAGE 31, CLOCKWISE FROM TOP LEFT Why, it's just like texting: reading a newspaper in a dangerous way.

Posing for the camera.

Judging a "bull."

Students in procession during a graduation ceremony.

Assembling.

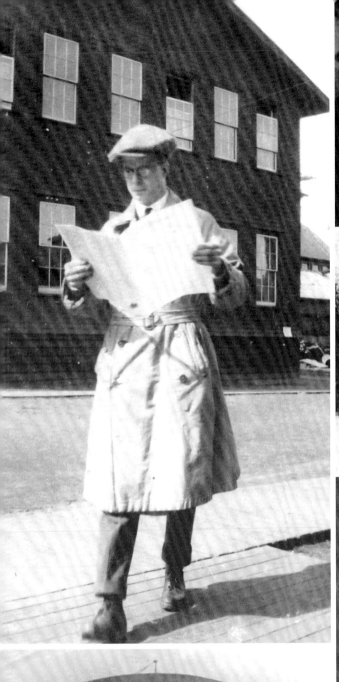

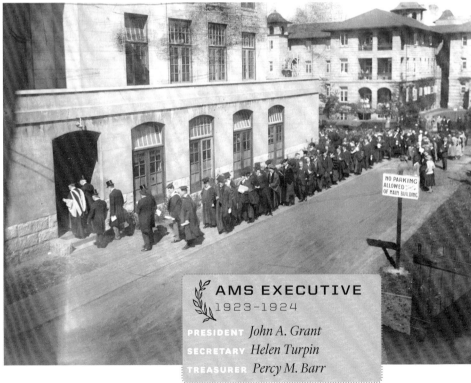

AMS EXECUTIVE
1923–1924

PRESIDENT *John A. Grant*
SECRETARY *Helen Turpin*
TREASURER *Percy M. Barr*

UBYSSEY EDITOR *A.L. Wheeler*

1924 TO 1925

Join the Team! As the last year at Fairview unfolded, Student Council and the *Ubyssey* became more exuberant (or hectoring) about college spirit and participation. Everyone should sign up for a sport, Council ordered, and everyone should root for the Varsity teams. Also, woe betide anyone who instead of playing for UBC signed up for a non-UBC sports team and played *against* UBC. The horror.

Said the *Ubyssey,* "It is almost unbelievable that any Varsity athlete would sign up for another club and play against his team-mates, when he knows his Alma Mater needs his services." Such an action is "childish and petty, and, further, it is disloyal."

See the sad saga of Louis Chodat in 1931–32 for more on this issue.

Hazing Gone? Not for the first (or last) time, the *Ubyssey* declared the end of hazing, that is, of physically dangerous initiation rites. Not that initiations were abandoned. Far from it. The first-year students were now required to wear green ribbons and caps and they had to learn the college yells. Those who refused to wear their ribbons were showing "disrespect for the great majority" and "a deplorable lack of pride in [the] university."

Gender Imbalance and Constitutional Change: The *Ubyssey* commented that women were under-represented on Student Council and saw the situation worsening as a result of a constitutional change reducing the number of Council members from twelve to nine. At the same time they warned voters not to support candidates just because of their gender: "Don't vote for a candidate because he or she is or is not a woman." The paper also warned against voting for a candidate just because they were in the same faculty as the voter.

No More Marshals: The constitutional change also did away with the marshals on the grounds that the position awkwardly separated disciplinary functions from event organizing. These powers were now to be combined in the hands of the student president in each faculty.

Be Good! Council issued a series of edicts against loitering, littering, talking in the library, making noise in the halls, writing on the walls, and gambling. The *Ubyssey* the year before had also warned against writing in the margins of library books.

Farewell to Fairview: Presumably written with tongue in cheek, the *Ubyssey* editorialized about missing the miseries of Fairview. Life will be too easy at Point Grey; there

The 1924–25 Council, with nine men and three women.

will always be seats in the library; no churches will have to be pressed into service for history lectures: "We have become too attached to our miseries to be very glad to part with them. And so this year's editorial is a wail for departed glory."

Arthur Laing: Visible in the bottom left of the Council picture for this year is Art Laing, president of the Agriculture Undergraduate Society, who went on to a career in politics, serving in the federal cabinet and also leading the BC Liberal Party. Then, in his last years, he became a bridge.

Council member Art Laing, after whom the Arthur Laing bridge is named.

AMS EXECUTIVE
1924-1925

PRESIDENT *A.E. ("Dal") Grauer*
SECRETARY *Elsie Rilance*
TREASURER *Lyle Atkinson*

UBYSSEY EDITOR: *T.W. Brown*

A CLASS IN NURSING.

33

1925-1935

IN POINT GREY

And so they reached the Promised Land at last. Or so the *Ubyssey* described it. But once there, they settled into the routine of being students and a student government, and they also realized that the land had not completely fulfilled its promise: for instance, there was no gym and no playing fields. After discovering that neither the University nor the provincial government would pay for such things (or at least not pay fully), the students organized, incorporated, fundraised, increased fees (when the University would allow them), and managed to get a gymnasium built, and some rather unsatisfactory playing fields, but not (at least not yet) the stadium they wanted.

And there were internal issues to deal with, such as discipline, and then the external world came crashing in under the name Great Depression, which almost caused UBC to close, and which caused the AMS to retrench, make cuts, seek economies.

And through it all the leaders exhorted and the membership went along, sometimes, or paid no heed, and there were snowball fights and snake dances and votes to overturn Council decisions and debates about war and peace. And the AMS introduced new services and saw the University take over some old ones. It was business as usual in the new home.

1925 TO 1926

Klahowya: "We have arrived!" the *Ubyssey* declared in its first editorial on the new campus. The editorial was entitled "Klahowya" (the Chinook term for welcome), but it went on to mix Biblical tradition with Indigenous by declaring jubilantly that the students had reached the "Promised Land" without losing a Moses or a Joshua.

The editorial then moved on from jubilation to exhortation, calling on the students to take part in activities beyond the classrooms, in the process mixing in yet a third tradition by alluding to UBC's Latin motto (*Tuum est*), calling it untranslatable and yet translating it to mean "it is up to you."

Another Indigenous Connection: Besides the use of Klahowya in the *Ubyssey* editorial, a term used before by the AMS as the name for celebratory weeks on Fairview campus, the AMS *Annual* this year announced a name change. Henceforth it would be the *Totem*. The editors thought such a name appropriate for a university that was already using terms like Capilano for its main cheer. They also noted that just as a totem

The newly christened *Totem*.

is "a record of a tribe's history," so this *Totem* would be "the record of our college history."

Refreshments Will Be Served: There was talk this year of establishing a Student Court to deal with discipline cases, and already in September the *Ubyssey* was registering the need for such a court by reporting on a "criminal" who was being charged with playing bridge for money, i.e., gambling in contravention of AMS bylaws. Though the defendant said the charges were a violation of his individual rights, a trial was going ahead. However, since there was not yet a court, the case was to be heard by a joint meeting of the Men's and Women's Literary Societies (!). Everyone was welcome to attend, said the *Ubyssey*, adding: "Refreshments will be served."

A week later the defendant was acquitted by reason of "insanity." The whole thing was treated as a bit of a joke, yet the push for a system of student-run discipline continued, resulting in . . .

The Vigilance Committee: In November 1925 Council decided to create a secret body known as the Vigilance Committee, consisting of ten men who would go undercover to try to catch smokers, loiterers, and other wrongdoers. The *Ubyssey* called the plan "obnoxious" and smack-

Besides the Indigenous, the Biblical, and the classical, perhaps another campus tradition was the automobilical.

ing of espionage. A general meeting of the students was called to vote on whether to abolish the new system, but voted in favour of keeping it. However, it was replaced the following year by the Honour System.

Lingering Initiation: Forms of initiation for the first-year students remained, notably the requirement to wear green armbands and rules against the newcomers smoking and sitting on steps. The *Ubyssey* mused about whether even relatively innocuous requirements like these were useful: they may encourage class spirit, but what about "alma mater spirit"? It is like the clash between nationalism and internationalism, they said.

British or American? An identity issue erupted this year in a perhaps unlikely arena: sports. After a long debate, the students voted to introduce American football to UBC. This despite the laments of the *Ubyssey*, which supported British rugby and feared the introduction of American ways, notably an emphasis on athletics at the expense of academics. The *Ubyssey*

also expressed displeasure over one-sided rooting at sports events, advocating instead for "British traditions of fair play."

The Cafeteria: In an early example of a long tradition, a service previously offered by the AMS (the old cafeteria at the Fairview campus) was taken

TOP American-style football at UBC in 1939.

BOTTOM The new "caf" in the basement of the Auditorium.

The Auditorium in 1927.

over by the University, which now ran "the Grill" in the Auditorium building. Students complained that the prices were higher and also objected to the rule that every-one, even those bringing their own lunch, had to eat in the new caf (as they persisted in calling it) to avoid causing litter around campus. Long lines resulted because there were only four hundred seats to serve fourteen hundred students, all of whom were supposed to eat during the same lunch hour at noon.

A Place of Their Own? There was talk of raising money for a Women's Union building, where the female students could hold events and have a refuge. The sororities contributed. This was an issue that remained

at the discussion stage for several years, but student attention (and funding) shifted to building a gym and then to building a place for all students, a Student Union build-ing—but that didn't happen until the thirties.

In the meantime, the AMS and other student groups (e.g., the *Ubyssey*) made do with space in the Auditorium building, including of course the cafeteria, which one (pre-sumably male) contributor to the *Ubyssey* complained was being taken over by the women, who he said were using the space "as a sort of Women's Building or School for Scandal or anything but a dining room."

A Poet: The *Ubyssey* editor Earle Birney went on to become a noted poet.

AMS EXECUTIVE
1925-1926

PRESIDENT *Thomas G. Wilkinson*
SECRETARY *Dorothy E. Brown*
TREASURER *Gordon Abernethy*

UBYSSEY EDITOR *A. Earle Birney*

1926 TO 1927

No Pep: In October the *Ubyssey* bemoaned the decline of pep meetings and college spirit, saying things were not as they had been in the glory days at Fairview (though when they were in Fairview, the *Ubyssey* complained about a lack of pep there). In any case, in October 1926 at Point Grey the *Ubyssey* spoke of the "student body, that mysterious, much mutilated being," which instead of going to pep rallies, "sat itself down in the Library and refused to do anything but study." (For shame.)

The paper added: "Despite the fact that this is the fourth week of the term, nothing very interesting has occurred. Neither have the students been very much alive."

Homecoming: November 1926 marked UBC's first Homecoming Week, which the *Ubyssey* hailed as a chance to tighten the bonds between the undergraduates and the alumni. Celebrations included a bonfire and a theatre night. The *Ubyssey* called it the "first real indication of life and activity among the undergraduate body." There was also a rugby match, rugby still being the major sport (as opposed to football), and on Thanksgiving Monday (which in those days fell in November) the freshmen gave the alumni a tour of the new campus.

Rugby: Showing the continuing importance of rugby was the prominence given to a game between the senior rugby team and the touring New Zealand Maori rugby team. The *Ubyssey* made it front page news, and UBC President Klinck ordered classes cancelled so students could watch the game. The result, a 12-3 loss for UBC, was hailed as a moral victory bringing UBC international athletic prominence.

MUSSOC: The Homecoming theatre night featured entertainment provided by two AMS student clubs: the Musical Society (in later years referred to as MUSSOC) and the Players Club. Founded in 1916–17 as the Musical Club, MUSSOC became notable for putting on operettas and musicals, and lasted until the 1990s.

A MUSSOC production of *Iolanthe* in 1944.

Arts '20 Relay: The relay had continued for several years, but in 1926, with the move to the new campus complete, it was decided to abandon it in favour of a race around a track at the new campus. In 1927, controversy erupted over whether to revive the original tradition, and in the end the old race was brought back, but with a difference: instead of running from Point Grey to Fairview, the runners went from Fairview (Willow and Tenth Avenue) to Point

The mysterious student body holed up in the Library instead of having fun.

A runner in the Arts '20 relay race in 1930.

Grey. The race continued this way until 1940, then stopped during the Second World War. Revived in 1969, it continued into the nineties.

Students Alive After All? After a year of what the *Ubyssey* editor himself called "destructive criticism" about lack of spirit, the actions of Council, the role of the Rooters Club, and so on, the students struck back, sending in a rash of letters objecting to the paper's negativity.

Ballot Stuffing: Finally at the end of the year, some excitement: someone stuffed the ballot box with forty-two fraudulent votes in the presidential election. A search was on for the culprit; some commented that the incident showed the lax security in elections; the president-elect (Leslie Brown) resigned because he feared

his election was tainted, even though Student Council declared that it was confident all the fraudulent votes had been accounted for. He was later declared elected by acclamation.

And More Scandal: In the midst of the controversial election, Council provoked more controversy by refusing to appoint as the next *Ubyssey* editor the candidate put forward by the outgoing editor and the AMS Publications Board (James Sinclair). Instead, it named Jean Tolmie, who refused to serve because she had not been endorsed by the Publications Board. Eventually, Council agreed to appoint James Sinclair, but because he had just won a seat on Council he now declined to serve, and in the end Jean Tolmie became editor after all.

James Sinclair went on to become a leading figure in the federal Liberal Party, serving as a cabinet minister in the 1950s, but

his greatest claim to fame may be as the father of Margaret Sinclair, who married Prime Minister Pierre Trudeau in 1971. He thus also, posthumously, became grandfather of another Prime Minister in 2015, when Justin Trudeau won that year's federal election.

Jean Tolmie was the first female editor of the *Ubyssey*.

🌿 **AMS EXECUTIVE**
1926-1927

PRESIDENT *John Craig Oliver*
SECRETARY *Kathleen P. Baird*
TREASURER *Harold McWilliams*

UBYSSEY EDITOR *Edmund Morrison*

1927 TO 1928

No More LSD: No, not the drug (it hadn't been invented yet), but the Literary and Scientific Department, the AMS body responsible for overseeing the student clubs, and often referred to as the LSD (from the beginning the AMS has had a penchant for acronyms and abbreviations). The LSD had been around since 1920, but there were complaints about it, and it was restructured this year and renamed the Literary and Scientific Executive (LSE). It later was replaced by the University Clubs Committee (the UCC) and then by SAC (the Student Administrative Commission).

Musqueam Connection: In one of the earliest interactions between the University and the Musqueam People, the second annual Homecoming ceremony saw the appearance of a Musqueam chief and the donation of two large Musqueam carvings, which were later placed in the University's Botanical Gardens. The AMS participated by hosting a tea for the Musqueam delegation.

Musqueam carvings in the gardens: one on the far left, one in the background at the right.

Mamooks: After that meeting with actual Musqueam leaders, the AMS returned to what might be called its imaginary connection with the First Nations by renaming its Rooters Club "Mamooks," a Chinook term which they translated as "Plenty of Pep and How," but which actually means making or doing. The club survived for decades, serving as the publicity arm of the AMS (putting up posters, organizing the yell leaders, and so on).

Initiation Woes: Despite plans for a "safe and sane" freshman orientation this year, the result was what the *Ubyssey* called a fiasco. Plans for a giant soccer or rugby game (it's

LSD at the AMS in 1923.

The Mamooks club in 1944.

unclear which) ended up with "a fight for a rugby-ball between mobs of over four hundred." Two students were taken to hospital. The *Ubyssey* found it ironic that there were more injuries this year in what was supposed to be a safe initiation than in all the years of "barbarous hazing."

The Gym: The students continued to press for a gymnasium, but met resistance from the University and the provincial government. A plan to raise student fees, coupled with a loan from the government, was rejected by the government. A later plan was rejected by the University's Board of Governors.

Soldiers on Campus? Plans for a revival of the Canadian Officers Training Corps (COTC or often just OTC) were hotly debated. Council expressed a favourable view, but a general meeting of the students voted against it. The University eventually established it anyway.

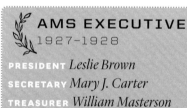

AMS EXECUTIVE
1927-1928
PRESIDENT *Leslie Brown*
SECRETARY *Mary J. Carter*
TREASURER *William Masterson*

UBYSSEY EDITOR *Jean Tolmie*

1928 TO 1929

A Society and a Gym: After the close of the 1927–28 year, on April 27, 1928, to be precise, the Alma Mater Society became an officially incorporated society, primarily with a view to raising money for construction projects, and during 1928–29 it made arrangements to float a loan and issue bonds to cover the cost of, finally, building a gymnasium for campus.

Broken Windows: In what the *Ubyssey* called an annual event, the students in Science (which meant Engineering back then) waged a snowball fight against Arts students, resulting in black eyes, cauliflower ears, and broken windows. All together fifty windows were broken that winter, and only one student came forward to claim responsibility, leaving the AMS to pay for most of the repairs out of its general coffers. The *Ubyssey* saw this as a failure of the honour system.

A Successful Initiation? On the other hand, the *Ubyssey* was satisfied with the year's initiation of the frosh, saying it avoided both extreme hazing and the "pseudo-initiations" of the immediately preceding years. This year the frosh had their hair bleached, their faces massaged with cold cream, and their clothes "decorated" with various colours; then they were made to crawl on their hands and knees through a building before being turned out into the street. All this, said the *Ubyssey*, put them through "the first steps in the laborious process of civilization." Well, maybe.

Peace and War: While lectures were being held on campus on the dangers of war and the need to work to protect the peace, the Canadian Officers Training Corps (COTC) began functioning on campus again, to the chagrin of many who condemned it as a sign of militarism. Also condemned was AMS president Ross Tolmie for sitting on a COTC committee despite the vote the previous year by the student body to oppose the COTC on campus.

Paid Managers? Council hired a curator-bookkeeper this year and debated whether to revamp the AMS financial system by hiring a business manager. It referred the matter to the student body, but several general meetings on the matter failed to reach quorum, and Council in the end decided on its own to try the system temporarily in 1929–30.

Fraternities: The Inter-Fraternity Council sought more independence, prompting the *Ubyssey* to invite comments on whether fraternities and sororities were of value to a university. Most who commented expressed ambivalence, praising fraternities for providing social connections but warning that they could gain too much power and also encourage exclusivity and snobbery.

Just Joking: In one of the first examples of a long AMS tradition, a joke candidate was put forward in the presidential elections: Rufus W. McGoofus, who called for one-cent candies in the cafeteria. McGoofus seems to have been entirely fictional, an invention of the *Ubyssey*'s Muck-a-Muck page (a regular humour page), unlike later joke can-

President Tolmie: criticized.

Now the AMS was legal.

43

Mucking around with the presidency.

didates who were flesh and blood. And he kept reappearing, running again in 1932 on a platform of abolishing lectures.

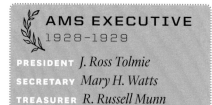
1929 TO 1930

In Business: The AMS named its first business manager, introducing an elaborate system of financial accounting administered by paid staff. The *Totem* hailed the system as a "great success" with an assured future, but it ran into opposition in the 1930s and disappeared for a while before reviving after the Second World War.

Hints of a SUB? The *Ubyssey* complained that rooms formerly used by the students had been taken over by faculty members and suggested that new buildings were needed on campus. It did not explicitly call for a Student Union building (that would not become a goal till the next decade), but it later praised the campaign for a Women's Union building (which never came to fruition) and noted that it had repeatedly been up to the students themselves to take action to build new facilities, the latest example being . . .

The Gymnasium! Finally, UBC got a gym. It officially opened on Saturday, November 9, 1929, during Homecoming Weekend, thanks to the efforts of the Alma Mater Society, which made the financing arrangements after being turned down by both the government and the University. Not the first time (or the last) that it would be up to the AMS to provide services or facilities.

Even before the gym officially opened, however, there was controversy, because the Vancouver basketball league in which the UBC team competed objected to UBC using its own gym, preferring that all games be played downtown. A compromise was eventually reached.

The first gym.

It should be noted that in these early years not only was it the AMS that built the athletic facilities, but until 1950 it was the AMS that ran the varsity athletics program.

We Are, We Are, We Are the . . . Engineers, that is. Adopting a traditional engineers' drinking song, the Engineers of UBC (or Sciencemen, as they were called then) took to chanting this ode to their drinking prowess as early as the 1920s, with one of the earliest mentions of it appearing in the October 22, 1929 issue of the *Ubyssey*. That issue contained a front-page article describing an epic battle between Sciencemen and Artsmen over the desecration of an Arts pennant. The result: several Artsmen were deprived of their trousers, which were run up a flagpole as a sort of trophy, and as the five-to-one bell for class rang, the Sciencemen celebrated their victory over their "white collar" opponents by singing their song: "We are, we are . . ." etc.

Debates, Decline, Disagreements . . . Revival: Student Council and the debating club (known as the Debating Union) conducted a months-long dispute over how to organize debates. Debating was a popular activity in the early years of the University, with both men's and women's debating clubs (known as the Men's and Women's Literary Societies) and international competitions against American and British schools, including Oxford. This year there was even a visiting debating team from New Zealand.

Horticulture class.

But this year also saw the dissolution of the Women's Literary Society, a mass resignation of the executive of the Debating Union over differences with Council, and a decline in attendance.

In January, the *Ubyssey* noted a general ebbing of interest in debating throughout Canada, and blamed AMS Council for making things worse. But a month later the Debating Union was reorganized, turnout increased at debates, and all was suddenly right with the debating world.

Lips That Touch Liquor: Three students were fined $25 each and barred from dances until the end of second term for being "under the influence of liquor" at an Agriculture ball in January. This was in violation of AMS Bylaw 19 at the time, which forbade drinking of "intoxicating liquors" on campus and at any University function and also forbade appearing at functions while "showing any trace of such intoxicating liquors." The AMS remained a prohibitionist organization until after the Second World War, but in later years adopted rather a different approach, opening pubs and lounges beginning in the 1960s.

If $25 seems like a lot for the time, it was. Tuition was $100 for the year, and the AMS fee was $10.

Agriculture Students: Besides hosting dances that led to unfortunate punishments for intoxication, the Aggies kept busy in classes like horticulture and pomology.

Pomology class.

Jobs for Students: Council established a Student Employment Committee to help students find jobs, beginning a long tradition of AMS involvement in assistance for job seekers.

In Court: The AMS gets sued! For the first time (but not the last). And all because of an initiation gone wrong. Seems that the snake parade at the end of freshman initiation (a snake parade being a massive crowd of students stampeding through downtown Vancouver) resulted in an innocent bystander being run over (not by a car; by the stampeding students). He broke his leg, and he sued.

The case did not actually go to court. The lawyer for the AMS,

A much milder snake parade by the Engineers in 1950.

Sherwood Lett (yes, that Sherwood Lett, the first AMS president), helped negotiate an out-of-court settlement for what the *Ubyssey* called "a great deal of money" (the sum of $500 was mentioned).

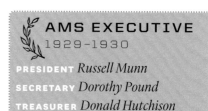

AMS EXECUTIVE
1929-1930

PRESIDENT *Russell Munn*
SECRETARY *Dorothy Pound*
TREASURER *Donald Hutchison*

UBYSSEY **EDITOR** *Roderick A. Pilkington*

1930 TO 1931

Too Much Spirit? After years of exhorting students to get out of the library and take part in athletics and other extra-curricular activities, the *Ubyssey* this year, following the lead of Student Council, shifted course dramatically and endorsed a new set of Eligibility Rules. The aim of these rules was to "eliminate that undesirable type of undergraduate who attends the university without having scholastic achievement as his main object."

The idea was to make sure that only full-time students who were passing their courses could take part in sports and other activities. This would enhance UBC's prestige, said the *Ubyssey*, and make sure it did not become a place known primarily for sports and social activities.

But What about Women's Basketball? The apparent turn away from extra-curricular activities did not stop the *Ubyssey* from hailing the return of the women's basketball team from Prague, where they had won the world championship.

Meanwhile the previous spring the men's basketball team had won the Canadian championship. A good year for hoopsters.

Oh, Initiation! The *Ubyssey* depicted the horrors of freshman initiation with a cartoon this year,

Athlete or scholar: which should a student be?

The world champion women's basketball team being fêted on its return from Prague.

The horrors of initiation.

but did not seem overly concerned about the goings-on, which included paddling of first-year students, smearing their faces with ointments, paints, oils, and even acids, then parading them in their pyjamas. The paper did shake its head over the "Battles of the Lily Pond," encounters in which sophomores and freshmen tried to toss each other into the pond in front of the library (or was it the pond in the Botanical Gardens? it's not clear). The paper also lamented the burns that occurred at the traditional bonfire when someone tossed gasoline-soaked rags into the flames, but overall it pronounced this year's initiation "a fairly successful business."

And a Snake Parade! Psst, wanna go to a snake parade? After the previous year's debacle, leading to an injured bystander and a lawsuit, and under pressure from the University, AMS Council declined to authorize a snake parade this year, which didn't stop students from organizing an unauthorized one. The *Ubyssey* seemed not too upset at the unauthorized parade, reserving its condemnation for the University's role in the matter, saying it was a threat to the "principle of student self-government." It would not be the last time there would be tensions between the University and the AMS over excesses at first-week events.

New Building Project: The AMS held a Special General Meeting at which students voted in favour of an immediate $5 increase in their fee in order to fund a stadium on campus. However, the Board of Governors refused to approve the increase, on the grounds that fees cannot be altered mid-year. This led to tensions with AMS Council and the

Ubyssey, which said that student self-government was under attack. In frustration, the paper published a cartoon showing various issues on which the University had overridden the wishes of the student body.

The *Ubyssey* depicts the "Authorities" threatening the tree of student desires.

Freedom of the Press: The *Ubyssey*'s critical approach to authority, in particular an editorial criticizing professors for criticizing the *Ubyssey*, resulted in the paper's editor (Ronald Grantham) being suspended by UBC president Klinck. After some apologies and negotiations, Grantham was reinstated and the right of the AMS

UBC president Klinck.

to run the paper was confirmed. But AMS Council then asked for Grantham's resignation because of his lack of "tact," and he was replaced by Himie Koshevoy.

Ubyssey editor Grantham.

New Building Project Redux: The stadium plan was not dead; the Faculty Association and the Board of Governors donated $5,800 for playing fields, leaving it up to the students to raise money for a grandstand. The students solicited donations, held benefit events, and even started a beard-growing campaign, raising thousands of dollars in the spring term. Meanwhile work began on the playing fields.

The Depression: The Great Depression went almost unmentioned this year, except that one argument for building playing fields was to provide work for the unemployed. Also, the government talked of reducing enrolment because of the economic situation, prompting objections from the *Ubyssey*.

Women Smoking: The Women's Undergraduate Society voted against allowing women to smoke on campus,

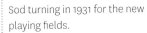
Sod turning in 1931 for the new playing fields.

on the grounds that it would tarnish the reputation of the University.

AMS EXECUTIVE
1930-1931
PRESIDENT *Donald F. Hutchison*
SECRETARY *Margaret O. Muirhead*
TREASURER *S.T. Fraser/*
Jack Thompson

UBYSSEY EDITOR
Ronald Grantham/Himie Koshevoy

1931 TO 1932

With a Song in Our Heart: The University got a song of its own ("Hail UBC"), lyrics and music by Harold King, an education student and member of the AMS Musical Society, thus filling a need, especially for sports events. The chorus begins, "Hail UBC/Our glorious University," a somewhat awkward rhyme, and includes both the Chinook greeting, *Klahowya*, and the University's Latin motto, *Tuum est.*

Hail, U.B.C.

A song for the Thunderbirds (except they weren't called Thunderbirds yet).

The Depression Hits Home: Barely mentioned in previous years, at the beginning of 1931–32 the Depression was still someone else's problem. In the fall the Women's Undergraduate Society (WUS) launched a clothing drive for those affected by the recent economic difficulties. "We are making an endeavor to help the more unfortunate members of the community who have been harder hit by the depression than ourselves," said the WUS president.

But by January it was the students themselves who were hit. Rumours began to fly about cuts by the provincial government, which might result in the closure of certain departments (Agriculture, Nursing, and Commerce were mentioned). There was even talk that the University might shut down.

The students organized, launching a publicity campaign to enlist public support for the notion that the University was essential to the province. As in the days of the Great Trek, a petition was started (garnering seventy thousand signatures), and there was large-scale public support (from the archbishop of Vancouver to the Trades and Labour Congress), but this time the government did not give in. Major cuts were made to the University budget, resulting in layoffs and a reduction in library hours. There was even a plan to merge Agriculture and Applied Science, which the Agriculture students objected to but which won support in some AMS quarters, causing internal division

Students rallying the public to fight the cuts to education.

among the students. (The plan did not go ahead.)

AMS Services: When not dealing with the funding cutbacks, the AMS spent time on various services, initiating a book exchange of second-hand books (four thousand were exchanged), starting a medical insurance plan for athletes, and getting involved in a reorganization of the campus employment bureau.

They Do Things Differently Here: The visiting editor of the student newspaper at the University of Toronto was shocked to discover that at UBC the male and female students sat together in the cafeteria and the library. He also noted how different it was that the students at UBC were the ones raising the money for campus buildings and that there were no residences for students on campus (those wouldn't come till much later). The students were younger too: admission age at UBC was sixteen.

A gathering of students in the University Auditorium in 1925. A similar meeting took place in 1932 to protest that year's cuts.

governance at UBC, an AMS committee warned against "the undue power and influence" the business manager might exert on the student executive. It recommended changing the position's title to business secretary and excluding it from Council.

Coincidentally (or not), the business manager, Arnold Henderson, resigned at the end of the year and was replaced not by a new business manager, but by an accountant, Sutherland Horn.

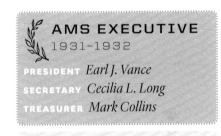

AMS EXECUTIVE
1931–1932

PRESIDENT *Earl J. Vance*
SECRETARY *Cecilia L. Long*
TREASURER *Mark Collins*

UBYSSEY EDITOR
Himie Koshevoy/Wilfred Lee

Eligibility, Shmeligibility: Poor Louis Chodat. Ruled ineligible to play for UBC sports teams under the new eligibility rules for students, he decided to play for two non-UBC teams (in rugby and basketball). Uh, uh, uh, said Student Council, fining him $5 for playing for non-UBC teams. When he refused to pay the fine, the AMS asked the University to suspend him, which it did.

The *Ubyssey* commended the AMS and the University for these actions; the AMS in this situation had shown that it had real power, said the paper, though noting that the general student body was more on the side of the "offender" and conceding that it was "pretty hard luck" for him.

Beware the Paid Staff: In one of the earliest investigations of student

A UBC rugby player in 1930. Presumably not Louis Chodat.

1932 TO 1933

Depression Woes: The Depression meant funding cuts, layoffs, and a drop in enrolment, resulting in less money in fees for the AMS. The reduction in fee revenue, and also a desire not to be seen to be partying in the midst of hard times, led the AMS to retrench in several areas. Several dances were cancelled, including the annual Science Ball, much to the chagrin of the Sciencemen. There were no intercollegiate athletic games, and there was even talk of cancelling the *Totem*.

Cutting Too Much? Somehow the result of the retrenchment was an AMS surplus of $3,900. The *Ubyssey*, which had originally congratulated AMS treasurer Mark Collins for keeping a tight rein on the budget, now questioned what he had done, wondering about the point of accumulating a surplus of student funds. The paper asked: Does the AMS exist for the sake of the students, or the students for the sake of the AMS? A letter writer criticized the AMS for being "tight-fisted."

Collins responded by saying the surplus was misleading; it was more a contingency that would be spent in the course of the year.

Treasurer Mark Collins.

Student Self-Government? It turns out that even at this late date AMS Council minutes were being submitted to UBC's Faculty Committee on Student Affairs, which returned one set "with a reservation" about the number of dances the AMS was set to approve. The *Ubyssey* noted that if Council did not reduce the number, the Faculty Committee would (in order to keep embarrassing reports about excessive social activities out of the regular Vancouver newspapers).

Always Look on the Bright Side: The *Ubyssey* noted that one result of the cutbacks was a reduction in the number of professors, which meant that one of the University's faculty lounges was being offered to the AMS for the use of the students.

On the other hand, a reduction in the number of janitors meant the campus did not look as clean as previously: litter was accumulating.

Whither the Stadium? The students had raised $20,000 for a stadium, but all that had been built was a playing field, and it was in bad condition, a "mud hole" said the *Ubyssey*, because of an inadequate drainage system that had been installed in what had formerly been a swamp. The AMS asked the Board of Governors to levy a new student fee to pay for improvements, but the Board said no, so the students launched a campaign for voluntary donations to raise the $1,400 needed.

Election Controversy: Treasurer Mark Collins won election as AMS president, but then resigned because of election irregularities. Council called a by-election, but no one but Collins sought to run, and he became president after all.

The *Ubyssey* noted that for some years a preferential system of voting (rather than first past the post) had been in use, though it was nowhere authorized in the constitution.

Swastikas? The *Totem* this year for some reason adopted swastikas as a design feature on some pages: not exactly the Nazi version, but the left-facing ones found in some Asian and Indigenous contexts. Still, this was the year Hitler took power, and one wonders what they were thinking.

Notables: Nathan Nemetz, a leading light as a debater on campus, went on to a distinguished law career, becoming Chief Justice of British Columbia and also chancellor of UBC.

AMS EXECUTIVE
1932–1933

PRESIDENT *William H. Whimster*
SECRETARY *Rosemary E. Winslow*
TREASURER *Mark Collins*

UBYSSEY EDITOR *F. St. John Madeley*

LEFT The playing field being built.

ABOVE Strange symbols in the 1933 *Totem*.

1933 TO 1934

How the Thunderbird Came to UBC: The UBC sports teams had no nickname, the *Ubyssey* sports department suddenly realized in the fall of 1933. The teams were known as the Blue and Gold (UBC's colours) or the Varsity or UBC, but they didn't have a name like Tigers or Lions, the way other schools did, something to strike fear into the opposition.

So the sports writers (notably Clarence Idyll) started a campaign to give the teams a name. The *Ubyssey* held a vote, and the winner was . . . Seagulls! No, no, no, said the *Ubyssey*; we can't name our teams the Seagulls; we'd look ridiculous: Vote again. And so they did, and chose Thunderbird, the mythical creature from Indigenous culture.

In 2014, feeling sorry for the poor Seagull, who had been so cruelly deprived of victory eighty years before, the AMS Communications Department created Gus the Seagull as the mascot for the new Student Union Building (a.k.a. the AMS Student Nest), but Thunderbird remains the official name and mascot of UBC's sports teams.

Clarence Idyll brought the Thunderbird to UBC.

LEFT The Thunderbird logo.

RIGHT Gus the Seagull.

The World Beyond: The Depression continued to make its presence felt: enrolment was down again, and the AMS had to reduce its budget. Beyond that, there was a growing interest this year (and the year before) in political developments overseas, with debates and lectures about Italian fascism, the rise of Hitler, and "the Moscow road." Closer to home, the *Ubyssey* editorialized about anti-Asian, especially anti-Japanese, discrimination, noting that Japanese Canadians were still denied the vote. This didn't stop the paper from continuing to publish a long-running serial about a fictional Chinese villain named Chang Suey, who in one episode is chased by the Queen of the Apaches.

War or Peace? Concern about overseas developments, especially the drift to war, led some students to begin organizing for peace. In February, a new student organization, the UBC International Relations Group, was able to convince local churches to let its members speak from the pulpits on the threat of war and the need to work for peace.

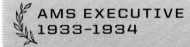

Playtime: Despite the hard times, two AMS clubs mounted big entertainment productions. The Musical Society put on *The Mikado*, Gilbert and Sullivan's operetta set in Japan (an oddly appropriate, or inappropriate, choice given the discussions this year on anti-Japanese discrimination). Then the Players' Club put on a lavish production of Bernard Shaw's *Caesar and Cleopatra*.

Too Many Clubs? AMS Council decided to look into the proliferation of student clubs, expressing concern that there were now forty-one, some of which were quite small and inactive. (By 2014–15, the number of clubs would rise to about four hundred, though it's true that was for a campus population of fifty thousand students rather than the fifteen hundred in 1933–34.)

Besides official AMS clubs, there were more informal groupings, like the Science Girls Club (later known as the University Nurses Club).

LEFT 1934 production of *The Mikado* by the AMS Musical Society.

RIGHT Nursing students wearing Science Girls Club sweaters.

AMS EXECUTIVE 1933–1934

PRESIDENT *Mark Collins*
SECRETARY *Isobel M. ("Peggy") Wales*
TREASURER *Jack A. Shaneman*

UBYSSEY EDITOR *Norman Hacking*

1934 TO 1935

The Main Library in a 1935 blizzard: broken windows still to come.

What Do They Put in Their Snowballs? Some not-so-proud traditions continued this year. In the fall, though there was no old-style hazing (much to the dismay of the *Ubyssey*, surprisingly), the newer tradition of fights between sophomores and freshmen continued, with dunkings in the lily pond and competitive bonfires. In January after a snowfall the Engineers and Artsmen fought snowball battles, breaking scores of windows, which the *Ubyssey* almost tried to justify. "A window or so is bound to be broken in the excitement," the paper editorialized, and joked about improved ventilation.

But the paper did worry that the University authorities, who had already expressed dismay over student fighting, might step in and threaten "Student Self-Government." It was up to Student Council and its Discipline Committee to keep a lid on things, or power would shift away from the students, the editorial writers warned.

Meanwhile, the *Totem* at the end of the year summoned up the long-standing pseudo-Indigenous motif, saying it was up to the "wise men of the village" to curb the enthusiasm of "the younger men of the tribe."

War or Peace, Round 2: There was more campaigning against militarism this year. New organizations formed, including an Anti-War Council, spearheaded by groups such as the Student Christian Movement. The anti-war groups denounced "the menace of imperialist war" and found themselves denounced in turn as communistic, echoing an earlier charge from a former attorney-general of the

province (R.H. Pooley) that the University was teaching communism. That charge prompted a rebuttal from UBC President Klinck.

Gowns and Gowns: In the fall the senior class voted to wear academic gowns, much to the amusement of the *Ubyssey*. (The gowns turned out to be too expensive, however, so nothing came of it.) However, gowns of a different sort made an appearance the following spring, when the idea of electing a queen for the Junior Prom was introduced. This ran into a slight snag when bal-

"OFFICER, LOOK!"

GOWN KITS

Do You Feel Self-Conscious About Your Gown?

Illustrated on the left is the suave omlette-dish-disguise-kit-case for the introspective student. To the right is our distingue sports model for Sciencemen and Aggies.

This guarantees complete inconspicuousity in street cars and beer parlors.

LEFT Communism on campus?

ABOVE The *Ubyssey*'s humour page makes fun of the academic gown idea.

UBC president Norman MacKenzie with a later campus queen.

Did Someone Mention the Stadium?
The stadium meanwhile remained in the planning stages. A general meeting of the students voted to repair the playing fields first before embarking on the construction of a grandstand.

A Female President? No, not this year. But for the first time since the First World War, a woman (Peggy Wales) ran for the office. Unlike Norah Coy in 1917–18, however, she lost, and it would be the 1980s before another woman became president by winning a campus-wide election (though in the 1950s and again in the 1970s a woman became president after a resignation).

lot stuffing was discovered during the voting, but it began a long tradition of campus queens.

If Only Someone Had Fallen In: The snowstorm in January led to extensive flooding, partly stemming from the drainage system at the site of the planned stadium. The results included the washing away of two bridges and the creation of a huge chasm on campus, which drew the attention of many curious students. Indulging in some black humour, the *Ubyssey* said that if only someone had fallen in, it would have brought lasting fame to their Alma Mater.

Peggy Wales.

Phrateres: A more successful accomplishment for the women of UBC was the establishment of a chapter of Phrateres, an American organization for women both in and out of sororities. The *Ubyssey* wondered about the point and foresaw problems, but Phrateres lasted into the twenty-first century.

Phrateres in later years.

Corn Flakes and *Reader's Digest*: The *Ubyssey* ran a survey and announced that most students ate Corn Flakes for breakfast (though one respondent said she preferred "Gripe Nuts," which the paper found amusing; there were lots of spelling mistakes, they said). Students drank Coke and ginger ale and beer (men only), and read *Reader's Digest*. The paper pronounced itself pleased that most of the students had bank accounts and insurance policies.

AMS EXECUTIVE 1934-1935

PRESIDENT *R. Murray Mather*
SECRETARY *Isobel M. ("Peggy") Wales*
TREASURER *James M. Malkin*

UBYSSEY EDITOR *Archie Thompson*

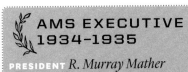

The campus chasm.

1935-1945

OLD AND NEW

Tuition protests, a lack of student housing, overcrowded buses, a new student union building that kept being delayed: one might think this was 2015, but instead it was the late 1930s. Some things never change, it seems, but in some ways the Alma Mater Society before and during the Second World War was quite different from the AMS in the twenty-first century.

For one thing it was much less independent. The UBC president was still the honorary AMS president. Student Council minutes had to be approved by a University committee. The phrase "Alma Mater" (not something heard anymore) was used in an ambiguous way so it was hard to tell whether it referred to the student society, the University, or both. Indeed, the AMS and the University were very much part of the same organism in those days, with much less separation than in later years.

And then there was the World War. That was different, though it is surprising how distant it remained for most of the war period. The First World War seemed to hit home harder; there was much more focus on the casualties then. Of course, there was much talk of the war effort, and students did go off to fight, but a lot of the focus was on whether the students who remained behind were draft dodgers. And by the last year of the war other issues entirely dominated the agenda, many of them about changes that would make the AMS much more like the AMS of later years: Council reform, the introduction of referendums, a push for lower bus fares, and so on.

So this decade was a transitional period, from a simpler time obsessed with borrowing Indigenous trappings to something more recognizably modern. And it brought UBC its first student union building, even if it was four years late.

1935 TO 1936

A Student Union Building: Suddenly there were plans to build a student union building on campus, to be called Brock Hall, after the Dean of Applied Science, Reginald Brock, and his wife, Mildred, who died in an airplane crash in the summer of 1935.

The *Ubyssey* editorialized that such a building would provide a "focal point where U.B.C. life will centre." Writing in the *Vancouver Sun*, Alan P. Morley (a UBC student journalist given a regular column in the *Sun* called "The Students' Angle") said that especially in the absence of student residences such a centre was needed to make UBC less of a "daytime college" and to help mature the new students, "smoothing off their rough corners."

Money was taken from the funds raised for a Women's Union building, the project from the 1920s that never came to fruition, and a campaign was launched to raise additional money by way of dances,

sports events, and direct donations. The Engineers held a lottery for a puppy. Still, the AMS was falling short of the $30,000 they had committed themselves to, so at a general meeting at the end of the year the students agreed to float a bond issue for $10,000.

The plan was to complete the building in 1936, in time for UBC's twenty-first anniversary. It would be a sort of "coming of age" project, since twenty-one was the age of majority in those days. But in the end, it was not till 1940 that Brock Hall finally opened.

Reginald Brock, Dean of Applied Science, after whom Brock Hall would be named.

Student Power: The students lobbied for a longer lunch hour and a proper intramurals program, as well as the hiring of two physical education instructors, and the University agreed.

The Auditorium in 1935: who should get to use it, the students or the Vancouver Institute?

Lack of Student Power: The students complained in vain about the giving away of space in the Auditorium to the Vancouver Institute when it was needed for a student event. And the students also complained about the new adult education program UBC introduced, which meant that regular professors would be away from campus for weeks at a time in order to teach on Vancouver Island or in the Interior. "The registered students at the college pay high fees for the privilege of a higher education," said the *Ubyssey*, commenting that

Dr. G.G. Sedgewick, noted UBC professor and head of the English department. He was one of the professors who was to be away from campus teaching adult education courses.

an extension system was all well and good, but it shouldn't be done at the expense of the regular students.

A Different Class: Speaking of privilege, the *Ubyssey*, in noting that the annual snake parade was treated with kid gloves by the police, contrasted with the much rougher treatment accorded to a march of the unemployed a few months earlier, said, "We happen to be a privileged set instead of social outcasts" and thus are "humored when we choose to paint the town red." But it warned students not to try the patience of those who helped pay for their education.

An Oxford Class? In a debate reminiscent of the one a couple of years before in which the Oxford Union resolved not to fight for King and Country, UBC students voted against the idea of fighting Italian aggression in Ethiopia. But this manifestation of pacifism was rare in 1935–36, in contrast to the year before, prompting the *Ubyssey* to lament the passing of the days when student peace societies would rail against the menace of war.

No More Fighting (sort of): After years of rowdy behaviour at initiation events and of dunking parties and other physical conflicts between students on campus, the Senate stepped in and ordered a ban on any "clash of students" that might become "injurious to any person or property." The *Ubyssey*, which in previous years was rather tolerant of the rowdiness, this year condemned it as "hooliganism."

That was in September. By February, after a snowfall, however, the students were at it again, holding a snowball fight (Engineers against Artsmen) that broke fifty-one panes of glass in campus windows, causing damage of $200 ($3,535 in present-day dollars) and attracting the attention of the downtown press. The *Ubyssey* was furious, condemning the "stupidities" of "pampered and ungrateful students."

Slates: As election time rolled around in March, the *Ubyssey* complained that there were too many candidates running, confusing the electorate. It would be better to simplify things by a party system, the paper said, a suggestion that got taken up with a vengeance in later years: "slates" became so powerful in the 1990s that no independent candidate could get elected. (Slates were banned in 2004, returning the AMS to a system of voting for independent candidates.)

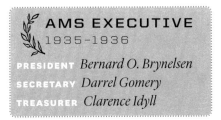

AMS EXECUTIVE
1935-1936

PRESIDENT *Bernard O. Brynelsen*
SECRETARY *Darrel Gomery*
TREASURER *Clarence Idyll*

UBYSSEY EDITOR *John Cornish*

TOP The campus in June 1936, having survived the winter snowball fight. The Main Library in the distance, Arts and Agriculture closer up.

BOTTOM And the Science building on Main Mall, which had featured so prominently in the Great Trek, now very peaceful.

61

1936 TO 1937

A Bunch of the Boys: Despite a ban by both the Senate and Student Council, students held a snake parade downtown in October, disrupting traffic, yelling, singing, causing damage, and resulting in one serious injury when a student had his arm pushed through a car's windshield. The *Vancouver Sun* ran a headline saying, "Student May Lose a Hand" (but he didn't).

The one bit of silver lining was that a campaign sprang up to raise money for the injured student (Donald Parham), which led to the creation of an Injured Students' Fund.

More Boys' Antics: Even before the snake parade, UBC students attracted unwanted attention from the regular press because of a series of near riots on campus resulting from fighting between frosh and sophomores. Students threw ink bottles, eggs, fruit, and sandwiches,

and even used a fire hose, resulting in what the *Province* newspaper called "black eyes, torn shirts and watery destruction."

The *Ubyssey* called it a "deplorable exhibition" and said the problem was that the old style initiation activities, such as competitive bonfires, had been banned, leaving the students with no organized outlet for their enthusiasm.

New Clubs: Two major clubs were founded this year. What had previously been an informal group of Chinese students became an official AMS club, eventually to be known as the Chinese Varsity Club.

And the year also saw the formation of the Film Society (later known as Filmsoc), which quickly gained four hundred members and began showing offbeat movies, such as *Thunder over Mexico* (based on the work of the Soviet director Sergei Eisenstein), *The Plow that Broke the Plains* (a documentary on the agricultural problems in the US Dust Bowl), and a film version of the opera *Fra Diavolo*.

Election Slates: Again there was talk of the possibility of students organizing into parties or "slates" to run in the AMS elections. But nothing came of it. Instead, the elections suffered from a severe case of apathy. The president and three other members of Student Council were chosen by acclamation.

Where Are the Buildings? Students asked what was happening to the project to build a student union

Construction finally got underway on the stadium.

building. What's happened to our money, they said? And there were questions about the long-delayed stadium project.

The stadium moved forward more quickly: a general meeting at the end of March approved a second bond issue to raise another $40,000 for it, and construction began in the summer. The Brock Hall student union building did not move forward quite as fast. All the AMS president could report was that somewhat less than half of the money required had been raised.

He also reported that since the arrival at the new campus students had raised $138,000 for campus buildings and facilities (from the gymnasium in the 1920s to the playing fields, stadium, and proposed new student union building of the 1930s).

1937 TO 1938

The Stadium: The big story first term was the long awaited opening of the stadium on October 2. Paid for with $40,000 raised by the AMS and constructed over the summer, it hosted two games on opening day after a ceremony attended by the provincial minister of education. "This is unique among educational institutions," the minister said, referring to the student role in raising money for UBC's buildings. AMS president Dave Carey said the stadium was a monument to the students, and a conference of the National Federation of Canadian University Students praised UBC's students for taking the initiative in projects like these.

The stadium lasted until 1968, when it was demolished to make way for the second student union building (the Old SUB).

Crisis: The big story of the second term was the crisis initiated when the Board of Governors, citing overcrowding and a lack of facilities, introduced a $25 tuition increase and announced a limit on registration of two thousand. (After dropping in the early years of the Depression, UBC enrolment had rebounded to nearly 2,500 in 1937–38).

The students mounted a protest campaign, calling for the provincial government to provide more funding and for the Board of Governors to postpone the tuition increase. The first head of the campaign committee was Morris Belkin, who went on to become a noted businessman (the Belkin Art Gallery is named after him and his wife). Another notable on campus at that time, Norman DePoe, who went on to become a respected CBC reporter, suggested that the AMS and the University should both look into other sources of revenue, such as business revenue, a suggestion not acted on at the time but which became the modus operandi in later years.

Student Council asked to see the University's financial statements. The *Ubyssey* said it was time there was a student on the Board of Governors, a suggestion that would not be acted on until 1974.

No Politics Please, We're Students: A request from some students to form a Conservative club prompted Council to issue an order banning all political clubs, on the grounds that they might unduly influence campus politics. The *Ubyssey* found the suggestion ludicrous and decried Council's actions as a violation of democratic rights. A compromise was then reached in which all political groups could combine into a single Political Discussion Club, which promptly split into Conservative, Liberal, Socialist, Communist, and other factions.

On the Air: The AMS launched a weekly half-hour radio show, called *Varsity Time*, on the local radio station CJOR, in an attempt to create some positive publicity for the University and its students. The following year *Varsity Time* was replaced by a full-fledged AMS club, the Radio Society, which began planning several shows and recruiting on-air talent, writers, and technicians. Eventually, this would lead to the creation of a student-run radio station, CiTR.

The stadium.

A Death in Spain: World events were rather in the background this year, but the *Ubyssey* did note the death in Spain of a UBC graduate who was fighting in the Spanish Civil War on the side of the Loyalists.

Debaters Win: For the first time UBC students won the prestigious McGoun Cup for the western Canadian debating championship. The UBC students, one of whom was Morris Belkin, defeated teams from Alberta and Saskatchewan on the topic of the effectiveness of the League of Nations.

Science Wants Out: For the second year in a row, students in the pure sciences asked to be recognized as distinct from Arts students. In 1936–37 they asked for a separate science faculty; this year they merely asked for a separate science degree. "We don't want a mere arts degree," one of them said. "We don't take cinch courses like history and economics."

However, science and arts remained combined in the Faculty of Arts, and students in physics and chemistry continued to receive BA degrees, until the 1960s.

TOP A Radio Society show in 1939.

BOTTOM Radio Society members on the air in 1941.

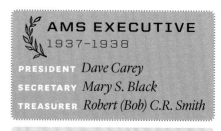

AMS EXECUTIVE
1937-1938

PRESIDENT *Dave Carey*
SECRETARY *Mary S. Black*
TREASURER *Robert (Bob) C.R. Smith*

UBYSSEY **EDITOR** *Kemp Edmonds*

1938 TO 1939

Freshmen sporting dunce caps.

It's Not Easy Being Green: Bonfires were revived, but paradoxically initiation was more peaceful this year (though one student did get slightly burnt at the fire thanks to the ill-advised use of gasoline). There were the usual fisticuffs and tossing of eggs and fruit, but for the first time no property damage. But the poor frosh had to go around in green dunce caps.

Crisis, Part Two: The AMS campaign committee visited the premier in Victoria and had some success, convincing the government to remove the cap on enrolment and increase funding for the University. However, the tuition increase remained in place, leading to calls for a refocusing of the committee's efforts, and at the end of the year the committee was dissolved and a new one put in its place.

One step taken to reduce the pressure on UBC's facilities was to move the start of classes back from 9:00 to 8:30 a.m. (which, with some wartime exceptions, remained the start time till the end of the century, after which it was pushed back even further, to 8:00 a.m.). Another step was to shorten the lunch hour, reducing it from an hour and a half, which provoked protests from the students, who said this made it difficult to take part in intramural sports and other extra-curricular activities.

The Union Building (a.k.a. Brock Hall): The *Ubyssey* lamented that "Union Building" had come to mean "hope deferred," but finally this year funding was secured: $25,000 from the University to go with $50,000 from the AMS. Plans were to begin construction, at last, in the summer of 1939.

Before the money came through, AMS Council passed a motion saying it would look into commercial ventures to pay for the building. However, the Faculty Committee on Student Affairs refused to approve the motion, again demonstrating the limits of student self-government. Plans for the union building included a dance floor, an assembly hall, Council offices, and a dining room. Also space in the basement for the COTC.

65

Gowns Again: The *Ubyssey* editor, who spent much of the year upbraiding the students for poor manners, complained that Council members had abandoned the practice of wearing academic gowns to Council meetings. The result, she said, was disorder—and yet she also complimented Council for getting so much done (Brock Hall, the campaign, etc.). Perhaps the gowns just got in the way.

Thievery Again: Concerned about an outbreak of vandalism and petty theft, Council ordered a crackdown by the Discipline Committee and, oddly, the Big Block Club (the club made up of winners of athletic rewards). The library was especially hit hard this year: books were stolen and mutilated, and the main door was broken no less than five times.

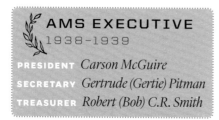

AMS EXECUTIVE
1938–1939

PRESIDENT *Carson McGuire*
SECRETARY *Gertrude (Gertie) Pitman*
TREASURER *Robert (Bob) C.R. Smith*

UBYSSEY EDITOR *Dorothy Cummings*

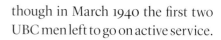

1939 TO 1940

War! The Second World War began the same month students returned to school. The main effect was an upsurge in enlistment in the Canadian Officers Training Corps (COTC) and a decision by the students to donate money to the Red Cross. As the *Ubyssey* commented, however, students on the West Coast were not bothered by "ration cards, blackouts, air raid sirens or . . . air raids." The war was still far away,

UBC's COTC in training.

though in March 1940 the first two UBC men left to go on active service.

CSA: The Canadian Students' Assembly (CSA), was a national student group to which UBC students belonged. It sparked huge controversy by coming out against conscription, leading to charges that it was anti-war and subversive. Student Council suspended its UBC branch, but then reinstated it. The *Ubyssey* at first joined the chorus of attacks, but by the end of the year was saying that the main threat to democracy lay with the CSA's opponents.

Slates (for Real, Maybe): One aspect of the CSA controversy was the accusation during the annual AMS elections that the CSA was assembling a slate of candidates to contest the election and take over control of the AMS. In response to this notion, for which there was actually no evidence, students in the fraternities organized a slate of their own, or so the *Ubyssey* said, muttering darkly about this being like Tammany Hall (the notorious American political machine). Four fraternity men did end up getting elected.

Brock Hall: On a happier note, Brock Hall finally opened at the end of January, though its first weeks were a bit of a letdown. Where are the students, the *Ubyssey* asked? There's a beauti-

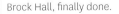
Brock Hall, finally done.

a cartoon imagining a table collapsing in the cafeteria and drowning a student in garbage:

HORRIBLE FATE OF JOE GLOTZ — CRUSHED TO DEATH WHEN KAF TABLE COLLAPSED.

The *Ubyssey*'s cartoonist joins the anti-littering campaign.

ful new building, and no one is using it. Restricted hours may have been part of the problem, or perhaps it would just take students a while to discover a new place to socialize.

Not Gowns Again: Yes, according to a *Ubyssey* article saying there was a campaign to get students to wear them. The article is notable for being written by one Pierre Berton, who went on to fame as a popular historian and broadcaster. He also tried his hand at cartooning this year, portraying his fellow members of "the Pub"—which in those days

meant not a drinking establishment but the AMS Publications Board, in charge of the *Ubyssey*, the *Totem*, etc.

Meanwhile, gowns did at least make it back to Student Council.

Photo ID: The AMS introduced photo ID this year in an attempt to prevent fraudulent misuse of the AMS Pass, introduced a few years earlier to let students get discounts on event admissions. The pass also functioned as a library card, so seems to be the origin of the AMS/ library card that lasted through the century.

Clean Up Your Mess! Student Council launched a campaign this year to get students to take more pride in the appearance of their campus by not littering cigarette butts, matches, bottles, papers, and so forth in the cafeteria, the common rooms, and the classrooms. Joining in the spirit, the *Ubyssey* ran

Pierre Berton's "Pub" cartoon.

AMS EXECUTIVE
1939–1940

PRESIDENT *John Pearson*
SECRETARY *Ruth Hutchinson*
TREASURER *Evan apRoberts/ Jack Stevenson*

UBYSSEY EDITOR *John S. Garrett*

1940 TO 1941

Beast Mode: Pierre Berton seemed to be everywhere this year. Besides being a major contributor to the *Ubyssey*, he was also an announcer on the *Varsity Time* radio show produced by the fledgling Radio Society. To cap it off, he made a memorable appearance in the *Ubyssey*'s annual joke issue as the rampaging beast threatening the library in a clever bit of photo montage done well before the days of Photoshop.

And Others: Pierre Berton was not the only notable to emerge from that year's *Ubyssey*. He made the biggest splash in later life (with his books on the building of the CPR, his appearances on the popular CBC quiz show *Front Page Challenge*, and so on), but the paper in 1940–41 also boasted columnist Lister Sinclair, who went on to become a CBC personality, and Eric Nicol, who wrote humour columns for the paper under the pen name Jabez, and who later became known for his numerous humour books. He also wrote the farce *Her Scienceman Lover*, which became a mainstay on campus for decades. And there was also reporter Les Bewley, who went on to become a noted (someone would say notorious) British Columbia judge and newspaper columnist.

Less Beastly: Pierre Berton at work.

Totie: Also everywhere this year, at least in the *Totem*, was a stylized, animated totem pole known as Totie, the *Totem* mascot who decorated many pages in the annual. This was part of the long-running Indigenous

BEAST STALKS CAMPUS

The Ubyssey

PUBLISHED TWICE WEEKLY BY THE PUBLICATIONS BOARD OF THE UNIVERSITY OF BRITISH COLUMBIA

VOL. XXIII.   VANCOUVER, B. C., FRIDAY, MARCH 28, 1941   No. 40

COLONEL SHRUM FIRED

With Enthusiasm For Training Corps

● **"I AM FIRED** with enthusiasm over the way the C.O.T.C. has been carrying on lately "Colonel G. M. Shrum told the Ubyssey Thursday.

At the same time Colonel Shrum denied rumours that the Corps would be sent to Manchuria to quell an impending evolution.

"I am totally ignorant," the Colonel asserted. "Of any move of this nature.

The Colonel branded recent letters to the editor of the Vancouver Daily Province, which charged apathy on the part of University students as being "rotten" to the Corps."

'So many students have rushed to join up with the Corps that we just don't know our own strength

Quits

—photo by the late Bill Grand.
Dr. Kaye Lamb: "I think something has come over the library."

Sciencemen Invent Beast In Spare Time

● **Terror struck the campus** late Thursday when a huge monster escaped from the Science building and bounded across the campus in mighty leaps, leaving a trail of devastation in its wake.

Berton as the Beast.

theme among the students, elaborated this year by the *Totem* editors, who went on at length about how the *Totem* was a "tribal record" produced in the "Publications tepee."

This year the mascot (actually introduced the year before under the name Sho-You-Hwa) wore a steel helmet, thus combining ancient Indigenous with modern military.

Life While at War: In the first term the *Ubyssey* said the campus was only "lightly affected" by the war, but things became more serious as the year progressed. There was talk of

Totie, the AMS mascot.

how military training might affect the students: if a full summer of training was demanded of all the men, many of them would not be able to take the summer jobs they needed to pay for continuing their education. It was also suggested that students in some disciplines (notably engineering) would serve the war effort better by continuing their

studies, perhaps even accelerating them, rather than being trained to become foot soldiers.

The war also meant a reduction in inter-collegiate sports and some other extra-curricular activities, but Council was dedicated to maintaining regular activities as much as possible, though both the Players' Club and the Musical Society said they might have to put on all-female productions since the male students were too busy with compulsory training to take part in plays or operettas.

Who's in Charge Here? Questions were raised at an AMS general meeting about who was running Brock Hall and the other two student facilities (the gymnasium and the stadium). Where

A soldier and two co-eds: the lighter side of war.

was rental revenue going? Who decides on bookings? A motion was passed directing Student Council to seek greater control. The *Ubyssey* said the students should never have just handed the buildings over to the University. The

AMS president said in fact there was joint control through various committees. It was all very confusing.

The good news, though, was that Brock Hall was better used this year, in part because Council persuaded the Board of Governors to allow it to be kept open in the evening. There were mixers held there, and the Junior Prom. Clubs could also meet there in the evenings.

Who's in Charge, Part Two: The student body and the *Ubyssey* were also upset by the departure of Sutherland Horn, the long-time accountant for the AMS. Again the circumstances were confusing; there were charges that Council this year had not given the accountant sufficient authority, but this was denied. The importance of the permanent staff for maintaining continuity was brought up.

In the event, Horn returned after only a short absence, but then left for good in 1943.

Student Housing: There were still no student residences on campus, but this year saw four student housing co-ops formed off campus, three male and one female. Four years earlier there had been a similar co-op (Salisbury Lodge). It had disappeared, but there were high hopes for these four new ones.

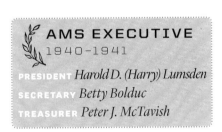

AMS EXECUTIVE
1940-1941

PRESIDENT *Harold D. (Harry) Lumsden*
SECRETARY *Betty Bolduc*
TREASURER *Peter J. McTavish*

UBYSSEY EDITOR *Jack Margeson*

1941 TO 1942

March March March: The war continued like a muffled drumbeat in the background this year. There was drilling and fundraising and at the end of the year an air raid drill. Also an armoury. With the expansion of the war to the Pacific, UBC students (or at least the *Ubyssey* editors) now felt different: from something far away, the war now seemed closer to home; it was as if they were on the front line.

Japanese Canadians: The declaration of war between Canada and Japan also led to a major issue for UBC's students of Japanese origin. Like other Japanese Canadians, they were forced to leave the coast for internment camps inland and thus had to abandon their studies. In 2012, in an attempt to redress this wrong, UBC granted honorary degrees to the seventy-six Japanese Canadians whose studies had been cut short in 1941–42.

The Lighter Side: Students attempted to retain their sense of humour despite the war. The *Totem* commented that the students training in gas masks looked like men from Mars, and after the air raid drill the *Ubyssey* commented slyly that some of the couples who went off into the bushes in accordance with drill procedures didn't come back for some hours.

Her Scienceman Lover: Pierre Berton was gone, but Eric Nicol and Lister Sinclair teamed up with the Players Club to put on one of the most successful productions in its history: Nicol's play, *Her Scienceman Lover.* Directed by Sinclair, the play was such a hit that an encore performance was demanded, and the Players Club kept putting it on for the next thirty-eight years as a "Welcome to the Frosh" tradition.

Student-soldiers training in the new Armoury.

A cartoon portrayal of *Her Scienceman Lover* from 1952.

Aliens? No, just UBC students in gas masks in front of the Main Library.

More on the Light Side: One of the first joke clubs was formed: the Club for Tired Old Business Men. And in what seems to have been another first for clubs, this year saw a Club Week in which clubs were urged to reach out to prospective new members.

Continuity: The AMS worried about continuity because of the continuing saga of its accountant, the head of the permanent AMS staff, who left, then returned, then left again. Without continuity from him, it was suggested that a special advisory body consisting of the past five AMS presidents be created to advise Student Council. Rules were also passed calling for the newly elected president and treasurer to attend meetings of Council even before taking office and for the last meeting of the old Council to be a joint one with the new Council, all to aid in transitioning and smooth functioning of the Society.

Clean-up: The AMS Discipline Committee cracked down on litterers this year, holding hearings for three students charged with leaving papers and bottles in the parking lot. When one of them didn't show up, she was charged with contempt and fined $2. The penalty for the littering was suspension of the AMS Pass, depriving the guilty parties of AMS discounts.

Paying the Executive: For the first time the AMS, at a general meeting, approved payments to at least some of the AMS Executive: the president and the treasurer, along with the *Ubyssey* editor. The argument was that because of their duties, these individuals could not work at paying jobs, so payment was necessary to allow everyone to seek to fill these positions, including those who would normally work to pay for their tuition.

It is noteworthy that the AMS in this era regularly managed to gather one thousand students or more for several general meetings a year. In later years this would become virtually impossible, despite (or because of) the greater number of students on campus.

Blame the Writer: The *Ubyssey* reported in October that librarians were still upset with an article on the John Dos Passos book *1919*, which the *Ubyssey* had run in its Literary Supplement the previous March. The article, by Lionel Salt, described the book as being "dirty" and went into some detail to explain how. The result was a run on copies of all of Dos Passos's works at the UBC library, many of which were never returned.

Despite this, the library decided this year for the first time to allow students to browse in the reserve stacks rather than having to submit call slips for specific books.

UBC MEN IN ACTIVE SERVICE: 300

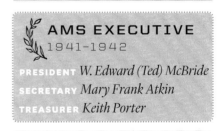

AMS EXECUTIVE
1941-1942
PRESIDENT *W. Edward (Ted) McBride*
SECRETARY *Mary Frank Atkin*
TREASURER *Keith Porter*

UBYSSEY EDITOR *Archie Paton*

1942 TO 1943

Draft Dodgers? Students were exempt from the draft, which prompted accusations that they weren't contributing significantly to the war effort. Words like "draft dodgers" and "slackers" were used. There was also talk at this time that the government might shut down the Arts faculty in favour of disciplines more closely allied to war work.

The *Ubyssey* took great offence at this sort of talk, and in fact the government officially declared that it was against shutting down Arts. The *Ubyssey* took this to be official endorsement of the idea that university work was important, both during the war and looking ahead to postwar reconstruction.

The government did say that it would not continue to exempt "incompetent mediocre" students, and the *Ubyssey* noted the extra effort put in by students at exam time to make sure they got passing grades.

The Women Get More Involved: At the urging of the women themselves, UBC this year introduced compulsory war work for the female students, including training in first aid, home nursing, map reading, motor mechanics, and munitions inspecting. The following year a Red Cross corps was formed, and the women got snazzy uniforms.

Female Firsts: Mamooks, the pep club, recruited female cheerleaders for the first time, ending the tradition of male-only yell leaders. The moribund Arts Men's Undergraduate Society decided to invite women to join, in an effort to revive itself, in the process becoming simply the Arts Undergraduate Society (or AUS). And a woman ran for AMS president for the first time since 1935 (but she lost).

Transit Woes: Wartime gas rationing meant fewer students drove to campus, which caused overloading of the buses on the one bus route to UBC (from 10th and Sasamat). Not all students could get on the bus they needed to catch to make it to class on time. Because of this phenomenon (what a later age would call pass-ups), UBC decided to stagger its course schedule, beginning some classes as early as 8:10.

Food Woes: Rationing also hit food supplies, causing concern that the

The Red Cross corps marching across campus.

Women sewing for the war effort.

cafeteria would soon be having meat-less days and might run out of coffee.

Sit Properly! The AMS Discipline Committee cracked down on students sitting on the arms of chairs in Brock and on students gambling in the cafeteria.

The Fee Is Too D–n High: Graduating students protested the $15 graduating fee and asked the Board of Governors for an accounting. The Board refused, and the graduating students threatened not to pay, but in the end gave in after asking the AMS to look into the question further. A compromise was reached in 1945 under which students would pay $3 a year instead of a lump sum in their final year.

Some Serve More than Once: Sherwood Lett, the first AMS president (who had already served in the First World War), was injured in the Second while serving as a Brigadier at Dieppe. But he recovered and returned to action in Normandy.

And in Other News: The AMS cut back on social activities, eliminating some of its formal dances. UBC president Klinck warned against initiation foolishness, and first week was quite quiet; however, brawling erupted a month later, when the Engineers attacked a meeting of Arts students.

The Parliamentary Forum experimented with Mock Parliaments. Pierre Berton visited and found a "pall of seriousness" on campus. The Great Snow Storm of '43, combined with a lack of fuel, shut the University down for ten days in January.

And after finding that not many students were using Brock Hall at night, evening openings were ended except for Wednesdays.

UBC MEN IN ACTIVE SERVICE: *667 (as of September 1942). Dead, missing in action, or in prisoner of war camps: 68 (as of spring 1943)*

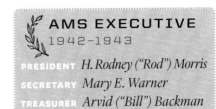

🌿 **AMS EXECUTIVE**
1942–1943
PRESIDENT *H. Rodney ("Rod") Morris*
SECRETARY *Mary E. Warner*
TREASURER *Arvid ("Bill") Backman*

UBYSSEY EDITOR *Andy Snaddon*

1943 TO 1944

Hello Sailor: The navy came to campus this year. The air force too. The Armoury was expanded. It seemed as if the students' commitment to the war was deepening. And yet after a while it all seemed to fade into the background. The biggest war issue at Christmas seemed to be the question of who would pass their exams and who would not. UBC at this time had a system of dismissing students who did not achieve a high enough average in December; unlucky students would become BACs (Bounced at Christmas). This was bad enough in ordinary years, but in 1943–44 it meant losing one's deferment and being exposed to the draft.

So there was anxiety in the air, almost as if the stories of students wanting to escape the war were true. But there was still drilling and fundraising, and sailors on campus who were learning "knots and splices, bends and hitches." And a great

many UBC men were already overseas, many of them never to return.

Brock and the Caf and Who Owns the Tables? One effect of the war was to reduce the number of janitors (they presumably were off fighting). This led to problems keeping Brock Hall open. It was also behind the renewed call for students to pitch in to keep the campus clean, a problem that was especially keen in the cafeteria, where Student Council threatened to rescind the right to reserve tables for those who were too messy. The table reservation issue would loom larger later in the decade.

Frats: The fraternities and the sororities were the main groups reserving cafeteria tables (and coming under fire as a result). The frats also had to weather charges of violating their own rules on "rushing" (i.e., recruiting), and the *Ubyssey* published a poll showing a near even split among the students over whether the fraternities had any value. Fraternities would become increasingly controversial over the next decade.

You've Come a Long Way, Baby (or Not): After much debate, the AMS sent delegates off to a Western Universities Conference. The delegates came back noting that they were somewhat out of step with opinion elsewhere. Whereas delegates from other schools argued that universities were for the students, the AMS delegates emphasized the responsibilities of students to their university, adding that student government must cooperate with the Administration and was not independent.

TOP Naval cadets.

MIDDLE Air force cadets.

BOTTOM Army cadets.

74

They Shall Not Pass

Not a call to arms, but a fear about Christmas exams.

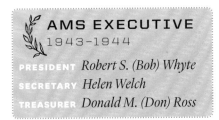

A student thrown in the pond for initiation in 1941: a rarer occurrence in 1943.

The Shape of Things to Come: But if the AMS seemed behind the times in some ways, it was also floating ideas that foreshadowed later developments. Council pushed for reduced bus fares for students (shades of the twenty-first-century U-Pass), the *Ubyssey* suggested holding a plebiscite (shades of the referendums that would become a natural part of the AMS landscape in later years). Even the obstinate delegates to the Universities Conference suggested that it might be time to follow the lead of other schools and put student representatives from each of the faculties on Student Council, a proposal that would take almost two decades to implement (at this time Council was a small group, the Dirty Nine some called it, elected at large across campus).

Progressives: A new discussion club was formed this year with the aim of pushing the University to offer "progressive leadership" to the rest of society. One of the founders of the club was Bruce Yorke, later a housing activist and Vancouver city councillor associated with the Coalition of Progressive Electors (COPE).

Trouble in the Office: Sutherland Horn left again, leaving the AMS without a manager to run the office, and Council decided there was no need for such a manager: the students could run things themselves. It would save money, they said. The *Ubyssey* agreed that it would save money, but said the cost in inefficiencies and inconvenience was too high.

An End to Foolishness? Initiation was quiet this year. Too quiet, said the *Ubyssey*: where is the green of yesterday? There was only one case of someone being dunked in the Library lily pond. But not to worry: in November a three-way brawl between Arts, Agriculture, and Engineering became so boisterous that the noise forced some lectures to be curtailed. This inflamed the *Ubyssey*, which criticized the "childishness" and worried about the reaction downtown from taxpayers who might not take kindly to the draft-exempt students spending their time in such activities.

Then in February snowball fights caused three broken windows. *Plus ça change . . .*

AMS EXECUTIVE
1943-1944

PRESIDENT *Robert S. (Bob) Whyte*
SECRETARY *Helen Welch*
TREASURER *Donald M. (Don) Ross*

UBYSSEY EDITOR *Margaret Reid*

1944 TO 1945

The War Is Over, Isn't It? Well, not quite, but everyone was acting as if it was. UBC installed a new president, Norman MacKenzie (replacing Leonard Klinck), who told the students the war was drawing to a close and it was time to look forward. He foresaw an era of growth, and the *Ubyssey* agreed, urging him to look into opening new faculties (medicine, law, etc.). The provincial government agreed too, promising $5 million for expansion, which the *Ubyssey* said would be very useful in putting up the new buildings needed because the number of students had increased again, causing strain on facilities.

As a sign of the growth of the University, so many students showed up at Brock Hall for the annual frosh reception that the old tradition of Student Council members introducing each individual freshman and "freshette" to the senior UBC administrators had to

be abandoned halfway through to leave time for dancing.

The War Is (Almost) Over, Part Two: The *Ubyssey* decided it didn't have to worry about paper rationing any more, and went from two issues a week to three. Food rationing eased in the cafeteria. A Red Cross blood drive for the war was disappointing, perhaps because of a feeling that the war was already won. And generally speaking the students and the AMS were moving on to other things.

Everything Old Is New Again: Snake parades were back. There were at least three of them, including one by Arts and one by Science in addition to the general one in September. The AMS revived an old accident insurance plan for injuries to students. The Brock Dining Hall reopened after a two-year closure, and the National Federation of Canadian University Students was revived, with AMS president Dick Bibbs becoming its president.

UBC's President MacKenzie greeting first year students at the frosh reception.

Dick Bibbs, president of the AMS and of the national students' federation.

Join a Club! Somewhat reminiscent of old-time college spirit editorials, the *Ubyssey* bemoaned the fact that there were students on campus who did little more than frequent the library and the lecture halls. Become a well-rounded person, the paper said; don't be a "satchel slave"; learn to interact with the others. The focus, however, unlike before the war, was more on individual improvement rather than on serving the collectivity (or tribe). Indigenous

Satchel slaves? Students studying in the library in 1949.

was Herb Capozzi, who was a leading figure on the freshman basketball team, and who went on to a career in pro sports, first as a player in the Canadian Football League, then as general manager of the BC Lions. He also served as an MLA in the provincial legislature.

At Least They Weren't Texting: Campus litter continued to be an issue, and the *Ubyssey* came up with a new theory to explain it: it was because students wouldn't sit down to eat but persisted in eating while walking, then tossing their lunch papers away wherever they happened to be on campus.

references were in decline, in fact, and perhaps where all this was heading was the era of self-help and individualism.

Here Today, Gone Tomorrow (but Here the Day after That): The recently created Arts Undergraduate Society (AUS) got shut down by AMS Council on the grounds that the Arts students were showing little interest in it. Infuriated, the Arts students organized their own election to keep their organization going, then held a pep meet and, in January 1945, put together what seems to have been the first Arts Week, featuring an appearance by African-American singer and actor Paul Robeson, who was in town to perform in *Othello*.

Reforming Council: There was talk again of introducing faculty representation on Student Council, but again it did not come to pass. Instead, the AMS created an Undergraduate Societies Committee (USC) to give a voice to the individual faculties, while modestly expanding the number of seats on Council from nine to eleven by adding a coordinator of activities and a sophomore member.

And the Frosh? With very little fanfare (it seems to have begun in 1942) the first-year class began electing their own executive, including a frosh president. The 1944 president

Paul Robeson (centre) on a 1946 visit to UBC, with UBC president Norman MacKenzie, right.

The War Memorial Gymnasium, paid for largely by the students, built in the late 1940s and early 1950s.

1945-1955

It was the best of times, it was the worst of times. So prosperous a time that no one cared about issues, the *Ubyssey* said one year. But that wasn't entirely true: the Cold War made its way onto campus and stirred debate about Communism and free speech. And racial discrimination came out of the shadows, thanks to AMS complaints and Ubyssey exposés about the fraternities and sororities.

The students kept building things (a gym), began to venture into business (a barber shop), and even survived a fire. And there were internecine fights (Engineers against frosh, Engineers against the *Ubyssey*, Engineers against Allan Fotheringham) and discussions about structure and autonomy and fees and apathy. Of course, apathy. So a decade like any other.

1945 TO 1946

Students to the Left of Them, Students to the Right of Them: UBC had never seen so many students: 5,200 showed up in September, and another 1,200 (mostly ex-servicemen) arrived in January. The library was crowded, the buses were crowded, everything was crowded.

One of the downtown papers wrote a piece about the supposed division between the more mature returning servicemen and the younger, female "bobby-soxers" and other "kids." The *Ubyssey* responded by deriding the idea, but felt compelled to revert to the topic more than once, so there may have been something to it.

One good thing about the situation was that the influx of students meant an increase in fees to the AMS, which was able to pay off more of its loan for Brock Hall. It also meant more work for Student Council, which in those days met every Monday at 7:00 p.m. and sometimes worked until one in the morning.

Residences: One result of the influx was a scramble to find housing. UBC finally opened some student residences, repurposing old military huts at Acadia Camp and Fort Camp. At Acadia Camp there were both men and women, and even families.

And Other Things: The *Ubyssey* worried that the campus was too dark,

Woman at an Acadia Camp hut in 1951.

especially in the parking lot, where there were more and more cars; and they called for a new bus route to campus along West 41st, something that would eventually come to pass. There was also talk of expanding Brock Hall, but that project soon got overshadowed by the massive new project that would dominate the next five years:

Another Gym! There was talk in the fall of erecting some sort of memorial in honour of the war dead, but it was all very mysterious until February, when it was announced that the memorial would be a new and larger gymnasium. The students took the lead on fundraising, and among the students the most active group was a new campus club with a quirky perspective on life:

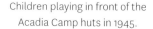

Children playing in front of the Acadia Camp huts in 1945.

The Jokers! Founded in the fall with the slogan, "Come and make an ace of yourself," the Jokers tried to liven up campus with their offbeat brand of humour. Members, all of whom were made vice-presidents, walked around carrying yo-yos. They organized goldfish swallowing contests to raise money for the new gym, along with a carnival, an egg auction in which students could buy eggs to hurl at one of the Jokers, and a roller-skating marathon for which the slogan was: "Break a Limb! Support the Gym!"

Students to the Left, Students to the Right (Part Two, Political Version): Sid Zlotnick of the left-wing Labour-Progressive Party (LPP) got in trouble with the Discipline Committee for distributing leaflets. No publica-

tions allowed unless approved by Student Council, the committee said. Zlotnick then lobbied to allow a Labour-Progressive campus club to be formed. Council hesitated. We don't have political clubs, they said, but let's ask the Board of Governors. The Board said, This is a student matter; you decide. Grant Livingstone, a Conservative, said if the LPP can become a club, so should other political groups.

Still uncertain what to do, Council decided to hold a plebiscite of the whole student body; this was the first referendum in AMS history, and it resulted in a 2:1 vote against political clubs. Politics would have to wait for another day.

Shave and a Haircut: Two Bits. Well, really four: it cost fifty cents

to get a haircut at the newly opened barber shop in Brock Hall, a business project spearheaded by AMS president Allan Ainsworth and treasurer Garry Miller. (Oddly, Garry Miller's grandson, Tristan Miller, would occupy a similar position in the AMS more than sixty-five years later as the vice-president finance. Is there a finance gene?) Meanwhile, the barber shop, run by Peter Van Dyke, was still going strong into the '60s.

We Are, We Are, We Are . . . the AUS? The Arts Undergraduate Society fell on hard times again, finding it difficult to get their members out to

The Thunderbirds play the Harlem Globetrotters—and win! That's Pat McGeer, in the air on the left.

Notables: Pat McGeer, later a BC cabinet minister responsible for higher education (and a favourite target of the *Ubyssey*), was a star basketball player for the Thunderbirds, helping the UBC team defeat the visiting Harlem Globetrotters in January 1946.

vote. The ever-helpful Engineers sent two hundred of their members to an Arts election meeting. Only fifteen Arts students showed up, so the Engineers happily elected themselves to all the positions on the Arts executive. (Of course, this was all ruled out of order, but it did not bode well for the AUS.)

1946 TO 1947

Is This Any Way to Build a Gymnasium? The drive to raise money for the War Memorial Gym bogged down this year. Less than half the money needed was raised. The *Ubyssey* said the campaign was not supported by all or even most of the students, and ran a letter that asked why the gymnasium of a public institution should be built "from the proceeds of raffles, rummage sales and beauty contests."

This wasn't entirely fair. The students also voted to raise their fees and dedicate $5 each to the gym, and at the end of the year there was talk of raising money by issuing bonds. But the letter-writer's main point seemed to be that such a project should be paid for by public funds; these, however, were not forthcoming, so despite talk of drawing up architectural plans, the project languished.

Coming Soon to a Campus Near You: Tim Buck, that is, leader of the Labour-Progressive Party (previously the Canadian Communist Party). Invited by the left-wing Social Problems Club to speak at UBC, he was at first barred by Student Council on the grounds that UBC's students had voted a year before in a plebiscite not to allow political clubs on campus. Besides, said AMS president Ted Kirkpatrick, allowing Tim Buck to speak would be "detrimental" to the good of the University.

The *Ubyssey* noted that the plebiscite had not banned political speakers, just political clubs. Other groups spoke up in favour of allowing the speech, and Council backed down. Tim Buck spoke to two thousand students in the auditorium, and UBC survived.

TOP Communism!

MIDDLE AMS president Ted Kirkpatrick: Tim Buck would be "detrimental."

BOTTOM Students in the Auditorium in the 1940s.

Louis Chodat's Revenge: Back in 1931–32, Louis Chodat was fined and suspended for playing on non-UBC sports teams. This year the Discipline Committee came down on several athletes doing the same. But this time the actions prompted opposition. The Discipline Committee itself said the rule needed to be changed. There was talk of discussing it at the Annual General Meeting. Eventually, it would disappear.

Musqueam Land: The Indigenous theme returned this year, with the fraternities and sororities staging a Princess Ball, by which was meant an "Indian" Princess Ball, complete with costumes meant to depict Indigenous maidens and warriors: buckskins, tom-toms, etc. Later in the year a *Ubyssey* columnist produced a humorous piece about the "Thunderbird tribe" (meaning UBC's students). The most interesting part of it was his statement that the Thunderbirds had "swiped" Musqueam land, one of the earliest references in the *Ubyssey* to the true history of the area.

Baby Steps? The *Ubyssey*, which had previously described the new Undergraduate Societies Committee (USC) as an infant tangled in its diapers, now said it had graduated to short pants. There was still confusion about its role and composition, however. There were questions about whether it would become a rival to Student Council or, on the other hand, have nothing to do. It would eventually become the model for a reformed Student Council, but that would not be for more than a decade.

Permanent Staff? The debate over hiring a general manager revived this year after several years in which the student treasurer and president tried to run things, with the assistance of typists and other office staff. Noting that the AMS had become a $200,000 business, the *Ubyssey* said a manager was needed to make things more efficient. Opponents of the move worried that such a manager might take away from student autonomy, which was clearly not complete yet because someone felt it necessary to say the manager should be paid by the AMS rather than the University.

The Annual General Meeting in March created a committee to look into the issue over the summer.

Prime Minister in Waiting: A young man known as "Chick" Turner showed up on the *Ubyssey* sports staff this year. He would later become a member of Student Council. But he became much better known in later life as Prime Minister John Turner, serving in that post in 1984.

"Chick" Turner.

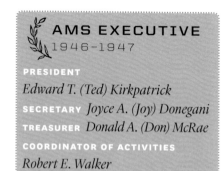

1947 TO 1948

Separatists? The Engineering Undergraduate Society clashed with AMS Council over the size of the EUS budget, and the *Ubyssey* warned darkly against "separatist tendencies" among the Engineers.

Communists? The year saw a long drawn-out saga, never really resolved, about whether UBC's students should support the plan for the National Federation of Canadian University Students to affiliate with the left-wing International Union of Students, which some saw as Communist-dominated. General meetings to discuss the issue missed quorum or ran out of time, and the issue was left hanging.

Meanwhile Communist leader Tim Buck came to speak again, and was jeered, hooted at, and shot at with pea-shooters; he even suffered the indignity of having dead cats tossed at him.

Earlier a Communist club, or at least a Labour-Progressive one, was allowed on campus after the students reversed their plebiscite decision of 1945-46 and said political clubs could be formed after all, under certain conditions. The Liberals, the Progressive Conservatives, and the CCF (socialist forerunners of the NDP) all established themselves.

Putting the Mock in Mock Parliament: Some students found all this politicking too much and formed joke groups to enter UBC's long-running Mock Parliament. Representatives of the real parties deplored the disrespect of such groups as the "Whig Union of Socialist Tories, excepting Stalinist-Trotskyites" (WUSTEST, for short).

Jokers: Meanwhile the granddaddy of joke groups, the Jokers, had fallen on hard times and were in danger of losing their club room in the Brock. In protest, they occupied the office of the AMS president, Grant Livingstone, and then camped outside Brock Hall, where they hanged the president in effigy, attaching a sign saying, "Livingstone, we presume." Their leader even fought Livingstone in a boxing match.

AMS president Grant Livingstone:
Fighter against Jokers and Communists.

USC: The still fledgling Undergraduate Societies Committee, now called the "idiot child" of student government by the *Totem*, made a grab for power this year, trying to establish itself as equal to Student Council. This struggle would last another decade.

Can't We All Get Along? Trouble erupted this year in the cafeteria of all places, as some students complained that other students were hogging space by reserving tables. The matter even went to AMS Council, which deplored the use of tables for "strictly social purposes," a statement that the *Ubyssey* said was aimed at the fraternities and sororities. Council members angrily denounced this interpretation of what they meant and banned the paper from the next Council meeting, an action the *Ubyssey* denounced as unconstitutional. Councillors said the *Ubyssey* had created a "misimpression." The *Ubyssey* said it was clear what was meant.

In the end Council decided that the table reservation issue was out of its jurisdiction and passed it on to the University administration.

War Memorial Gym: Almost forgotten this year was the gym project. There was a ceremonial sod-turning on Remembrance Day, but the funds to go forward were insufficient; soaring construction costs meant the project was short $140,000. Meanwhile the scope of the project was reduced: gone was the plan for a swimming pool, but there was still going to be a boxing ring and bowling alleys.

TOP Registering in the Armoury, 1957.

MIDDLE Writing an exam in the Armoury, 1970.

BOTTOM A book sale in the Armoury, unknown date.

And in Other News: There was a dispute over enforcing the prohibitionist liquor regulations. A member of Council quit in the middle of a Council meeting. There were complaints about holding the annual Fall Ball in the campus Armoury instead of downtown. And a letter-writer told AMS leaders that a lot of students came to UBC to study and were not interested in petty political squabbles. All in all, a somewhat testy year, which may explain the creation of a Flying Club. What better response to all this testiness than to just fly away.

But Wait, the Armoury? Yes, with the end of the war, the military training facility was put to other uses, from registration to exam-writing and even book sales.

AMS EXECUTIVE
1947–1948

PRESIDENT *Grant B. Livingstone*

SECRETARY
Katherine ("Taddy") Knapp

TREASURER *Robert S. (Bob) Harwood*

COORDINATOR OF ACTIVITIES
Robert Bagnall

UBYSSEY EDITOR *Donald Ferguson*

1948 TO 1949

Still debating: Harry Rankin, far left, at an AMS Debating Society event in 1979.

Communists? The Cold War made its presence felt this year as worries about Communism surfaced on campus. Former AMS president Grant Livingstone returned from Europe to announce that the International Union of Students was Communist-dominated. A recent law school graduate was denied admission to the bar on the grounds that, as a Communist, he was "not of good repute," prompting protests on campus. Student members of two left-wing campus clubs picketed downtown against arms shipments meant to be used against Communists in China. And Council refused to approve a Peace Council club, saying it might be a "Communist Front organization." Even the Student Christian Movement came under attack for alleged Communist sympathies and members.

The most surprising turn the commotion took was when the Canadian Legion became embroiled in a debate over whether to support the Communist law student. The debate was initiated by another law student, Harry Rankin, who went on to become a well-known political figure in Vancouver: a founder of the Coalition of Progressive Electors (COPE) and a long-time city councillor.

Capitalists? After a year in which it seemed that the AMS was rolling in money because of increased enrolment, this year reality set in. There had been so much overspending ("optimism," one report called it) that the AMS had a $20,000 deficit ($194,000 in 2015 dollars). Treasurer Paul Plant called for austerity measures and slashed budgets. At the end of the year he asked the students to agree to a $4 increase in the AMS fee (which would have raised it to $20). But the students, in a referendum, said no; in fact, they lowered it to $15.

In an earlier referendum (the two referendums this year were the second and third in AMS history) the students voted to restore the business manager system, one argument for which was that it would introduce better fiscal control and thus save money. No more leaving things to the student president and treasurer.

AUNTY'S AT THE DOOR

The deficit problem through the eyes of the *Ubyssey* cartoonist. Note the looming threat of the UBC administration in the background.

Remember the Gym! The War Memorial Gym project seemed stalled for most of the year, but in February, after lobbying by the students, the provincial government promised a $200,000 contribution, not just for the gym but for women's residences and two academic buildings. The students would still end up paying almost half the cost of the gymnasium, prompting the *Ubyssey* to say: "Someday soon students

87

at the University may grow tired of providing facilities for UBC's department of physical education."

(But in fact students contributed funds, by self-imposed fees, for a new arena in 1961 and the aquatic centre in 1975. Only in 1989 did they balk at paying for something, the Student Recreation Centre, and it didn't matter, because the University simply imposed its own ancillary fee on them.)

Real First Nations Representatives: Perhaps marking the beginning of the end of pretending to be their own tribe, the students arranged with Chief William Scow of the Kwiksutaineuk people to attend the Homecoming football game, at which time he donated a totem pole and also granted permission for the use of the Thunderbird name (which UBC's sports teams had been using since 1933).

Chief Scow's son Alfred was an Arts student at the time, and he went on to become the first Indigenous British Columbian to graduate in law and become a judge. The AMS awarded Alfred Scow its Great Trekker award in 1995.

Dance, Dance, Dance (but No More Jokes): The Jokers sadly faded away, but in January 1949 the Dance Club started up. It became popular almost immediately and was still going strong in 2015 despite the appearance of many rival dance groups on campus over the years, from square to swing to salsa.

Notables: Ron Haggart, the *Ubyssey* editor, and Val Sears, the managing editor, went on to distinguished careers in Canadian journalism. Regular columnist Les Armour went on to a notable career in philosophy.

Gendered Elections: For the first time in years a male student, Bob Currie, ran for secretary (but lost). On the other hand, a woman (Margaret Low-Beer) won the election to become head of the Literary and Scientific Executive, the body overseeing clubs, becoming the first woman to do so.

AMS EXECUTIVE
1948–1949

PRESIDENT *David M. (Dave) Brousson*
SECRETARY *Nancy M. Davidson*
TREASURER *Paul S. Plant*
COORDINATOR OF ACTIVITIES
John N. ("Chick") Turner

UBYSSEY **EDITOR** *Ron Haggart*

The Dance Club in 1978.

The totem pole donated by Chief Scow stood in front of Brock Hall for many years.

1949 TO 1950

Old Soldiers Never Die: The number of veterans on campus was dwindling. They had passed through the system and were moving on. The *Ubyssey* lamented this, saying there would be less seriousness on campus, and soon there would only be "playboys" left. Recognizing the realities, the UBC branch of the Canadian Legion began discussing whether to disband. It decided not to, and in fact its president won the AMS presidency in February, but eventually it would fade away.

Kidnapped! The Engineers ambushed the *Ubyssey* editor in February, shaved the head of an assistant (the future philosopher Les Armour), and took over the paper for a day. It seemed mostly in fun, but did reflect some antagonism between the "Redshirts" and the newspaper. There was also of course the ongoing tension between the Engineers and the Arts students, which in ear-lier years burst out in brawls but this year got sublimated into an election call by one of the presidential candidates for a "holy war" between Arts and Engineering. (No such holy war took place, and the candidate lost.)

Underway: Finally construction began on the War Memorial Gym. Tenders also went out for the building of women's residences, and the University talked about building residences for men as well. The *Ubyssey* decried the sex segregation as Victorian, saying residences should be for both men and women.

Work begins on the gym.

Quorum, Quorum, Who's Got the Quorum: Although general meetings still tended to meet quorum (one in the previous year drew five thousand students, or more than 50 percent of the students), the AMS decided to reduce quorum this year from one-third to 20 percent. This was the beginning of a trend. By 1980, in a period in which quorum had become increasingly elusive, the requirement was down to 10 percent. It was reduced to 2 percent in 2008 and 1 percent in 2013, but still it seemed impossible to get enough students out to conduct official business. Finally, though, in 2014, for the first time in almost forty years, quorum was reached at an annual general meeting.

We're in the Money: After the previous year's deficit shock, Treasurer Walter Ewing, with the assistance of the newly appointed business manager, H.B. Maunsell, kept a tight grip on the AMS purse strings, so much so that by the end of the year there was a $5,000 surplus, replaying the situation from 1932–33. Also as in 1932–33, the *Ubyssey* disapproved, saying the point of having money was not to hoard it but to support student activities. But Ewing remained cautious, and a new literary magazine (the *Thunderbird*) got cancelled; there was also a fuss over spending $50 to hold a reception for some visiting Austrian student performers and over spending $800 for an engineers' conference.

However, Council did vote to lend $10,000 to the Varsity Outdoor Club for its cabin on Mount Seymour, the beginning of a troubled relationship between the club and the AMS over ski cabins.

Walter Ewing, the cautious treasurer.

Louis Chodat's Revenge, Part Two: Once again the issue of UBC students playing for outside sports teams came up. The rule that got Louis Chodat fined and suspended in 1931–32, and which was discussed again in 1946–47, came to a head this year when Council asked the University administration to enforce fines and carry out suspensions for such "delinquent" athletes.

The request never got to the University, however. A general meeting voted to throw the rule out, or at least to modify it so that all such an athlete had to do was give notice that he wanted to play on an outside team. No permission would be needed in future, just notice.

Ban the Bomb! The Peace Council got approved as an AMS club in late December, much to the disgust of the *Ubyssey*, which objected to the approval being put through when no one was around and also to the fact that the decision went against the wishes of a general meeting the year before. But the Peace Council got to work, and its first campaign was a petition against nuclear weapons. The *Ubyssey* declared this naive, saying a piece of paper wouldn't stop anything.

Separatism: Social Work students, who spent much of their time off campus, complained that they were

TOP Students lounging.

BOTTOM Lining up for registration in the Armoury.

getting little for their AMS fee and talked of somehow withdrawing from the AMS. As a compromise, Council voted to refund their fees.

Meanwhile, regular students strolled across campus or measured the height of trees and surveyed forests (if they were Forestry students). Or they studied in the Ridington Room or, in these days before the Knoll, lounged on the lawn in front of the Old Administration Building, near where the Sedgewick and Koerner libraries would go up in later years. And of course they stood in line.

TOP Surveying the forest.

MIDDLE Measuring a tree.

BOTTOM Strolling.

1950 TO 1951

President Donaldson.

A Woman President: Nonie Donaldson unexpectedly became AMS president in the fall, when John Haar took up a scholarship in Texas and stepped down from the presidency. A quirk of the AMS constitution meant that in such a situation the head of the Women's Undergraduate Society took over the office at least temporarily, and Council and a general meeting passed votes to have her continue through the term.

At the end of the year the *Ubyssey* said she'd done a great job even though some at the time had been aghast at the thought of a "mere woman" being president. Donaldson herself had said that she wanted to prove that "a woman [could] handle the job."

Despite the plaudits for Donaldson, there was unseemly haste at the end of the year to amend the constitution so this could never happen again. A new post of vice-president was created so that a "man" could step in next time. True acceptance of women presidents would have to wait till the 1980s.

The Times They Are A-Changin': In other ways, though, this was a pivotal year. Separatist rumblings from the students in various faculties came to a head over a plan by the Engineers to issue their own yearbook, the *Slipstick*. The *Ubyssey* was appalled, calling the plan "a body blow to student unity." There were concerns about effects on sales and advertising for the *Totem*. Compromises were agreed on, but the bigger issue as the 1950s began was what was going to be the relationship between the students in their individual faculties and the central AMS.

The Times They Are A-Changin' (Maybe): The *Ubyssey* and several student clubs came out this year in favour of changes to the Indian Act to extend Indigenous rights. On the other hand, the fraternities and sororities followed very old AMS ways by making "Totem Land" the theme of their annual Mardi Gras ball and transforming the downtown Commodore nightclub into an "Indian village" where non-Indigenous people could dress up in Indigenous costumes. But they did at least involve some actual First Nations representatives this time, including a chief from the Capilano reserve.

The Gym! Yes, at long last, the War Memorial Gymnasium, first dreamt of in 1945–46, opened its doors on February 23, 1951 for a basketball game at which President Donaldson threw in the first ball. The building still wasn't paid off, though, so the students launched a pledge campaign asking for donations of $3.43 per person.

The first volume of *Slipstick*, the Engineering annual, April 1951.

The War Memorial Gym.

Women's Residences: And three residences for women also opened: Mary Bollert Hall, Anne Wesbrook Hall, and the Isabel MacInnes Building.

One of the new women's residences.

But Oh, the Athletic Program: Apathy seemed to be reigning supreme with Varsity athletics. Not enough students attended the games. Not enough players tried out for the teams. The downtown newspapers worried that it could be the end of football at UBC (shades of worries to come in 2013). The *Ubyssey* called for athletic scholarships. What actually happened was a restructuring of finances and a call for the University to hire a full-time director of athletics to run the program. (The University did hire a director, marking the beginning of the end of AMS control over intercollegiate athletics.)

And the Bookstore: Thinking that prices in the UBC Bookstore were too high, Council ordered an investigation, only to be stymied because the University declined to release its financial statements. But the University did agree to take over the second-hand book program, making it easier for students to sell their old textbooks.

Old Traditions: The *Ubyssey* worried that initiation traditions were disappearing. The frosh had hardly any regalia to wear this year, they lamented, and they weren't turning out for frosh events. But the Engineers came to the rescue during Club Day, already a tradition itself, diverting the frosh from club recruitment into the lily pond.

New Traditions: The AMS initiated its Great Trekker award for graduates who had gone on to distinguish themselves and serve the community. The first recipient was Joseph Brown, who had taken part in the

Initiation activities.

1922 Great Trek and gone on to work in alumni development. The award is still going strong today.

The Engineers held a generally acclaimed fundraiser for the March of Dimes; even the *Ubyssey* had nice things to say about it, praising their mortal enemies in Applied Science for an event that included an auction (the Arts Building "sold" for $25), a cigar-smoking contest (sigh), and a chariot race. Chariot races remained popular for decades, but eventually came under fire for being too violent.

Still with the Engineers, one of them had the bright idea of naming their annual ball Godiva's Gallop, after Lady Godiva, the famous naked lady from medieval England, who somehow captured the imagination of Engineers not just at UBC but elsewhere in Canada and beyond. The *Ubyssey* commented dryly that the Engineers were not able to produce

anyone in authentic Godiva costume—but that would come, much to the displeasure of others on campus.

The fairly new tradition of referendums continued with the students voting in favour of UBC introducing "objective" courses on religion (though most of them said they wouldn't take them).

The Varsity Outdoor Club opened their ski cabin on Mount Seymour.

And the Engineers attempted their second kidnapping of *Ubyssey* editors, but the result was a messy "newspaper war," followed by lectures from Council, apologies from both sides, and a move to investigate how the *Ubyssey* Publications Board functioned.

And for a failed attempt to start a tradition there was the Kickapoo rabbit hunt, initiated by a new club on campus, which seemed to be trying to take over from the defunct Jokers. (The hunt did not involve a real rabbit.)

AMS EXECUTIVE
1950–1951
PRESIDENT *John L. Haar/ Noreen A. ("Nonie") Donaldson*
SECRETARY *Jo Ann Strutt*
TREASURER *John MacKinnon*
COORDINATOR OF ACTIVITIES *James Midwinter*

UBYSSEY EDITOR *Vic Hay/Ray Frost*

1951 TO 1952

A Feisty Year: Council fought the president, the *Ubyssey* stung the Board of Governors, the Kickapoos demanded retribution from the *Ubyssey*, Council tried to decapitate the *Ubyssey*, and of course the Engineers went a-kidnapping. Not to mention Council versus the University over fees, and as the year wound down, the Aggies taking on the *Ubyssey*, and Council versus the fraternities.

Hunt the Lyon: AMS president Vaughan Lyon had to survive a vote of non-confidence at Council, and when that failed there were rumours that disaffected councillors would try to remove him at an upcoming general meeting—but that didn't happen. What the antagonism was about is hard to discern. There were charges that he acted without Council approval (never a good idea as later presidents would discover), but the *Ubyssey* said the real issue

AMS president Vaughan Lyon.

was political: people didn't like the fact that Lyon was the former head of the campus Liberal club.

Put on Your Armour: Next under fire was the *Ubyssey* editor, Les Armour, who inspired an attack from the Kickapoo Club of all places for allegedly not providing sufficient publicity for one of their pep meets, which consequently lost money. The Kickapoos asked that the *Ubyssey* be made to pay for the losses, and Council at first voted to support them, until cooler heads prevailed.

Later in the year Council tried to fire Armour but backed down in the face of protests by the rest of the *Ubyssey* editorial staff and on the eve of a general meeting that went ahead and voted to support the editor. The reasons for this attack were

Ubyssey editor Les Armour.

unclear too, though Armour's left-wing views probably had something to do with it.

And finally at the end of the year, the Agriculture Undergraduate Society complained that the *Ubyssey* had messed up the special Aggie edition of the paper. *O tempora, o mores.*

Allan Fotheringham: Later to become a respected columnist on such publications as *Maclean's* magazine, Allan Fotheringham began his career at the *Ubyssey*, where he delighted in mocking the Engineers. They took their revenge, however, by kidnapping him, taking all his money and his coat, and abandoning him in Horseshoe Bay, from whence he returned with great difficulty. The police were called, but dismissed the incident as a prank.

Allan Fotheringham.

Fees, Fees, Fees: At the very end of the 1950–51 year, the University announced a $30 fee increase, much to the disgust of AMS Council and the *Ubyssey*. In 1951–52, when the University refused to release financial statements justifying the increase, the *Ubyssey* suggested that something underhanded was going on at the Board of Governors, causing much offence and resulting in a retraction. UBC president MacKenzie seemed to suggest at one point that the increase might be reversed, but it wasn't, and the students were left to grumble.

Meanwhile the AMS was talking about raising its own fees, largely because it had been unable to repay a bank loan it had taken out to finance the War Memorial Gym. The previous year it had collected donation pledges from students, but many of them had not actually paid what they said they would.

Bigoted? Us? Council took on the fraternities this year after years of distant rumblings over their practices. Charges of religious and racial discrimination were levelled, and eventually a general meeting passed a motion calling on the University to require all fraternities to remove discriminatory clauses from their constitutions.

Battle of the Sexes: "Female triumphed over male," said the *Ubyssey*, reporting on the election of Jane Banfield to the new post of vice-president, which she won by defeating a male rival. (So much for the notion that creating the vice-presidency would ensure that the next time a president resigned he would be replaced by a man.)

Presidential First: In retrospect what looks like even bigger election news was the victory of Raghbir Basi in the presidential race. Basi, a native of the Punjab, became the first person of colour to be AMS president, something not mentioned in the news coverage for some reason, though it was mentioned in passing during the debates over discrimination in the fraternities to show that AMS attitudes did not accord with those in the fraternities.

Raghbir Basi, AMS president-elect.

And Another First: Long before the radical sixties, the issue of student representation on University committees emerged when residents of the Fort Camp men's residence complained about conditions there and Student Council asked for representation on the UBC Housing Committee. UBC president MacKenzie said he was open to the suggestion.

AMS EXECUTIVE
1951–1952
PRESIDENT *Vaughan Lyon*
VICE-PRESIDENT *Phil Dadson*
SECRETARY *Anita Jay*
TREASURER *Phil Anderson*
COORDINATOR OF ACTIVITIES
Jack Lintott

UBYSSEY EDITOR *Hugh Cameron/ Les Armour*

1952 TO 1953

A Boring Year: Or so said the *Ubyssey*, complaining that the students were more interested in the candidates for Mardi Gras Queen than in the pressing issues of the day. It was certainly a year of queens: the *Totem* Queen (the *Totem* was seeking the most photogenic beauty on campus), the Frosh Queen, the Homecoming Queen. The Homecoming Queen candidates were even used as a lure to try to encourage students to attend the Homecoming football game: athletic events were still not drawing crowds.

Even the speeches of visiting politicians were dull, said the *Ubyssey*, calling them "symptomatic of a stagnancy which the general prosperity of a nation always seems to bring." Indeed. It was still the fifties after all.

Joe Schlesinger: Perhaps in an attempt to liven things up, *Ubyssey* editor Joe Schlesinger ran for AMS president this year, the first time that happened. He lost, though, and returned to journalism, later becoming a respected CBC television reporter.

Ubyssey editor-in-chief Joe Schlesinger.

The Mardi Gras Queen (Shary Pitts) being crowned by UBC president MacKenzie in 1952.

Kidnappings: The Engineers were at it again, trying to kidnap the president of the Nursing Undergraduate Society. Foiled at this, they were mocked by the *Ubyssey*, and so went and kidnapped columnist Allan Fotheringham—again!—this time chaining him to the iconic Birks clock downtown. Later they also kidnapped editor-in-chief Schlesinger, who, however, escaped.

Athletics: The athletics program was still in the doldrums, and the AMS began to realize that it had handed over control of it to the University administration. Some clamoured for a return to student control, but that was not to be. This didn't mean the AMS stopped paying for athletics, and there were debates over how much of the AMS fee should go to support intercollegiate sports, but control over these sports was now essentially gone.

Athletic Scholarships: The debate over funding athletics included discussion of introducing athletic scholarships in the manner of American schools. The idea was debated at a general meeting, at which UBC's star football player, George Puil, spoke against the suggestion. In later years Puil went on to a long career as a Vancouver city councillor.

Girls Can Play Football Too: As part of the annual Engineers' fundraising event for the March of Dimes charity, there was the usual chariot race and also this time a football game between the Nurses and the women in Home Economics. This would become a tradition in later years, and would come to be called the Teacup Game.

The Russians Are Coming: After over a year of discussions, the students at a general meeting finally approved a plan to bring over an exchange student from the Soviet Union.

The Med Students Are Grumbling: Why should we pay AMS fees, they say, when we're never on campus? Council rejected the argument, but less than fifteen years later a fee exemption would come to pass.

Smut: And finally, the *Ubyssey* came out against smut, or at least against some of the magazines on sale in the bookstore (*Pic, Quick, Flash*) which featured suggestive photos of Marilyn Monroe and others. Such pictures, said the paper, cause eigh- teen-year-olds to become "hot and bothered," leaving them in no condition to attend physics labs. This seems a tad prudish, but perhaps they were joking.

AMS EXECUTIVE
1952-1953

PRESIDENT *Raghbir Basi*
VICE-PRESIDENT *Jane Banfield*
SECRETARY *Ann Willis*
TREASURER *Gerry Duclos*
COORDINATOR OF ACTIVITIES *Denny Silvestrini*

UBYSSEY EDITOR *Joe Schlesinger*

The first women's football game.

1953 TO 1954

A Sexy Year: The Kinsey Report on female sexuality came out this year, and UBC students engaged with it in a formal debate competition, in which victory went to the side arguing that the report was a threat to western civilization (!). But if sex was defeated on this occasion, which is how the *Ubyssey* put it, nevertheless it seemed very much in the news, or at least in the *Ubyssey*. Sex is more important than religion, the paper said. It also ran an article on excessive kissing in Brock Hall and suggested that the kissing booth at the annual blood drive was responsible for the record turnout of male blood donors.

Off with Her Head! Lots of queens around this year: Homecoming Queen, Mardi Gras Queen, Frosh Queen: in fact, two rival Frosh Queens (almost). The Frosh Undergraduate Society protested when one of the fraternities announced that they were anointing the Frosh Queen. That's just your fraternity's queen, said the official Frosh; we're going to choose our own. In the end, however, the official Frosh backed down, so no one ended up in the Tower, thankfully.

Alma Mating Society: One of the judges of the Homecoming Queen contest was former AMS president Nonie Donaldson, now referred to as "Mrs. Vaughan Lyon," because she ended up marrying her presidential successor. Mr. Vaughan Lyon did not attend, but two other past presidents helped out with the judging.

Not Again! The Engineers kidnapped Allan Fotheringham, by now the editor-in-chief of the *Ubyssey*, for the third time, perhaps because he said engineering did not belong in a university and kept referring to the Engineers as applied scientists, a term they disliked.

The Engineers also showed their displeasure with the *Ubyssey* by stealing one day's edition, though they later returned the copies.

Death of an Undergraduate Society: If the Engineers had to put up with constant provocations from the *Ubyssey*, not to mention getting fined by the new Student Court for damage caused during their kidnapping raid, at least they survived as an organization. Not so the Arts Undergraduate Society, which decided it had nothing left to live for, and so dissolved itself. (But it would be back.)

Student Court: There had been talk of having a Student Court for years, and in earlier decades AMS Council sometimes constituted itself as a court, but there was no actual court until this year, when despite worries that it would just be a playground for law students, Council finally created one. It was of course subject to appeal to the University's administrative body, the Faculty Council (the AMS still did not have full autonomy), but it got into action right away, fining the Engineers and hearing complaints about drinking on campus and unauthorized pamphlet distribution.

Nurses promoting the blood drive in 1954.

Frats and Religious Clubs: The issue of religious and racial discrimination in the fraternities continued to simmer. Council pushed the University's Faculty Council to crack down on them, which it refused to do. Council then turned its attention to AMS religious clubs, suspending two Christian clubs for not allowing non-Christian members. The suspension was lifted by a general meeting.

Apathy, Lethargy, and What Is the AMS, anyway? Not for the first or last time, both Council and the *Ubyssey* complained about a lack of student interest in the running of the Society, noting the number of Council seats that were filled by acclamation. The *Ubyssey* also did a survey that revealed that some students didn't know that being the AMS president meant being president of the student body.

Perhaps the fault lay with the proliferation of mysterious acronyms, which had become so widespread that the *Ubyssey* ran an "alphabet soup" contest, asking students to identify as many acronyms as they could, from MAD, PhUS, and CUS to SCM, NFCUS, and the like.

Hard to Say Goodbye: Eric Nicol, the star columnist from the 1940s, was back, helping to put together the first Blue and Gold Revue, featuring a cameo appearance by UBC's President MacKenzie playing a freshman. Nicol even found one of his columns for the Vancouver *Province* reprinted in the *Ubyssey*. It was an unusually serious one for the

humourist, attacking McCarthyism, and it may have helped encourage some students to burn an American editor in effigy. "It's the first time I've ever succeeded in writing inflammatory material," Nicol said afterwards (so he hadn't lost his sense of humour after all).

And in Other News: The *Ubyssey* managed to annoy another set of students, those in Home Economics, by refusing to run their articles on the grounds that they were not up to a university standard.

Looking Forward: One of the earliest mentions of teaching evaluations came this year when the AMS began talking of conducting them. Meanwhile the *Ubyssey* began talking of a Second Trek to demand better funding for higher education. And there was discussion of whether the students would pay for a roof for the new outdoor pool UBC was building for the Empire Games (they wouldn't, but eventually they did pay for a whole new indoor aquatic centre).

President MacKenzie, centre of seated group, as a freshman at the first Blue and Gold Revue.

Notables: Ron Basford, later to be a federal cabinet minister, was active in the campus Liberal club and the Civil Liberties Union. Pat Carney, later to be a federal cabinet minister and senator, worked for the *Ubyssey*.

AMS EXECUTIVE
1953-1954

PRESIDENT *Ivan Feltham*
VICE-PRESIDENT
W. Richard ("Dick") Underhill
SECRETARY *Ann Cooper*
TREASURER *Allan ("Al") Goldsmith*
COORDINATOR OF ACTIVITIES
Mike Nuttall

UBYSSEY **EDITOR** *Allan ("Al") Fotheringham*

1954 TO 1955

Brock Burns: On the evening of October 25, 1954, as Council members gathered for their weekly Monday night meeting and *Ubyssey* staff members prepared to put out the next day's paper, a fire broke out in Brock Hall, probably caused by a cigarette. Everyone evacuated the building safely, and many stayed to watch, and thus were able to see the roof fall in around 7:00 p.m.

The students immediately began a campaign to raise money for repairs, and temporary accommodation was found for the AMS offices, the *Ubyssey*, the Brock barber shop, and a variety of clubs. By January 13, the *Ubyssey* was able to report that the Brock was back to normal, "except that it has no roof."

The new roof was already underway, however, and there were even plans to start building what became known as the Brock Extension, all with student funds, as the University said it was unable to contribute.

The Brock Hall fire, during and after.

Baru Because: AMS elections were dull in 1955, causing the *Ubyssey* to pine for the more exciting days of the year before, when the campaign of Clive ("Baru") Nylander had livened things up with slogans such as "My Baru Heaven," "From Here to Barubity," and the enigmatic "Baru—Because." Nylander lost, however, which is perhaps why the new year's candidates aimed for more sobriety.

Bigots Beware: No dullness on the fraternity scene, with the *Ubyssey* going on a campaign against those fraternities that continued to discriminate against "Non Caucasians." They made such a fuss about it that Council (largely composed of fraternity members) censured them.

This didn't stop the paper. They next went after the sororities, which had proclaimed themselves better than the fraternities because, unlike their male counterparts, they had no "Non Caucasian" clauses in their constitutions.

However, the *Ubyssey* engaged in some investigative reporting and discovered that the sororities were also restricting the number of non-whites, by the simple expedient of not mailing them the application forms. In defence of the practice, UBC's Dean of Women said they were probably acting on the belief that Asian girls weren't interested in sororities.

Hijinks: The traditional women's Hijinks party had finally disappeared by this year, but the students were still intrigued by exotic dressing up, something a later age might call cultural appropriation. This year at the Mardi Gras Ball the theme was Africa, and some of the students dressed as Mau Mau terrorists(!). No pseudo-Indigenous themes this time, and such things did seem to be fading, though the Chinook term Siwash was briefly adopted by a not very successful campus literary journal.

Who's in Charge Here? The *Ubyssey* complained that one of its reporters was excluded from a meeting of the Men's Athletic Committee (a body now run by the University) and also complained that the students were not getting clear information about how the fees they were paying for athletics were being used. The problem, said the paper, was that the students had given up control of the athletics program, but that had probably been inevitable

Helen Mawdsley, the Dean of Women.

because it had become too big for them to run anymore.

Who's in Charge, Part Two: If athletics was something that had just recently passed from student to University control, discipline was something that had always been ultimately within the University's jurisdiction. However, now that the AMS had finally set up a Student Court, there was a bit of an outcry when one of its rulings was amended by the Faculty Council (the University's administrative body).

The case in this instance was another Engineers' "riot," in which, in response to an uncomplimentary article in the *Ubyssey*, some Engineers went on a rampage and trashed the newspaper's office. There was also an attack on the Mardi Gras Ball and a basketball game.

Student Court found two Engineers to blame and fined them $5 ($45 in 2015 dollars) and also, oddly, found two *Ubyssey* columnists partially to blame. The Faculty Council stepped in and issued penalties of expulsion against all four (but then suspended the sentences). AMS Council complained about the Administration "going over the heads of Student Court."

Who's in Charge, Part Three: The Undergraduate Societies Committee made another attempt to wrest power from Student Council, but Student Court said it was Council that was supreme. Eventually, people would realize that trying to have two ruling bodies was a bad idea, though they would try it again in the late seventies, with SAC and Council (it didn't work then either).

This was just one of the issues that was raised about the AMS constitutional structure this year. President Dick Underhill commented that the AMS had outgrown its "Town Hall" origins and should no longer rely so much on general meetings. A move away from general meetings was indeed what happened in subsequent decades, and probably to a much greater extent than had been envisaged by the president.

Let's get away from general meetings, said AMS president Dick Underhill.

AMS EXECUTIVE
1954-1955

PRESIDENT
W. Richard ("Dick") Underhill
VICE-PRESIDENT *Wendy Sutton*
SECRETARY *Faye Fingarson*
TREASURER *Ronald Bray*
COORDINATOR OF ACTIVITIES
Jerome Angel

UBYSSEY EDITOR *Peter Sypnowich*

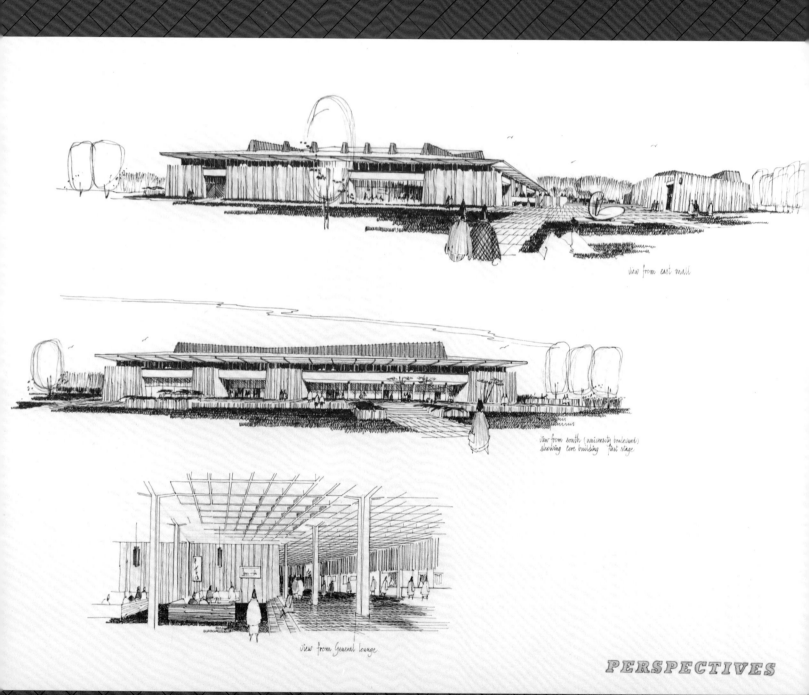

view from east mall

view from south (university boulevard)
showing core building first stage

view from General Lounge

PERSPECTIVES

Plans for the new student union building:
Kenneth R. Snider's winning entry in
the architectural competition.

1955-1965

TRANSITIONS

There was rowdiness, there were also stunts, though at times the *Ubyssey* complained that nothing was happening. It was a transitional period, with the conformist fifties mentality only slowly giving way to the rebelliousness of the sixties. Sex and drugs raised their ugly heads. There was talk of educational reform and calls for more student power (more faculty power too).

The students backed Mac (UBC president Macdonald) and then opposed him. The faculty opposed him too. Communist Party leader Tim Buck kept visiting campus, but the real radicalism was coming from a different direction, not from the proletariat but from a youth culture just beginning to find itself.

And through it all the AMS grew, the student body grew, there were plans for a new student union building, and the AMS began to become more professional.

1955
TO
1956

Sound and Fury: It was another of those years full of squabbles, involving the Engineers (of course) and Council, the revived Arts (and Science) Undergraduate Society, the *Ubyssey*, Student Court, and even, mysteriously, the Aggies. Not to mention Tim Buck and rowdy sports fans.

The Buck Stops Here: Canadian Communist leader Tim Buck made another visit to campus and was pelted with fruit for his pains. The *Ubyssey*, the University president, and others were appalled at the attack on free speech, and some of the perpetrators were even brought before Student Court for "conduct unbecoming" a student. One was found guilty and fined $3.

Student Court: The newly established Court was busy this year. It also imposed a fine on a rowdy football fan who had caused mayhem south of the border as part of the annual "Bellingham Invasion," and fined another student for ballot stuffing in the AMS elections. It also looked at charges and counter-charges involving Arts and Engineering students, and Student Council, over advertising for the annual Engineering ball, the disappearance of the Engineering edition of the *Ubyssey*, and associated issues.

Real Money: Meanwhile, for stiffer fines than the students themselves handed out, one had to turn to the University, which was collecting money over parking violations: some students owed more than $40 (over $350 in today's dollars), though amassing this much was something of an achievement, since individual fines were even lower than what the AMS imposed ($1 for a first offence, $2 for a second).

Parking: Did someone mention parking? This was one of the issues of the day, in a year in which the *Ubyssey* complained that there were no issues. There's not enough parking space, the paper worried, especially noting the disappearance of spots thanks to the construction of the new Education building. There was a bus stop, of course (with a new Bus Stop Cafe being built beside it, along with a new bookstore), but the focus in those days was not on public transit, but the automobile. One-third of the students drove to campus, a much higher percentage than in the environmentally conscious twenty-first century. (Of course, there was no U-Pass then.)

TOP Education before parking? For shame. (The new Education building, 1956.)

BOTTOM The old bus stop, with the old bookstore beside it.

Money, Money, Money: A proposal to pay all Student Council members got shot down at the fall general meeting. Leading the opposition was law student Rafe Mair (later a provincial politician and radio talk show host). Why not pay every club executive too, he asked sarcastically?

The Return of Arts: After disbanding a couple of years before, the Arts

Undergraduate Society returned, now called the Arts and Science Undergraduate Society to acknowledge the presence of chemists and physicists in its membership. It returned with difficulty, however, struggling to meet quorum and having to put up with "helpful" interventions from Engineering students.

Those Engineers: Even when working in a good cause (raising money for charity), the Engineers pushed the envelope by pieing and spitting: they held a spitting contest in which unwary bystanders who stood too close were "driven back with somewhat dampened spirits," as the *Ubyssey* put it.

And On a More Positive Note: The first Student Leadership Conference was held at Camp Elphinstone on the Sunshine Coast. UBC won the right to host an international stu-

BELOW A spitting contest in 1951.

dent conference (the Pacific Student Presidents Association). The AMS started a new literary magazine, *Raven*, and extended its accident insurance coverage from athletes to all students. And perhaps most important of all the students voted money for . . .

The AMS Art Collection: The AMS had acquired a painting in 1948 by E.J. Hughes (*Abandoned Village*). Now it acquired another, *Northern Image*, by Lawren Harris of the Group of Seven, and set up a committee with funding to oversee what was to become a sizable collection, still in place in 2015, when it was installed in new quarters in the AMS Student Nest.

Brock Extension: Long before the Nest (the third student union building), the AMS was still working on its first, the Brock, and planning an extension to house more club and meeting space. There was even talk of a bowl-

TOP The *Raven*, a literary magazine started by the AMS, being read in a classroom.

BOTTOM Lawren Harris in 1948 unveiling the first piece in the AMS art collection: *Abandoned Village* by E.J. Hughes.

ing alley, but that would have to wait till the second student union building (and the War Memorial Gym).

Sports: The rowing team did well, making it all the way to the Henley Regatta in England, but the football team was abysmal, despite the efforts of Don Coryell, a coach who went on to a distinguished career in the NFL. The *Ubyssey* suggested that the Thunderbirds would be better off playing Canadian teams than trying to compete in the American Evergreen Conference.

UBC's rowers finished second in England's Henley Regatta.

Snarl: The football team tried to promote itself with "Snarl" cards, including their schedule and the text: "You can't win. Snarl! Life at UBC is trying." An odd slogan because after all life at UBC wasn't all that trying. And yet the slogan made it into the Homecoming Parade:

Snarling at Homecoming.

That Vile Rag: Out of nowhere (well, Ontario) the *Ubyssey* found itself attacked as "the vilest rag you can imagine, and the best argument for censorship that could be produced": and this in one of their relatively innocuous years. The attack came from the faculty advisor to a student newspaper in Windsor, who apparently didn't like the freedom out West. The *Ubyssey* ran with the description and would often describe itself in later years as "the vilest rag west of Blanca" (referring to the street bordering the campus).

A Joke (We Hope): The debating club held a formal debate between students and professors on the topic, "UBC would be better off without students." The profs said that without the students they wouldn't have to miss their lunch breaks explaining the obvious, the administration

could save money on classrooms, and the library would be much more pleasant. And they won. Hmm.

And then there were the mysterious Aggies, who wrote letters to the *Ubyssey* apologizing for burning copies of the paper. Why is not clear; something to do with their Farmers' Frolic dance. Sweet mystery of life, or the energy of Youth.

AMS EXECUTIVE
1955–1956

PRESIDENT *Ronald Bray*
VICE-PRESIDENT *Ron Langstaffe*
SECRETARY *Helen McLean*
TREASURER *Geoff Conway*
COORDINATOR OF ACTIVITIES
Donald McCallum

UBYSSEY EDITOR *Stanley Beck*

TOP A 1950s classroom in the new Buchanan building. Wouldn't be needed if not for students.

BOTTOM Exam rooms wouldn't be needed either.

1956 TO 1957

Trek II (The Sequel): "Perhaps it's time for another Great Trek," said the *Ubyssey*, noting that UBC was bursting at the seams and in dire need of more funding. They weren't a voice crying in the wilderness either. The UBC president and AMS Council both called for more funding, and some students were ready to re-enact the glory days of 1922. Not all, though: at one major protest event a sudden snowfall prompted some members of the student body to fire snowballs at a venerable Trekker from 1922 and to generally disrupt the proceedings.

But students did gather 86,000 signatures on a petition, even more than on the petition of 1922, and a delegation of AMS leaders went to Victoria and got to speak to the premier. There was a letter-writing campaign and a series of campus events: all that was missing was an actual march downtown, though one was threatened when the government seemed to be saying No to additional funding.

However, the government relented, sort of, and offered matching funds for anything UBC or the students could raise; this was treated as a victory, and the march was called off.

Now That's Trekking: But the really big trek of the year didn't involve UBC students at all, except as supporters and greeters. The students (and faculty) in the Forestry School at the University of Sopron in western Hungary fled en masse to Austria after the Soviet Union crushed the Hungarian uprising of 1956. When word first came of this, AMS Council seemed reluctant to act, but eventually it agreed to raise money for three students, which then became twenty students, and in the end turned into the whole Sopron Forestry School, which migrated to UBC.

But Isn't That Being Too Political? Some said AMS Council had no business involving itself in international politics like this. Some said charity begins at home: why not help local students before helping those from afar? But the general sentiment, perhaps aided by Cold War attitudes, was to aid the Hungarians and welcome them to a new land. When it comes time to act, the *Ubyssey* said, UBC students do act, and indeed it seems to have been pressure from below that got Council to do something about Hungary: that and the dedication of the AMS coordinator of activities Ben Trevino, who was also the moving force behind the Second Trek, and who went on to be elected president.

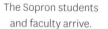

The Sopron students and faculty arrive.

Ben Trevino.

So Perhaps We Should Talk about Art Instead: This was a time of boosterism, conformity, and docility, said the *Ubyssey,* despite the Second Trek and the Hungarian affair. The only rebellious behaviour by the students, the paper said, is to walk on the grass and park illegally. But not so: some of them took it upon themselves to deface a modern sculpture that the University had placed on campus: *Three Forms,* the prize-winning creation of former UBC architecture student Robert Clothier, who went on to much greater fame as the actor who played Relic on the Canadian TV series, *The Beachcombers.*

Three Forms.

Or Music? What is this hateful noise that sounds like a toilet bowl with hiccups? asked the *Ubyssey.* We have to stop "the creeping rot of rock-and-roll at UBC," they said—by which they meant Elvis Presley.

Or Literature? Don't ban *Peyton Place*, said the *Ubyssey* when Canada Customs threatened to keep it out of the country. So no to Elvis, but yes to trashy bestsellers.

Well, How about Some of That Old-time Religion? The Inter-Varsity Christian Fellowship decided it was time to do some missionary work—but not in some faraway clime. No, no, it was time to bring the gospel to UBC, where the students, according to a totally unscientific poll conducted by the *Ubyssey*, were no longer interested in Christianity. Indeed, the *Ubyssey* called Homecoming festivities that year a celebration of "gay paganism." So Reverend John Stott spent a week on campus trying to convert the heathen—and in fact drew huge crowds.

Maybe Just Study in the Library? But the library, it turned out, was not primarily a place for studying these days, perhaps because of the lack of funding and lack of space. It was becoming a social spot, a place to meet, a place of conversation, which bothered those who did want to study. If only the extension to Brock Hall could be finished. Or that second wing of stacks. The new College of Education did open, but that mostly meant more students and especially more women, and bringing men and women together meant more "socializing."

But Don't Get Dunked in the Pond: Hazing seemed back with a vengeance this year. The Engineers especially had it in for the frosh, especially the female frosh (the "freshettes"), whom they hoisted into trees and sprayed with perfume. The Faculty Council stepped in and said, Don't do that.

Meanwhile about a hundred of the male frosh got dunked in a special tank the Engineers created (not wanting to use the library's lily pond anymore, or perhaps being forbidden to). The frosh retaliated by marching on the Engineering building and unleashing a battle of fire hoses. The place was flooded. The Faculty Council said, Don't do that either.

🌿 **AMS EXECUTIVE**
1956-1957

PRESIDENT *Don Jabour*
VICE-PRESIDENT *Murray McKenzie*
SECRETARY *Peggy Andreen*
TREASURER *Al Thackray*
COORDINATOR OF ACTIVITIES
Benjamin B. Trevino

UBYSSEY EDITOR *Sandy Ross*

1957 TO 1958

Twinkle, Twinkle, Little . . . Sputnik?

The Russians sent a rocket into space, and the rest of the world went mad, including UBC and the *Ubyssey*. "We're falling behind," people said. "We have to reform our education system." When the Russians sent a second rocket with a dog, the *Ubyssey* made jokes about "mutnik." When the Americans finally followed suit, the *Ubyssey* pretended to be relieved, but it seemed more than a pretence.

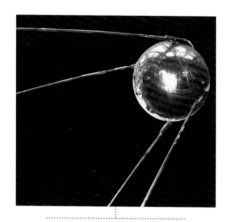

Sputnik.

Education, Education, Education:

The Sputnik controversy became part of a discussion that was already underway about education. Should the aim be to produce more scientists and technical people, or was something more well-rounded the goal? Should UBC introduce entrance exams and cater more to the intellectual elite? And where was UBC's new College of Education in all this? The new teachers' training program came under fire for being too theoretical, too focused on methodology, and just plain dull. The *Ubyssey* opened its pages to the dean of education, Neville Scarfe, who defended the program. People are always criticizing teaching programs, he said.

Phonies:

Even before Sputnik, the new editor of the *Ubyssey*, Pat Marchak, signalled a new focus for the year, her first editorial in September being a denunciation of "phonies," by which she meant students who didn't really deserve to be at university, non-serious students more interested in extra-curricular activity than academics. A serious student herself, Marchak went on to a distinguished academic career, eventually becoming UBC's Dean of Arts, and her editorial writing this year, including her piece on phonies, won her a national award.

At Christmastime, however, the *Ubyssey* announced ruefully that maybe its campaign had worked too well: no new reporters had signed up to work for the paper this year. (Were they all too busy studying?)

Award-winning Pat Marchak, *Ubyssey* editor-in-chief: thinking about phonies?

Donors:

Not willing to curtail enrolment and cater to an elite, UBC president MacKenzie called for money from new sources, and for the first time there was a campaign for private donations. More than $6 million came in, most notably from the Koerner family. The students helped out by going on a door-to-door blitz and also by raising their own fees by $5 a year, which was seen as not only important in itself, but as a way to encourage private donors—though some said, Why do we have to contribute extra? Where is the government?

Yes, Where Is the Government?

Well, the government finally visited campus, first in the person of Attorney-General Robert Bonner, and then when the premier, W.A.C. Bennett, showed up. Both encountered hostile audiences. Someone even threw a lunch bag at the premier (who promptly threw it back). He also announced an increase in funding.

And Where Are the Women?

Well, according to the *Ubyssey*, senior faculty in the English department had just been installed in the new Arts building, junior lecturers were "scattered across campus," and "women assistants were in huts." Hmm. (These were the old army huts that UBC used for years.)

Meanwhile the Brock Extension had also just opened, and the games room manager waxed lyrical about its tables for pool and ping pong, saying that even girls should come and use them. Double hmm. Well, it was another time.

Then there was a debate on AMS Council about whether to abolish the seat set aside for the Women's Undergraduate Society (WUS), a move the WUS naturally objected to, saying that women as a minority group on campus (as they still were then) needed a dedicated seat to defend their interests.

Women were also mentioned in the special Engineering edition of the *Ubyssey*, but we had better not talk about that: not for the last time the Engineers resorted to crude humour and demeaning portrayals of women, and found themselves roundly criticized.

But at Least the Students Found God: No, not that God, but the Gentleman of Distinction, or G-O—well, you get the idea. This was the work of the Women's Undergraduate Society and the Women's Athletic Directorate. Making a change from the annual search for campus queens, they held a contest for the most distinguished man on campus, someone who could set female hearts a-flutter by being "an unassuming athletic Apollo." Twenty-three contestants entered.

But Not Food: At least not good food. Students complained about cafeteria fare. The *Ubyssey* complained about the University's monopoly on food services. Students should at least be represented on the University's food committee, they said. Another alternative, of course, would have been for the students to get into the food business themselves, but that wouldn't happen for a few more decades.

Students in the cafeteria.

Nor Any Drop to Drink: What this campus needs is a pub, one columnist wrote in the paper, echoing the sentiments of the winning side the year before in a debate on allowing liquor on campus. But such a thing would have to wait for David Suzuki and the sixties.

There Was Still Art, Though: Student art, or student-bought art, in the AMS Art Gallery in the new Brock Extension. Well, it was not so much a gallery as a corridor, one commentator noted. Other commentators took to critiquing the art in the pages of the *Ubyssey*, but at the end of the year someone went further than that and vandalized several of the paintings. Shades of the Three Forms sculpture the year before.

The art gallery, or corridor, in Brock.

And in Other News: The AMS got in trouble with the local labour council for printing the *Totem* in the United States, two student Communists nearly got into trouble for trying to enter the United States, councillors got in trouble for making themselves eligible for the annual Honorary Activities Awards (they later reversed themselves), and the *Ubyssey* got in trouble for not providing enough coverage of clubs: indeed they were ordered by Council to provide more coverage, an order they resisted on the grounds of freedom of the press. (It would not be the last time Council and its newspaper clashed over clubs coverage and other things.)

Speaking of Clubs: A new one got off the ground (and into the water) this year: the Aquatic Society, or Aquasoc, for scuba divers (or frogmen as they were called then).

And then there was Fencing, a club that died out after a first appearance in the twenties, but which made a return after the war.

TOP Fencing at Totem Park in 1957.

MIDDLE Students in front of the Main Library.

AMS EXECUTIVE
1957-1958

PRESIDENT *Ben Trevino*
VICE-PRESIDENT *Ken L. Brawner*
SECRETARY *Barbara Leith*
TREASURER *George Morfitt*
COORDINATOR OF ACTIVITIES *Bryan Williams*

UBYSSEY EDITOR *Patricia (Pat) Marchak*

Meanwhile, for the less adventurous there were the joys of lounging on the lawn in front of the Main Library (this in the days before the construction of the Sedgewick and Koerner libraries pushed students to find other places in which to enjoy the outdoors).

The "frogmen" of Aquasoc, 1958–59.

1958 TO 1959

Fee Fight Ho-Hum: So read a *Ubyssey* headline in the early days of the fight against a $100 fee hike announced by the Board of Governors. At first the student opposition seemed weak, but by the end of the year 2,500 were marching on campus. There were calls for another Trek or even a student strike, but Council urged restraint, and Ben Trevino, architect of the Second Trek two years earlier, warned against overusing the term.

In the end the increase went through ("regretfully," said the Board) to cope with the lack of government funding, the increase in enrolment, and the need to pay higher salaries to faculty. The *Ubyssey* wrung its hands and said more should have been done, and perhaps its frustration led to its going a bit overboard in its annual joke or "goon" issue.

Goon Issue: The *Ubyssey* had a long tradition of publishing joke stories and even whole joke issues, especially at the end of each term, but this year they were felt to have crossed a line in an issue in which they not only satirized the government and the Board of Governors over the fee hike but mocked Eleanor Roosevelt, widow of the late American president, who came to campus to talk of world leadership and to open International House. And the final straw was an Easter section of the paper, which mocked religion in a way that many found sacrilegious.

Student Council stepped in and suspended the whole staff.

A Bad Year for Editors: Not only did the whole *Ubyssey* staff get suspended at the end of the year, but earlier the previous editor-in-chief and the city editor resigned after a missing artwork from the Brock Hall collection was discovered in their

The *Ubyssey*'s cartoonist saw the actions of the government and the Board of Governors as pushing students and faculty over a cliff. That's the smiling premier with a halo over his head and the Board of Governors represented by a man in a stovepipe hat.

Eleanor Roosevelt, the "internationally-known humanitarian," as the *Ubyssey* described her in a more sober moment.

possession. Just a prank, they said, but they were gone.

Art, Art: The Brock collection was much expanded this year thanks to a donation of paintings by *Maclean's* magazine which gave the AMS a notable collection of Canadian art by such artists as E.J. Hughes, Arthur Lismer, and Jack Shadbolt. And said the *Ubyssey*'s art critic, the "delight" of the collection was that it was right there on the walls of the Brock. "We can live with these pictures," he said. Perhaps the *Ubyssey* editor should have been content with that.

Women, Women: Before things got serious at the end of the year, one of the preoccupations on campus seemed to be how women looked. To be fair, there were also comments on how the men looked. And the conclusions were not flattering. At one panel discussion on campus a panellist called UBC's women "the scraggiest lot I have ever seen." The downtown papers said the women needed more charm, and indeed a charm school did appear mid-year, though some said UBC's women were not there to be models, but to get an education.

But should they be there at all, one wag asked in a letter to the editor? What's the point of educating women if they're just going to get married and not use their degrees? To which another letter-writer responded by saying some men don't use their degrees either. So there.

And the men came under fire for dressing sloppily, and the *Ubyssey* was happy to provide fashion advice and to open its pages to writers who bemoaned the fact that only the Law students habitually wore jackets and ties. Which led to someone saying it was a cultural thing: the British were much superior on such matters. And so on, until the fee issue forced such matters into the background.

And Where Will This All Lead To? Kissing perhaps. But not for nurses. A nursing student got suspended for two weeks for kissing her boyfriend in broad daylight at Vancouver General Hospital.

Or Perhaps Even Further? An announcement appeared in the *Ubyssey* about the formation of a Free Love Society and advertising its first meeting. Forty students showed up, all but four of them male, but the whole thing turned out to be a hoax (though not for the forty perhaps).

Jokes and Pranks: Besides the removal of the artwork and the *Ubyssey* goon edition, there was a mock coup d'état at an AMS General Meeting. Council members were kidnapped, and a Student Safety Committee declared that it was in control and going to introduce reforms about politics, religion, sex, and everything else. No one seemed to pay much attention.

And there were the usual dunkings in the lily pond and insults tossed at the Engineers (the *Ubyssey* continued to pursue its running feud with the men in Applied Science), but hazing was a bit tame: the paper complained that the frosh weren't fighting back this year, but were "masochistically submissive." On the other hand, the Engineers lightened up the year-end general meeting with fireworks and a stink bomb. And, oh, there were snowball fights.

But What about Culture? Well, the AMS did its part this year, inviting noted poets such as Stephen Spender, Langston Hughes, and Marianne Moore to campus. Also the Beat poet Kenneth Patchen. And a sort of Beat poet emerged from among the students themselves: one issue of the *Ubyssey* featured a poem on the editorial page. "Growl," it was called, playing off the well-known Beat poem of the time, "Howl." Author: George Bowering,

an Arts student who went on to a distinguished literary career.

Meanwhile the AMS Film Society pushed the limits by showing Nazi and Soviet propaganda films and also the risqué movie *Baby Doll*.

And the Rest of the Usual Suspects: Parking continued to spark complaints from those forced to pay fines (though one smart thinker said maybe the fines could help fill the University's funding shortfall). Some suggested fanciful alternatives to driving, such as a monorail. Or bike riding. Meanwhile there were also complaints about high bus fares, but no one connected the two issues.

A parking lot in 1960.

🌿 **AMS EXECUTIVE**
1958–1959

PRESIDENT *Charles J. (Chuck) Connaghan*
VICE-PRESIDENT *Jairus Mutambikwa*
TREASURER *John Helliwell*
SECRETARY *Wendy Amor*
COORDINATOR OF ACTIVITIES
Jim Horsman

UBYSSEY EDITOR *Dave Robertson/ Al Forrest*

And there were complaints about bookstore prices. *Plus ça change*.

Anticipating the Future: There was talk of a new student union building to replace Brock Hall. Also talk on the University's side about developing land and renting out property: one day there might even be a shopping centre on campus serving non-student residents. And perhaps inspired by the Suez crisis of a couple of years before, the *Ubyssey* opened its pages to a discussion of Islam.

Not on This Campus: The *Ubyssey* also declared its opposition to a series of phrases: "golly gosh," "gee whiz," "crazy man," and "thank you muchly." Anyone using these was not welcome at the paper. Instead, what was wanted were reporters who distrusted student leaders and could blow smoke through their ears. No mention of appropriating artworks or committing sacrilege, but those things came later.

1959 TO 1960

Poltergeists: That was the Film Society's explanation for why they were having so many problems this year: everything from poor sound quality to reels getting out of order to bad splices. They decided to hold a seance to deal with the unruly spirits, and things did get better for them as the year went on.

Cinema 16: A more this-worldly source of problems for Filmsoc was the emergence of Cinema 16, a new group wanting to show avant-garde and foreign language films, such as Marlene Dietrich's *Blue Angel*. Council was not keen to authorize a rival to Filmsoc, but eventually the two found a way to resolve their differences.

More Poltergeists? "Lost, one rabbit," said the ad in the *Ubyssey*. A six-foot high wooden rabbit advertising a production of *Harvey* (the play about a giant invisible rabbit) went missing. Three weeks later the rabbit showed up with no explanation.

Where, oh where, did Harvey go?
Or did he just turn invisible?

More Things Lost: This time the *Ubyssey* staff. In this case there was less mystery; at the end of the previous year most of the staff was dismissed because of the sacrilegious "goon" issue of the paper. This

year the paper had trouble finding experienced journalists. When they did find some, they didn't stay. It all added to the somewhat disorientating feel to the last year of the fifties.

She Sells Seashells: No, make that shoes. The frosh queen was selling shoes this year, right on the back page of the *Ubyssey*. (This was actually a tradition dating back at least a couple of years.)

Pretty girl, pretty shoes . . .
Is nothing sacred?

Pick a Card, Any Card: Meanwhile a Parapsychology Society was established and set out to discover whether any UBC students had ESP. They ran a test in the pages of the *Ubyssey* and announced that two students did indeed show signs of extra-sensory powers.

More? There were lily pond dunkings throughout the year, but not so much on official hazing day, and Student Council heard a report calling for an end to hazing (would this finally be the year?) because of the

The *Ubyssey* wonders where its staff has gone.

Do you have ESP? Take the test.

danger of injuries and the possible blow to the University's reputation, and also just because people weren't that interested anymore. Old traditions fading away.

And indeed the AMS did away with hazing day altogether starting in 1960–61: no more green beanies and other demeaning practices imposed on the frosh.

Anybody Seen the General Meeting?

This was the last year the AMS held two regular General Meetings. For a while there had been difficulties meeting quorum for the Fall Meeting, and more than once there had been attempts to abolish it, but without quorum what could they do? The *Ubyssey* said the Fall Meeting must be the only institution kept alive by a lack of interest. But finally the Spring Meeting mustered up quorum and passed a motion to abolish its Fall counterpart, though there were questions about procedures: were the rules really followed?

Rules, Rules, Rules: Council worried that the RCMP were cracking down on hitchhikers and that the City of Vancouver was cracking down on illegal suites (thus reducing the hous-

ing market for students). Council wanted to enforce its own rules against gambling in Brock Hall and the University's rules about silence in the library. It got confused over the rules on reports ("Do we vote to receive them or approve them?") and wished there was some way to make Council meetings shorter: one special meeting (the overlap meeting of outgoing and incoming councillors) lasted more than ten hours, from 3:30 in the afternoon until 2:00 in the morning.

Bigger Rules: There was also a commission established to look into the whole structure of the AMS. Our institutions don't match our growing size, said the *Ubyssey*. The commission came up with a suggestion to increase the powers of the Undergraduate Societies

Committee to give more weight to the individual faculties.

Bigger Buildings: Also needed, given a student population that for the first time exceeded 10,000 and was expected to hit 20,000 in another decade, was a bigger student union building. The Brock was too small and no longer central. A place with more food outlets would be useful too. It was important to create some sort of unity via a SUB to avoid the student body turning into "a disunified conglomeration of faculties," said the *Ubyssey*.

The Future: The *Ubyssey* also worried that there were too many women on Council: one day they might take over, foisting a pink SUB with frilly curtains on the unsuspecting men and turning the *Ubyssey* itself into a glamour magazine. Hmm.

The Present: The *Ubyssey* investigated male-female relations at the

Learning social etiquette? Life at Fort Camp.

Fort Camp residence. "By being exposed to the company of each other," the paper concluded, "men and women may learn social etiquette to a far better degree than by living in separate areas."

There Will Be Blood: Or there was, at the annual blood drive, but even that couldn't go smoothly. One letter-writer complained that there was too much heavy-handed publicity shaming people into donating—and even so the drive came up short of its target. Then there was confusion over which faculty had produced the most donations. Nursing? The Aggies?

And Poor Art: Art took a hit this year again. First, UBC's art gallery was robbed. Then the students' Brock collection was vandalized: someone smeared red paint over two paintings, damaging one beyond repair, though one wag commented, "How can you tell?" Everyone's a critic.

The Lionel Thomas mural, *Symbols for Education.*

But on a More Positive Note: The Lionel Thomas mural commissioned by Student Council went up on the exterior of Brock Hall. And a Sailing Club launched.

"THIS PAINTING is a masterpiece . . . now where is the one that got ruined?"

The *Ubyssey* cartoonist makes a statement about modern art.

🌿 **AMS EXECUTIVE**
1959–1960

PRESIDENT *Pete Meekison*
VICE-PRESIDENT *Pete Haskins*
TREASURER *Dave Edgar*
SECRETARY *Lynne Rogers*
COORDINATOR OF ACTIVITIES
Russell Brink

UBYSSEY EDITOR *Kerry White*

1960 TO 1961

And This Is What We'll Look Like from Now On: At least constitutionally. A new system comes in. No more electing the whole Council at large; now it will be rep by pop, or by undergraduate society. A Special General Meeting said yes yes yes, and we lived happily ever after. This after years of discussions and an emerging consensus that the "Ivory Tower" Council could only reconnect with the students via their individual faculties, such as Science and Arts.

Science and Arts: Speaking of Science and Arts, students in the pure sciences finally got their own undergraduate society (SUS), as what had been the Arts and Science Undergraduate Society (ASUS) split in two. No more including physicists and chemists among the Artsmen. And this two years before the University decided to split the Faculty of Arts and Science.

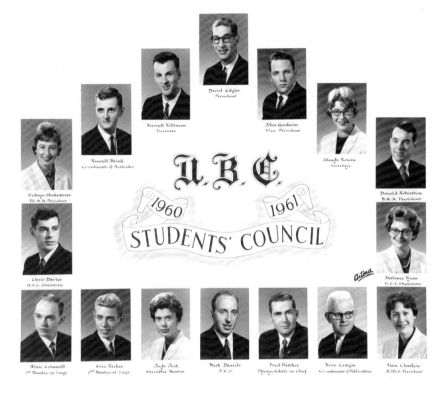

The old Council and the new.

University Boulevard around 1960.

And This is Where We'll Live (We Thought): On University Boulevard. Well, not right in the middle of it, but where it meets East Mall in what was then a parking lot (D lot). The students voted in a referendum to put a new student union building there, but in the end the SUB went elsewhere.

Parking: Meanwhile students were up in arms over the University's new approach to parking penalties. Now there would be not just fines but towing, done by Buster's Towing. The Engineers, among others, objected and launched a campaign to "Buck Fuster's." One student shied a rock through a tow truck's window and was fined for his trouble.

Bicycles? More as a joke than anything else, AMS president Dave Edgar took to riding a girl's bicycle, called the Jabberwockcycle. A *Ubyssey* columnist remarked that turning to bicycles could solve the campus parking problems and at the same time afford students some physical exercise and thus convince the University it was no longer necessary to continue compulsory courses in physical education (which the *Ubyssey* abhorred). But bicycles' time had not yet come.

Vandalism: Rowdiness was the order of the day on Homecoming Weekend, with drunken crowds tearing down the goalposts during the football game (during!), stealing a drum major's hat, and even making off with a referee's penalty flag. Not to mention careening wildly around the football field in a car. And it wasn't even the Engineers, somebody said.

"Drunking": The *Ubyssey* said the problem was that the prohibition against drinking on campus just meant that the drinking went on secretly and was done to excess (resulting in "drunking"). It was time to allow liquor on campus, some were saying.

Lost: But in the meantime there was drunkenness and disorder. Rowdiness. Rebels without a cause. The Engineers did get into the act, with some kidnapping, though they were relatively tame this year. The one kidnapping was "just a normal kidnapping," they said. And then the Engineers' president was kidnapped, by the Associated Women Students (formerly known as the Women's Undergraduate Society), though it was all in a good cause: the ransom was three hundred cans of food to go to charity. ("Keep him," the Engineers said good-naturedly, "and we'll donate 600.")

And Council felt out of touch and directionless, until the big Council reform finally occurred, and the *Ubyssey* reprinted an article from the *Alumni Chronicle* saying the campus spirit was gone.

Stop Talking to Us about Campus Spirit: So said some. We have studies to attend to, said a grad student. And one letter-writer said he was tired of the attacks on apathy. Apathy meant freedom for a person to do what they wanted and not have to take part in rah-rah events.

The *Ubyssey* still worried about spirit, though, such as the lack of attendance at football games. They decided the problem was an excess of clubs and cliquiness. The students have become too fragmented, "provincial," they said. There is no unity—but maybe the new Council system would unite the fragments.

Debauchery: Was it an attempt to revive spirit, or a sign of its decline that the *Ubyssey* ran a "Gam Gazers Game," in which readers were invited to match the legs of ten beauty contestants to their faces? And then there was dark talk of prostitution, and threats of slander suits. And a controversial debate about chastity that prompted protests in the provincial legislature.

Autonomy: Both the rowdiness and the governance problems led people to worry about AMS autonomy: If we don't fix things, the University will take it away. The University had already appointed a director of student affairs, which caused some alarm.

But autonomy was a strange thing in these days. It was more like the autonomy of a University department. The AMS was still subject to oversight by the administration (Council minutes still were sent over for approval), and when the administration wanted something done (like an end to noise in the library), they'd ask the AMS, which would say, "Ready, aye, ready." True independence would have to wait.

The flip side of this, though, was that the University would do things for the AMS, for instance cancel classes for an AMS general meeting, and the AMS sometimes seemed to think it was just an extension of the University, worrying about doing things which would give not the students but the University a bad name.

Student Power: On the other hand, there was an early glimmering of student power this year, with Council setting up a committee to look into what general academic and other University issues students should legitimately have a say in. Council said it wanted to find some way to let the University Senate know what the students thought on academic matters. (It eventually found a way.)

1961 TO 1962

Beds, Books, and Vandals: Back at the beginning of 1961, a new club on campus, the Intellectual Stunt Committee (ISC), took up an idea from South Africa and pushed a bed forty-two miles from the Peace Arch at the US border back to campus. All for charity, combining with a book drive by the UBC branch of the World University Services Committee (WUSC).

In the next few weeks bed-pushing became a thing across Canada (but we were first, the UBC pushers said), even drawing the attention of *Time* magazine.

And it worked too, though perhaps too well. WUSC had hoped for five hundred books to distribute overseas; instead it received seven thousand.

While it left its friends at WUSC to figure out what to do with the books (they eventually worked things out with WUSC headquarters in Geneva), the ISC moved on to other stunts, from attempting to traverse the Burrard Inlet in a bathtub to commandeering a tank and invading a general meeting to staging a mock coronation, which unfortunately brought out the Vandal in UBC's students . . .

King for a Day: Homer Tomlinson, self-proclaimed King of the World, was travelling around the globe to bring peace, and his travels took him to UBC, where he also claimed to be King of the University. Crowds came out to see him, but fearing for the safety of such an elderly gentleman (he was sixty-eight), Council secreted him inside the Brock.

But never fear, the Intellectual Stunt Committee came forward with their own candidate for king, seeking to perform a coronation ceremony in front of the crowds outside the Brock.

But along came the Engineers, saying, No king at UBC, and pandemonium ensued: eggs were thrown (there were charges that the Engineers had come armed with them), and the would-be ISC king was tossed in the lily pond. Damage to Brock Hall amounted to $80 (almost $650 in today's dollars).

More Vandalism: That was first term. Second term was Frosh Week, a new institution replacing the old first term hazing period. In its first year (1960–61) it seemed innocuous, but this year it turned into a war between the frosh and the Engineers, culminating in a "riot" at the Engineering building, which among other things featured a car being pushed through glass doors and fire hoses being deployed. But at least there was no hazing.

When not worrying what to do with seven thousand books, the UBC branch of the World University Services Committee sponsored conferences on such matters as the issues facing overseas students at UBC.

The *Ubyssey* cartoonist's view of the war between Engineers and frosh.

Those Engineers: The Engineers were active this year, as always. According to the *Ubyssey*, there were only three faculties with spirit this year: the Engineers, the Aggies, and the Forestry students. The Engineers went down to the University of Washington and hoisted their flag, and perhaps their biggest prank of the year was stealing 101 toilet seats from various campus buildings. They also kidnapped Arts students and carried them around campus in a cage, and of course there were plenty of dunkings in the lily pond. (But at least there was no hazing.)

In revenge, the Arts students devised a coffin supposedly holding the Engineers' president and dumped it in the lily pond. Someone also shaved the Engineers' president's head. Things were different in those days.

Those Aggies: The Agriculture students got in trouble for publishing something called the *Moobyssey*, which was apparently so obscene they got fined for it. No copies seem to have survived, so who knows what it contained?

Meanwhile the Forestry students contented themselves with winning the blood drive competition and the Ugly Man contest (another ISC stunt, meant to raise money for Tibetan refugees).

You're Going to Need a Bigger SUB: Student Council was expecting to spend $800,000 on a new building for the students to replace the Brock, but Porter Butts, an expert on such matters, came to town and said no way. For a campus this size you'll need to spend $5 million and build something six times the size of what you've been planning.

So back to the drawing board or to the fundraising circuit. The AMS approached the provincial government, but was rebuffed.

Meanwhile the other student building project, the new winter sports arena, did get outside funding, from the Molson family, but the AMS was dismayed when the University said that the $100,000 from the Molsons would be deducted from the University's contribution. Some asked why the students were paying at all (the AMS had pledged $250,000): shouldn't this be the University's responsibility?

The winter sports centre that the AMS helped to build.

Here I Park: One student refused to let his car be towed away this year, sitting in it and refusing to get out when it was targeted for illegal parking. The tow truck operator said he wasn't allowed to tow with a person inside; the RCMP showed up and a dean; but no one could convince the student to relent, and he eventually drove away unhindered.

Such civil disobedience did not become widespread on this or other issues. There were plenty of complaints about parking, especially when the University announced a plan to charge annual parking fees on top of its fines and towing. A report came out saying UBC's parking fines and towing practices went much beyond what was done elsewhere. The *Ubyssey* editorialized, students wrote letters to the editor, but no direct action ensued—except that students and faculty in Geography warned that the campus might turn into one giant parking lot and instead proposed introducing express buses to campus, and indeed by the end of the year an express bus route was in the works, to run on Broadway. Bussing before parking? (But in fact before bussing became the major alternative to driving, UBC invested in multi-storey parking garages, or parkades, to house the growing number of cars arriving on campus in the last few decades of the twentieth century.)

Ban the Bomb: An anti-nuclear club formed, but was unable to muster much support: about seventy students, not many more than had spontaneously gathered to lend support to the recalcitrant parker. The *Ubyssey* shook its editorial head and lamented the lack of interest in international affairs.

Communism: But there was still interest in Communism. Communist speakers kept coming to campus, only to be pelted with lunch bags and milk cartons. And this year some anti-communist groups formed on campus to warn against the "Red threat." The *Ubyssey*'s letter pages were filled. The Communists asked for courtesy. One letter writer, Ross H. Munro, who went on to become an expert on the People's Republic of China, said they didn't deserve any.

Student Power: And there were murmurings about what would later become issues in the struggles for a greater student voice in the University. The issue of student representation on University committees came up, especially representation on the parking committees and the committee overseeing the sports arena project. The AMS worried about being relegated to the status of junior partner—but in some ways it still clung to that status. When there was confusion over AMS eligibility rules for student elections, the AMS president asked the University to intervene to set things straight (the University declined).

But on the other hand the AMS felt strong enough to ask for an end to attendance rules and compulsory physical education and for the introduction of a second term

break; also more eating facilities, longer library hours, and interesting seminars.

Teaching methods were in the air: the *Ubyssey* ran articles about how discussions would be better than lectures, and complained about professors who read the same lecture notes year after year. They also ran an article about student evaluations, something not yet seen at UBC.

The AMS also sent a delegation to Victoria asking for more scholarships and an end to sales tax on textbooks.

Grad Students: Yes, UBC had grad students back then. Not very many (a few hundred), but this year they got their own building, thanks largely to the generosity of the Koerner family, and questions were raised about who should pay for what in running the building.

The issue of whether grad students should pay AMS fees also came up. They already were, but now that they had their own building, some argued they didn't need AMS facilities or resources, so should be exempt, and after all they had their own fees. The result was a referendum that exempted graduate students from AMS fees after their first year, an exemption that would subsequently be reversed.

International students also had a new building, opened by Eleanor Roosevelt on her visit in 1959.

Football: UBC's Thunderbirds won the Western championship and were hoping to play the Eastern champions (from Queen's), but Queen's balked, and there was not as yet an organized national structure (no Vanier Cup), so it was left there.

The new home for graduate students.

Frats: The discrimination issue still lingered. The last two fraternities known to have clauses restricting membership to "white Christians" removed them, but a Senate investigation later said three fraternities were still discriminating.

AMS EXECUTIVE
1961–1962

PRESIDENT *Alan Cornwall*
1ST VICE-PRESIDENT *Eric Ricker*
2ND VICE-PRESIDENT *Patrick Glenn*
TREASURER *Malcolm Scott*
SECRETARY *Lynn McDonald*
COORDINATOR OF ACTIVITIES
W. Douglas ("Doug") Stewart

UBYSSEY EDITOR *Roger McAfee*

TOP Students socializing at International House.

BOTTOM The Western champs.

1962 TO 1963

Let's Trek Again: The Twist dance craze came to UBC this year, and so did yet another Trek. This time the students had a twofold aim: calling for more money for the University and also supporting the call by the new UBC president John B. Macdonald for additional postsecondary institutions to be created.

Because the students took their inspiration from President Macdonald, this Trek became known as the Back Mac campaign.

I'm Their Leader; I Must Follow Them: President Macdonald actually seemed a bit embarrassed that his recommendations produced such enthusiastic support from the students. Don't be rash, he told them, but they marched and petitioned and sent telegrams, and meanwhile the government was already saying it was moving to create new colleges in the province, though as to more money for UBC, well . . .

That was at the end of the year. At the beginning the *Ubyssey* had complained that no one was doing anything. The campus was just a "passive vegetating sponge," one of its columnists wrote. Some vegetation, some sponge, as Winston Churchill might have said.

Beer! The Hotel Georgia, known jokingly as the downtown branch of UBC campus, closed its bar. Students were outraged. That's where we go to drink, they said.

"Bring Back the Georgia," a sign read at the AMS general meeting in the fall. The ostensible point of the meeting was to debate whether the frosh should have a special seat of their own on Student Council (the answer was yes despite the opposition of the Engineers, who said the frosh weren't mature enough). The Engineers

128

demonstrated their own maturity by delivering the AMS president to the meeting wrapped in toilet paper and then afterwards dunked as many councillors as they could find in their dunking tank.

The AMS president arrives at the general meeting dressed like a mummy, thanks to the Engineers.

Drinking: Did we mention that students indulged in drinking off campus? On campus too at traditional "boat races" (drinking contests) held at half-time at the annual Teacup football game between the women in Nursing and those in Home Ec. And yet officially the AMS remained a dry organization, warning attendees at the annual Frosh Retreat not to drink (though officials who issued the warning were themselves found to be drinking in private). Hypocrisy, said the *Ubyssey*. We need a campus pub, said the Science students. It's too difficult, said the AMS president. And so it would remain, but just for a few more years.

Cuba Sí? Missiles No? On a more serious note, the students showed

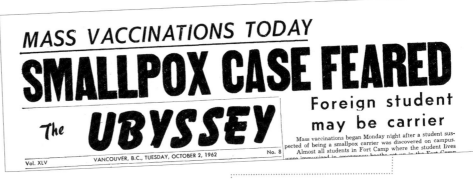

MASS VACCINATIONS TODAY

SMALLPOX CASE FEARED

The UBYSSEY

Foreign student may be carrier

Mass vaccinations began Monday night after a student suspected of being a smallpox carrier was discovered on campus. Almost all students in Fort Camp where the student lives were immunised in emergency booths set up in the Fort Camp

Vol. XLV   VANCOUVER, B.C., TUESDAY, OCTOBER 2, 1962   No. 8

Fears were raised about smallpox.

that they cared about international politics, especially when it affected their own survival, by turning out en masse (five thousand was the estimate) to hear professors talk about the Cuban Missile Crisis. The *Ubyssey*, which distinguished itself this year with some serious investigative journalism, sought to discover where students should go if the bombs started falling. Unfortunately, no one could tell them.

Smallpox! News that a student from Thailand had been hospitalized with a mysterious rash thought to be smallpox caused thousands of students to get vaccinated. It turned out to be a false alarm.

Have Soapbox, Will Rant: Someone who cared about everything, it seemed, was Dietrich Luth, described by the *Ubyssey* at one point as the person "disagreed with more than anyone on campus." Luth would stand up on his soapbox in front of the library and harangue listeners about nuclear disarmament, communism, elections, the Back Mac campaign, and the blood drive

(giving blood was good for your sex life, he said). Listeners responded with that UBC staple, fruit from their lunch bags (or even the whole lunch bag), and one time exceeded themselves by setting his soapbox on fire. Luth took it all in good humour, even seeming to be proud of the negative reactions he provoked.

Keep Us Safe! Meanwhile larger groups expressed concerns about campus safety, notably about the need for a crosswalk on Marine Drive and the lack of a campus ambulance. The University did put in a crosswalk. As to an ambulance, well, after a car crash in which injured students had to wait 40 minutes for help to arrive, the University produced a sort of ambulance (derided by the *Ubyssey* as a "truckwithfirstaidequipment").

The graduating class tried to donate a real ambulance, but the University said no, that would cause us too much operating expense. But wait, they said, we're building a hospital on campus, and then there will be plenty of ambulances.

Vote in a Lump, Vote Calathump: The National Non-Conforming Calathumpians arrived on campus. Yes, this was a thing. At first it seemed they were a serious group jumping into the religious debates on campus (provoked by one professor's publicly declared support for atheism), but then they seemed more like a joke group who decided to take part in the AMS elections when several of the positions seemed in danger of being filled by acclamation. The *Ubyssey* praised them for adding interest to the election, but they all lost.

Fraternities: The *Ubyssey* was less pleased with the role of the fraternities in the elections, accusing them of being an electoral machine that scooped up far more than their fair share of seats on Council. The fraternities hotly denied this, and the outgoing AMS president blamed the *Ubyssey*'s coverage for the lack of candidates in the new elections: fraternity people were afraid to run, he said.

Racial Discrimination: The fraternities also came under attack for noisy parties, but not this year for racial discrimination. Instead, the *Ubyssey* found such discrimination among the landlords in Point Grey, several of whom said they wouldn't rent to non-whites. The *Ubyssey* also revealed that many of the available rentals were substandard and said something should be done. Perhaps in response the City of Vancouver announced that they would be closing down many of such suites and rooms because they were illegal. Not perhaps what the *Ubyssey* had in mind.

Student on soapbox (probably not Dietrich Luth).

🌿 **AMS EXECUTIVE**
1962–1963

PRESIDENT
W. Douglas ("Doug") Stewart
1ST VICE-PRESIDENT
Peter B. Shepard
2ND VICE-PRESIDENT
Eduard M. ("Ed") Lavalle
TREASURER *Malcolm G. Scott*
SECRETARY *Barbara Bennett*
COORDINATOR OF ACTIVITIES
Bernie Papke

UBYSSEY EDITOR *Keith Bradbury*

1963 TO 1964

Those Engineers: The Engineers outdid themselves this year, pulling off stunt after stunt, from running forty-seven candidates for coordinator of activities in the AMS elections to posting a phony exam schedule that had panicky students running to the registrar about having to write four exams on one day. Not to mention the usual dunkings or "tankings" (their new word for watery immersion, because they now had a water tank to put people in), along with letting the air out of a patrol vehicle's tires (they got reprimanded for that one) and hoisting student politicians onto the roof of the library.

But their stunt to end all stunts involved campus sculpture . . .

It's Ugly, but Is It Art? What are these strange new forms on campus, people said in September. New sculptures. Rather ugly. More of this abstract art. Some people hated it.

Then one day the Engineers went out and smashed them all. Oh, those barbarians. How could they?

But wait, said the Engineers, calm down: that wasn't art; that was junk that we created ourselves. Apparently, you can't tell the difference. And now we've destroyed it, so there. Oh. A stunt with a point.

Anything You Can Do: Not wanting to be outdone, the Science students also staged a stunt with a point: a mock accident at the UBC gates at the campus entrance on Blanca Street, which they said were a hazard to traffic. The gates were later moved.

The Blanca entrance in later years: no more dangerous gates.

But Back to Those Engineers: The Engineers were after even bigger game than art appreciation at the spring general meeting. They proposed a motion to abolish the AMS. However, the motion never got discussed because the Forestry students let off smoke bombs, causing chaos and bringing the meeting to a premature end. What a circus, said the *Ubyssey*.

The Old Order Changeth: The AMS itself survived, but other things disappeared this year: the Undergraduate Societies Committee (made redundant by the transformation of Student Council into a body based on representatives from the undergraduate societies), the Associated Women Students (the former Women's Undergraduate Society, whose members no longer saw a point to it), and student control of the AMS administration: time to hire an executive secretary and other professional staff, the AMS decided, to lift the administrative burdens from the elected student politicians. The professionalization of the AMS.

Yeah, yeah, yeah: Some people weren't quite ready for the new, including the *Ubyssey*, which dismissed the Beatles as a passing fad. And the censors weren't quite ready for sex and nudity in the movies. A film produced by UBC student Larry Kent called *The Bitter Ash* and featuring wild goings-on at parties (Drug-taking! Adultery!) got banned in the downtown theatres, though it managed screenings on campus. And the *Ubyssey* was a bit confused

Larry Kent.

131

about marijuana: it ran a three-part series, most of which seemed sympathetic or neutral, but which ran under a headline saying that pot was a "deadly monkey."

Anti-Calendar? Where the *Ubyssey* was more on the cutting edge was with student evaluation of teaching. They ran articles on "anti-calendars" that elsewhere were coming out to rate professors and also ran articles discussing various departments (political science, chemistry). They also published a letter from sociology students complaining about boring professors and irrelevant course material, adding that too often professors were more interested in research than teaching. A sign of protests to come.

Anti-Administration? Where the *Ubyssey* also led the way was in the response to the unexpected tuition increase announced by President Macdonald in January. We backed you, they said (alluding to the previous year's Back Mac campaign), and now you do this. But mostly they criticized the government for not providing enough funding and seemed in the end to accept that the tuition increase could not be avoided.

This was not the position taken by AMS president Malcolm Scott, who used such intemperate language that President-elect Roger McAfee said one of his goals would have to be to repair relations with the University. And the tuition increase went through, of course.

The *Ubyssey* cartoonist calls for UBC president John B. Macdonald to change his mind about raising fees.

Intemperate? Us? Speaking of intemperate language, the *Ubyssey* got carried away in denouncing the influence of Quebec students on the newly created Canadian Union of Students (the former National Federation of Canadian University Students, just shorn of two initials). It even used a derogatory term for French-Canadians, and got censured for its pains. Meanwhile AMS Council tried to take a more conciliatory approach to suddenly resurgent Quebec nationalism, passing a motion recognizing Quebec as a separate nation within Confederation: more than forty years before the Canadian parliament did the same thing.

Loans and Rumours of Loans: Part of the issue with the Quebec students was the newly proposed Canada Student Loans program, which the AMS and the *Ubyssey* welcomed, but which faced opposition from Quebec, where it was seen as an intrusion by the federal government into an area of provincial jurisdiction. Meanwhile AMS Council mused about creating an emergency loan program for UBC students, and one AMS executive (Jim Ward) became a leading figure in a campaign to raise money for a school in Bechuanaland, in Africa.

Johnny, We Hardly Knew Ye: The biggest international story of the year was much closer to home than Africa. It was the assassination of US president John F. Kennedy, an act that shocked students and staff at UBC as much as anywhere. UBC shut down, as did an AMS referendum on the SUB. The *Ubyssey* spoke of a sense of loss that students felt. One reporter said, "It's like the world coming to an end." The paper speculated that this was because of his youth, or his seeming to be a symbol of Youth, of the New Frontier that would replace the old order.

The SUB: The world didn't actually end, but what was prematurely stopped, or at least postponed, was the SUB referendum, a strange two-headed creature that asked first if students were in favour of a new student union building and then, separately, whether they would pay extra to build it. Yes, said the students, let's build it. But no, we don't want to pay for it; build it with existing funds.

Memorial service for President Kennedy in the Armoury.

But that turned out to be impossible, so there was a second referendum three months later, and this time the students okayed a $5 increase in their AMS fee, and the SUB was good to go, with plans being made for an architectural competition, and talk of a special donation from religious sources for a Christian chapel as part of the project (that never happened). A site was finally settled on: at the old stadium.

Winter Sports: The other major student construction project of the decade, the Winter Sports Arena, opened and played host to the Canadian Olympic hockey team, a largely UBC endeavour under the guidance of Father David Bauer, a respected hockey coach who the year before had led UBC's hockey Thunderbirds to a Western championship.

Cancer Sticks: The US Surgeon General warned that cigarettes cause cancer, and UBC students began vowing to quit, though the *Ubyssey* noted there were still clouds of blue haze in the cafeteria and even at Council meetings. As for classrooms, as long as students used ash trays, that seemed to be okay. This was a part of the old order that would definitely change.

Symbols: The Arts Undergraduate Society instituted its Last Lecture program, seeking professors and others on campus to give a talk as if it were their last. Roy Daniells of the English department used his to call for a new Canadian emblem: the unicorn. Meanwhile, when a symposium called for Canadian historical figures to replace the Queen on Canadian currency, AMS president Scott objected, saying he didn't want any "Diefenbucks" (an

allusion to former Prime Minister Diefenbaker and his currency devaluation); nor would he like to see even Sir John A. Macdonald on our money. Oh, well, some things happen despite objections.

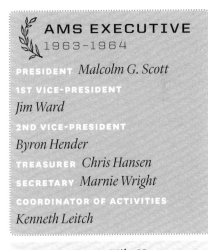

AMS EXECUTIVE
1963-1964

PRESIDENT *Malcolm G. Scott*

1ST VICE-PRESIDENT
Jim Ward

2ND VICE-PRESIDENT
Byron Hender

TREASURER *Chris Hansen*

SECRETARY *Marnie Wright*

COORDINATOR OF ACTIVITIES
Kenneth Leitch

UBYSSEY EDITOR *Mike Hunter*

133

1964 TO 1965

Leaders of the World, Unite! But they wouldn't. Instead, there was the future leader of the Communist Party of Canada (Marxist-Leninist) tussling with the future leader of the Progressive Conservative Party of Canada. And the AMS president tussling with the future Communist leader. In fact, everyone seemed to be tussling with him. And meanwhile the AMS president was staving off the first Council revolt since Council was transformed into a body representing the undergraduate societies: it had probably been only a matter of time till that happened.

The Bains of Their Existence: Hardial Bains, that is, a graduate student from India who involved himself in AMS activities, pushing the AMS to start an academic activities committee and talking about "intellectual revolution," from which he eventually graduated to proletarian revolution and the founding of a

new Communist Party, along with the BC Student Federation, which devoted itself to protests and demonstrations. That's not the way to get things done at UBC, said AMS president Roger McAfee: you need facts and rationality. And thus were the lines laid down between moderate and radical, a division that would persist among the students for decades.

Presidents of the World, Unite! This at least did happen: the undergraduate society presidents, who now made up the majority of Student Council, began caucusing before Council meetings. There's no need for that, said President McAfee, but the other presidents accused him of railroading policies through Council, not providing them enough background information or not giving them enough time to digest it when he did.

LEFT Hardial Bains: working for the revolution.

BELOW AMS president McAfee, left, looking at plans for the student union building.

"No railroading here." The *Ubyssey*'s satirical take on the clash between the AMS president and Council. (The cartoon is by Jeff Wall, who went on to a have a respected career as an art photographer.)

Kim Is Cuddlier: That would be Kim Campbell, who later became the first female leader of the Progressive Conservative party and the first female prime minister of Canada. But long before that she was the first female frosh president at UBC. For her pains she ended up being kidnapped by the Engineers (of course) and hoisted into a tree, but the Engineering president, out of chivalry or romantic interest, rescued her from his fellow Engineers, only to be dunked in the lily pond for *his* pains. Traitor, they said.

Once back on earth, the future prime minister was not shy about making pronouncements on every-thing from the superiority of women to the silliness of Hardial Bains. And when there was talk of new blue and gold ties for the boys, honour-ing UBC's colours, she said the girls should get blue and gold striped underwear. In your heart you know she's right.

K. CAMPBELL
Frosh

Lady Godiva: Anticipating the notion of striped underwear, the Engineers early in the year paraded an actual woman around as Lady Godiva. She wore a striped bikini under an Engineering sweater. Fairly tame. Things would get raunchier.

Psst, Wanna See a Dirty Book? If you wanted raunchy, you could always try to get a copy of Henry Miller's *Tropic of Cancer*. Unfortunately, it was banned in Vancouver's bookstores, but the UBC Library had a copy, as the *Ubyssey* helpfully reported. In Special Collections (of course). Call number PS3525 I56 T72. You can look it up.

Thefts: There seemed to be an epi-demic this year, so much so that Council announced a crackdown. Not that that helped. Everything from books and briefcases to rain-coats and umbrellas disappeared. Also wallets and purses, and a camera. Someone even stole eggs from the campus poultry farm, and someone else broke into a professor's office and stole forty math exams. Before that the giant Freddy Frosh balloon went miss-ing, and at the end of the year so did a giant ice sculpture. Cars or parts of cars also disappeared. And then there were the. . .

TOP Kim Campbell as frosh president.

BOTTOM Kim Campbell's campaign slogan.

Gates: Not the gates at the campus entrance, but new gates that were put up around the women's dorm in the new Totem Park Residence. An elaborate security system was put in place to keep the young women residents "safe." The young women themselves complained. So did residents of the older Acadia Camp residence, who said that the money could have been better spent upgrading the archaic conditions where they lived. A bunch of them marched to Totem Park and stole one of the gates.

SUB: Having obtained its funding, the new student union building was proceeding apace. An architectural competition was launched, and there was a plan to find a name. Thunderbird Union Building? TUB? No, that would never do. In the end, it was just the SUB.

That Ambulance Is Taking a Long Time Getting Here: Emergency response was an issue again. There was still no real ambulance on campus. The Nursing rep on Council complained. AMS president McAfee complained. The University posted emergency numbers on the campus pay phones: Fire 222, Hospital 333, Police CA4-1911. (911 hadn't been invented yet, nor cellphones.)

But Photocopying Has Arrived: The *Ubyssey* announced that there was now a Xerox machine in the library, so students would no longer have to copy things laboriously by hand (or steal them).

And Computers: For the library and the bowling alley, for questionnaires and exam schedules, and even for *Bird Calls* (the student telephone directory). All of which prompted the *Ubyssey* editor to pen a mock book review of the computer-generated *Bird Calls*, saying that its author (IBM 7040) was very logical and comprehensive but lacking a bit in humanity.

Sex, Drugs, and . . . Larry Kent's *Bitter Ash* returned to campus, as did his new film about adolescent sexuality, *Sweet Substitute*. A club formed to hand out birth control information, despite concerns this might violate the Criminal Code. They showed a film too, on human fertility. A Lutheran minister was reported as telling students he was in favour of same-sex marriages, but he later said he had been misquoted and really wanted to guide homosexuals back to "normal heterosexuality."

A UBC student was arrested for possession of marijuana and sentenced to six months in jail by former *Ubyssey* columnist and now judge Les Bewley, whose ruling was upheld on appeal on the grounds that it was important to "stomp out this incipient social evil."

The *Ubyssey*'s new Page Friday cultural section joined the fray by running a feature showing how to roll a joint.

Anti-Communism? Against the flow of the times, one might say, several anti-communist speakers showed up on campus, only

Kenneth R. Snider's winning design for the SUB.

to be heckled ("Better Red than Fred," said one banner at a speech given by an anti-communist named Fred Schwarz). In the name of free speech, the AMS even thought it was a good idea to invite American Nazi leader George Lincoln Rockwell to speak, but that fell through. And then old-time Communist leader Tim Buck made an appearance. But this was really not where it was at.

Where It Was At: Well, maybe it was really a mixed bag: *Roadrunner* cartoons and Bob Dylan songs. The first Vietnam protests and Engineering stunts. Bearded students and noise in the library. Traditional complaints about transit fares versus plans for anti-calendars. The old was still there, but things were stirring.

And the AMS was slowly changing too. The president and the treasurer were going to stay around and work in the summer. More professional staff were going to be hired. The Radio Society was talking of becoming a proper radio station. And AMS president McAfee intervened in a dispute between UBC Food Services and its student staff to reach an agreement on pay rates. The student society, one might say, was growing up.

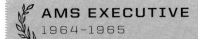

AMS EXECUTIVE
1964-1965

PRESIDENT *Roger McAfee*
1ST VICE-PRESIDENT *Bob Cruise*
2ND VICE-PRESIDENT *Byron Hender*
TREASURER *Kyle Mitchell*
SECRETARY *Marilyn McMeans*
COORDINATOR OF ACTIVITIES
Graeme Vance

UBYSSEY EDITOR *Mike Horsey*

1965–1975

REVOLUTION AND BEYOND

As Virginia Woolf might have put it, in or about September 1965 student character changed. The sixties burst upon the campus, and suddenly it was no more frosh queens—well, that's not true, there were still queens and dunkings and . . . but the whole atmosphere had changed: the Faculty Club got "liberated," people talked about LSD, people took LSD (and marijuana, of course), and the students marched and protested, and some called for the abolition of fees and student control of the University: students on Senate, students on the Board of Governors, students on committees, students everywhere where they didn't use to go.

And there was talk of changing society: feminism, environmentalism, cycling (and recycling). And changing the University: make it more relevant, not a place for churning out people with degrees who could fit into corporate society. Oh, and stop the war in Vietnam. The times they were a-changing. For real this time.

And yet, and yet . . . After the burst of energy, there was a cooling down period, what Stan Persky called the post-coital period. The revolutionary moment passed, and there was a reaction against all things political, a retreat, a stop.

Still. The campus would never be the same. The ferment gradually ebbed away, but attitudes had changed. People woke up. New issues came to the fore. The University and its students, like all of Western society, had entered a new era.

1965 TO 1966

What Do We Want? Free tuition, it seems. After years of asking for lower increases, the student leadership suddenly was saying, Forget that, there shouldn't be tuition fees at all. Fees prevent universal access. Everyone should go to university; there should be no barriers, nobody kept out for want of money, or for want of anything else, it seemed. No more social injustice.

When Do We Want It? Now! UBC president Macdonald said he could see the argument for free tuition, but the time was not appropriate. No, said the *Ubyssey* and student leaders like AMS vice-president Bob Cruise, the time is now! We will march to the courthouse and nail our demands to the door (who *are* these heretics?). We will refuse to pay our fees. Oh, my God, what is going on?

Well, It's the Sixties: It would seem so. Men's hair got longer, and they wore beards. Women talked of buying birth control pills. Even single women! The horror. But we don't give contraceptives to single women, said the health service. Oh, I'm married then, said the under-cover *Ubyssey* reporter (wink, wink). Well, that's all right, then: here are your pills.

And the paper talked about Bob Dylan and Joan Baez, and there were protests about Vietnam, and the Science students published the first UBC "anti-calendar," a collection of student evaluations of their courses: A *Rate My Prof* for the pre-Internet age. And the Arts students said they would do this too.

And the motto of the *Ubyssey* at the beginning of the year was from William Blake: "The tigers of wrath are wiser than the horses of instruction" (revealing both the political and poetic inclinations of that year's editor, future poet Tom Wayman).

Now, Now, Children: A government minister said fees were necessary to give students a voice in running the University. So just pay up and enjoy the nice celebrations for UBC's fiftieth anniversary.

Some of Our Leaders Aren't Leading Enough: While Vice-President Cruise pushed the radical agenda, where was AMS president Byron Hender? Joining Canadian prime minister Lester B. Pearson to break ground for the student union building: was construction finally about to get underway? Well, that's nice, but what about social injustice? The march, the fee strike?

Nope, None of That. Well, maybe if the students vote in a referendum. And then in another referendum. So the students marched, but did not strike, and President Hender ended up leading the march (but not the strike: there was no strike).

AMS president Hender (at the microphone) and Prime Minister Pearson at the ground-breaking ceremony for the student union building.

Even the Engineers got into the fee protest mood with their "well-hung student" poised above UBC president Macdonald.

New sorts of dancing: partners not even touching!

And Some Did Not Agree: Not everyone was a radical, of course. A dissenting group showed up at the march to protest the protesters. One cynic said yes, abolish their fees so they can afford haircuts and shaves.

But There's More: Once they got going, there was no stopping them. Give us a seat on Senate, said even the moderate Council. And the University administration, though not quite ready to do that, seemed so affected by all the pushback over fees that they promised that next time they planned an increase they wouldn't sneak it through in the summer (as had happened this year), but they would consult the students about it first. Consult the students: who ever heard of doing that? The world really was changing.

And not just in politics. Ballroom dancing was out, and in came the frug and the jerk and something called the watusi. And music was about to take off, like a plane, like . . .

The Jefferson Airplane! At UBC! Yes, the band that was to be a major sixties phenomenon showed up, singing their songs, inspiring madness. Or at least bell bottoms and psychedelic colours. And there was a Happening and Tarzan movies (Tarzan movies?) and the whole world seemed to be going crazy. It was wild, man. You know.

Oh, and there was an "allegorical and artistic atrocity."

The "atrocity."

Okay, Let's All Take a Breath: Not everything changed. The Engineers still did their stunts, there were beauty contests for campus queens, there was talk of progress on the SUB—but even there a radical group suddenly wanted to question the arrangements or the very idea of a SUB, and then there was a move to reform the way Student Council was constituted, and speakers showed up extolling the fight of the Viet Cong against the evil American Empire and telling students that LSD was a wonderful and harmless drug. Maybe everything *was* changed.

And Just to Cap It Off: The year ended with utter confusion over one of the Executive elections; for a moment it looked like everyone might get disqualified. And then the head of the Religious Studies department told students that God might be dead. And a student ran to be chancellor (he lost, of course, but still . . .).

Part IV: The February Revolution
(March 1917)

Alexander Kerensky,
Provisional Government

Vs.

Vladimir Lenin,
Bolsheviks

1966 TO 1967

No Room, No Room: The library was short of money, short of staff, and short of space, said the *Ubyssey*. So was the bookstore. And the TAs were cramped. Even the professors lacked space. But most of all the students had no place to lay their heads; or not very many places. We need more housing, they said, on campus and off. And to make their point a hundred of them slept overnight in tents on Main Mall. Later there was talk of starting a student housing co-op, which merged a bit with talk of an experimental college, something like Rochdale in Toronto, but nothing along those lines got off the ground.

Down with the Multiversity: But student activists were after bigger game than more residences. The whole nature of the University had to change, they said. Curriculum should be made more relevant and less lecture-oriented; the aim should be a true education, not a meal ticket. And the University should be democratized so that students could run it. There should be students on the Senate, the Board of Governors, committees. And the University was just the beginning. It was society that had to be changed, really.

A university, said the *Ubyssey*, should not be "an ever-expanding degree mill, punching out graduates like plastic cups and stuffing them into the convenient corporate pigeon holes."

Tent city.

Not so Fast: UBC president John B. Macdonald warned that the University was not an instrument of social change (why not, said the activists?). But he did agree to open his door to students wanting to drop in without an appointment to discuss whatever was on their minds. And then he just quit.

Shock and Disbelief: That's what everyone expressed when Macdonald resigned, so much so that the *Ubyssey* began to make fun of the response. Macdonald served a short term (five years) by his predecessors' standards, but there would never again be presidents serving for twenty years like MacKenzie and Klinck, and some would stay for even less time than Macdonald.

> **"There is unrest in all society and UBC is not exempt."**
> —JOHN B. MACDONALD, UBC PRESIDENT

People: Well, there was Stan Persky bursting onto the scene as a member of the new AMS club dedicated to raising money to support people charged with marijuana possession. From there he moved on to becoming president of the Arts Undergraduate Society (not without some issues over his eligibility: eligibility was a theme with Stan). As president he embarked on holding meetings in corridors and build-

WE NEED ❀ MORE HOUSING! ...NOW ○

ing an office for thirteen cents. Also promising an Arts anti-calendar and a newsletter, and generally bringing the new light-hearted activist ways into the halls of "bureaucracy": student leaders in those days were generally dismissed as bureaucrats (unless they were activists), and one analysis divided the campus population into Bureaucrats, the New Left, and the Don't Care crowd.

Other People: *Dennis Healy*, the forward looking Arts dean, who put some of the new ways of thinking about the curriculum into practice: introducing the inter-disciplinary program called Arts One.

David Suzuki, who as a young zoology professor also introduced educational innovations, including seminars at the Fraser Arms pub and overnight exams.

Malcolm McGregor, the head of Classics, who opposed Arts One ("I don't think this is education"), and who as director of housing denied that there was a housing crisis. A former sports editor of the *Ubyssey*, Dr. McGregor enjoyed writing letters to the editor of his former paper, chiding them for their coverage (and for misspelling his name).

Alexander Kerensky, a holdover from the Russian Revolution fifty years before, who showed up to tell students that despite wars and bombs, they should live by love. So a convert to hippiedom, apparently.

> **"The colours, the lights, the sounds!"**
> —GABOR MATÉ, *UBYSSEY* COLUMNIST

Malcolm McGregor, Classics professor and bane of the *Ubyssey*.

Gabor Maté, who tried to combine humour and politics in a *Ubyssey* column, at one point suggesting that a hippie version of the traditional Mardi Gras party put on by the frats could be called Mardi Grass.

Sharing: Bike sharing, umbrella sharing: there was talk of such things, but they would have to wait till the twenty-first century, if then, to come to fruition. There was also an early expression of concern over mental health, again something more focused on in later decades. This being the sixties, of course, some denied the existence of mental health problems: people aren't sick, society is sick. Schizophrenia is sanity, said one visiting speaker.

Timothy Leary: He wasn't on campus in person, but ads for a long-playing vinyl record of his on which he extolled the merits of LSD ran in the *Ubyssey*, and there was much talk of potheads and acid heads this year, and the controversial play known as *Marat/Sade* came to campus, as did Joan Baez, and people supporting American draft dodgers escaping the war in Vietnam.

Vietnam: The AMS even held a referendum on Vietnam, in which students voted to oppose the bombing (by the Americans) but voted in favour of continuing Canadian arms sales (to the Americans). Oh, well.

Referendum Happy: There was a referendum on an AMS fee increase, and then another (both failed). There was a referendum on whether to stage a strike to protest the lack of government funding (again the result was no, especially after Student Council changed its mind on whether a

The Wild Sixties on stage: the 1966 Freddy Wood production of *Marat/Sade*.

strike was a Good Thing). Instead of strikes and protests, someone said, it might be better to have a permanent lobbyist in Victoria, and hence was born a new position on the AMS executive: External Affairs Officer (later to become the Coordinator of External Affairs and then the VP-External).

> "Before we were primarily concerned with things like contests, carnivals, discounts, and sports—but we came to realize this had nothing to do with real life."
> —JOHN CLEVELAND, CANADIAN UNION OF STUDENTS

Marching: Council did go along with a march in Victoria organized by the new BC Association of Students, but it didn't seem to have much effect. The BCAS called for the abolition of tuition fees, but the minister of education said no. Some said the call for the abolition of fees reflected a something-for-nothing attitude, and indeed though student sentiment seemed to be turning increasingly pink, as some put it, some objected, and there was even the creation of the Blue Guard, a right-wing group, at UBC. It didn't seem to accomplish much, however. One letter writer to the *Ubyssey* also called for a passivist movement to counter all the activism, but he was probably joking. In any case, what would a passivist movement do?

Not everyone was for activist measures, as this *Ubyssey* cartoon humorously indicates.

> "Youth is no longer content to sit on the sidelines."
> —MARSHALL MCLUHAN, QUOTED IN THE *UBYSSEY*

The SUB: Oh, yes, the SUB. Whatever happened to it? Still no construction underway, but agreements were signed and tenders were put out. The *Ubyssey* would actually have been happy if it hadn't been begun at all, repeatedly calling it a White Elephant, a Big Mistake, and a playpen for the "bureaucrats." Radical Bob Cruise the year before had opined about it: Why so big? Why so expensive? And why so late? But it would come.

And More People Came: The Maharishi Mahesh Yogi. Buckminster Fuller and his geodesic dome. People praising Mao's Red Guards. The Beatles on celluloid, with a double bill of their movies shown on campus. And people praising the violent FLQ movement in Quebec. Let a hundred flowers blossom.

AMS EXECUTIVE
1966-1967

PRESIDENT *Peter Braund*
1ST VICE-PRESIDENT *Charles Boylan*
2ND VICE-PRESIDENT
Ian MacDougal/Carolyn Tate
TREASURER *Lorne Hudson*
SECRETARY *Gayle Gaskell*
COORDINATOR OF ACTIVITIES
Jim Lightfoot

UBYSSEY EDITOR *John Kelsey*

1967 TO 1968

The Year of Stan Persky: The revolution has begun, and it's being led by Stan Persky, said a writer in the *Ubyssey*, but it was a peaceful sort of revolution, full of love and caring, in the name of "human government." As president of the Arts Undergraduate Society, Persky said it was important to help people make friends and to discuss the larger issues, from death to love.

In more practical terms, he set about providing things for free: from rock concerts to lockers, causing some on Student Council to call him irresponsible and to try to cut Arts off without a penny. But that was okay, because Persky went to the Arts students to ask them to give him a special $2 fee just to use on Arts projects: the beginning of Undergraduate Society fees, or it would have been if AMS Council hadn't said, No, no, you can't do that.

Fed up with the AMS, Persky decided to cut diplomatic ties with it, as he put it (this meant he gave up attending AMS Council meetings), but he still came up with a scheme to get money from the AMS athletic fund to support an imaginary hockey league playing imaginary games in the Buchanan building. And then he ran to be president of the AMS. And won! Or he would have if Student Court hadn't declared him ineligible. Only third years could run for president in those days, and he was only in second. Very legalistic, he said, and pointed out that AMS treasurer Dave Hoye was also technically ineligible. Fair was fair, and Hoye was forced to resign. Hoye Vey, as the *Ubyssey* said (in another context).

And then to cap it off Persky got arrested downtown when the city decided to clamp down on "hippies" loitering near the courthouse. People protested: everyone from the Civil Liberties Association to UBC law professors to alderman Harry Rankin. But Persky himself went placidly to jail with a copy of Henry David Thoreau. That's the sort of revolutionary he was.

Persky went on to become a philosophy professor at Capilano University in North Vancouver, the author of many books on history and

Stan Persky, the advocate of human government.

Persky's quest for the presidency was thwarted by Student Court.

literature, and a frequent commentator on public affairs in the media.

And Then There Was Gabor Maté: If Stan Persky was the apostle of peace and love, Gabor Maté was more the hardliner. At a demonstration against Dow Chemical recruiters in the fall, Persky wanted to engage in dialogue to inform people about the uses Dow's products were being put to in Vietnam. Maté wanted to block the doors, to stop the recruiters from recruiting.

On the other hand, Maté wanted to open the doors to the UBC Senate. UBC had agreed to allow four students to sit on Senate, and Maté got to be one of them, but he and his colleagues did not want to simply be co-opted into a governing institution; he wanted to transform it, make it responsible to the University community, especially the students, and one way to do that was to end its secrecy (Senate meetings were closed in those days, and the student senators wanted them open to the public).

The Senate resisted, voted the idea down, sent it to committee, told the students to be patient, but in the end gave way. Indeed, the University gave way on many fronts this year.

Reforms: Besides opening the Senate and allowing students onto it, the University put students onto various advisory committees, eliminated the language requirement for undergraduates, lifted the curfew on women in residence, and when the students in architecture protested against certain curricular requirements, the University changed those too. They also backed down on talk of restricting enrolment, invited education students to make suggestions for changes to their program, and rolled out the first year of the experimental Arts One program of interdisciplinary studies.

And surely once the students saw all these reforms being made,

Architecture students in 1972.

they would calm down and end their discontent and never dream of something as radical as, say, occupying the Faculty Club. Well, time would tell . . .

Are the Old Times Gone for Good? Well, not entirely. The Engineers were still up to their tricks, dunking and kidnapping, and at what turned out to be the inaugural Shrum Bowl between the UBC and Simon Fraser football teams, they instigated a brawl that drew the attention of police and media.

Not all the protesting was political.

Science versus Arts: And it wasn't just the Engineers. Science students launched a water barrel attack on the Arts redoubt in Buchanan, even producing a confrontation between peace-loving Stan Persky and the first female president of the Science Undergraduate Society, Robin Russell, who, however, was able to smooth things over later by making a peace offering of chrysanthemums.

Feminism: The Russell-Persky confrontation led the *Ubyssey* to editorialize on the supposed inappropriateness of women in politics. Were they joking? They were a very radical publication by this point, but the interesting thing about this stage of radicalism at UBC was that it didn't seem to include feminism. The *Ubyssey* denounced the war in Vietnam and called for the democratization of education, supported Black Power in the United States and celebrated Che Guevara. But women?

Gabor Maté, the hard edge of the revolution. Maté would go on to become a well-known author promoting unconventional views on medicine, addiction, and child rearing.

They were still just pretty things to look at. The paper even continued its Christmas tradition of running a jigsaw puzzle of female body parts.

It was left to Gabor Maté to step forward and denounce this sort of thing as objectification and to say that it was time to stop focusing on women's looks and their roles as wives and mothers. He used some extreme language in presenting this analysis, provoking objections, but his general point won support from professors and students: feminism had finally appeared on the scene at UBC.

Mardi Gras: And then there were the frats. Still hosting their traditional costume ball, which got them into trouble this year for its "Deep South" theme, including a skit about Ku Klux Klan members lynching a black man. At a time of heightened unrest in the United States over civil rights issues, some found the Mardi Gras theme highly offensive. So the fraternities now won't discriminate in their constitutions, just in their hi-jinks, said one letter-writer to the *Ubyssey*. But this sort of thing seemed to be the wave of the past.

Co-optation, Thy Name Is Capitalism: The *Ubyssey* ran an ad for coats in which a woman was depicted holding a protest placard reading, "Demonstrate the swingin'est styles in college fashion." The protest wave was the wave of the future (or at least the present). Similarly, the AMS sought to have students join clubs by running an ad saying, "Tune in! Turn on! Drop in . . ." Timothy Leary, eat your heart out.

Going with the flow..

And What Else? Construction of the student union building was underway, though you would hardly know it from the *Ubyssey*. AMS Council experimented with weighted voting to give the larger faculties a fairer share of the vote on Council motions, but better ways would be found for this in the future. The Ladner Clock Tower went up, much to the dismay of the *Ubyssey* and other radicals, who thought it an annoying throwback and a waste of money that could have better been spent on student housing or books. And Stephen Scobie, who would go on to become a respected Canadian author, was writing film reviews in the *Ubyssey* saying that *Bonnie and Clyde* was the best film of all time. Here's looking at you, kid.

TOP The SUB goes up on the site of the old stadium.
BOTTOM The Clock Tower.

1968 TO 1969

It's a party, man. A band plays an unscheduled set during the Faculty Club occupation.

It's the Sixties, Man: Paris, Chicago, Berkeley . . . UBC? For a day at least, the day Jerry Rubin came to town. The leader of the Youth International Party (the Yippies), fresh from confrontations with police during the Chicago protests, showed up with his pig (a protest candidate in the 1968 US presidential election) and asked the students of UBC what they would like to liberate. "The Faculty Club," someone called out, and two thousand students invaded the professors' inner sanctum, liberating not only the space but the contents of liquor cabinets and the club pond (skinny dipping!). Someone even brought a band.

But What's It All About? The *Ubyssey* thought the occupation was an undeveloped expression of protest against oppression. Radicals, like the visiting Rubin himself, talked about rejecting traditional institutions, not accepting minor positions in the existing power structure, opposing corporate control of education and society, and revolutionizing society. Rubin also talked about having fun. "Free yourself," he said. Also: "Wherever you see a rule, break it."

No, But What Was It Really About? Well, the occupation of the Faculty Club took place against a worldwide backdrop of student unrest, and at UBC itself the AMS had produced a brief calling for a variety of educational reforms to make courses more "relevant" and to give students a say in running the University. Demands were in the air: There should be students on governing bodies, the students should have a say in making appointments, something should be done about overcrowding. Some said, We should not have to attend dull and boring courses. Indeed.

In fact, the University was already experimenting with new approaches to teaching (having already introduced the Arts One inter-disciplinary course the year before). It had also granted student representation on the University Senate, though radicals called the appointment of four student senators (out of eighty-one) tokenism.

Jerry Rubin, liberator of the Faculty Club.

Hare eventually resigned just seven months after taking office (making him the shortest-serving UBC president), and in response to AMS demands the committee to find a replacement for him included four students.

Can't We Even Open a Student Union Building without a Protest?

The big achievement of the AMS

And What Good Came of It? Well, the next day there was a giant rally (five thousand students) which called for a teach-in on educational reform, and there was indeed a teach-in the following week, endorsed by AMS president Dave Zirnhelt and UBC president Kenneth Hare. Zirnhelt, later an NDP cabinet minister, played a moderating role in the events, as did Hare, who seemed quite sympathetic to the students' demands, so much so that even the radicals said nice things about him, though adding that of course he couldn't really do anything because of the conservative power structure.

this year was the opening of the new Student Union Building (the SUB), finally replacing the overcrowded Brock Hall. The SUB opened in late September, complete with a bowling alley and listening rooms (where students could hear records played on turntables).

But some people were not happy over the lack of a pub in the building, and in this era of protests they decided to protest against the situation by drinking illegally in front of the building before it opened and then inside on opening day. No, no, said harried AMS president Zirnhelt; we're working on getting a liquor licence; this will spoil it all. But it didn't, and a licence was duly obtained, which led to the opening of . . .

The Pit: Yes, the famous AMS pub. Suddenly, the AMS was in the liquor business, and this after years of not even allowing people to show up at AMS functions with the smell of alcohol on their breath—because until 1968 students never drank (or had sex or did any of the other things that the sixties had to invent).

Of course, the Pit in 1968 was not what it would become. It became known in later years as the dark place in the basement, but in 1968 it was not even a place. More a concept, which was perhaps appropriate for the era. Although the plan all along was to build an actual pub, since no thought had been given to this in the original construction of the SUB there would have to be renovation, expansion, work, delays . . . It would take five years for the Pit to get a permanent home. Until then it was really more a series of beer gardens held upstairs in the SUB party room or ballroom.

And Did We Mention David Suzuki? Yes, the noted environmentalist who began his career as a UBC zoology professor, and who in October 1968 published a piece in the administration's newspaper (*UBC Reports*), saying that what the campus needed was a pub. Seeing a kindred spirit, the AMS appointed him to their committee looking into a pub, and it was Suzuki who came up with the idea of naming the place the Pit.

They Did What? In the midst of protests and resignations, the Engineers tried to lighten the mood by carrying out one of their pranks: stealing the Nine O'Clock Gun from

TOP The listening lounge.

BOTTOM The bowling alley.

David Suzuki.

WHAT THIS CAMPUS NEEDS

IS A PUB

BY DR. DAVID SUZUKI

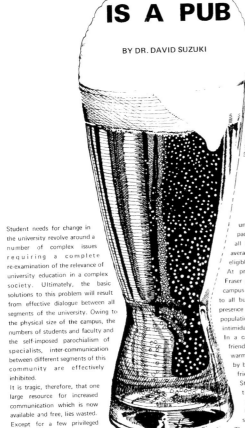

Illustration by Bob Field

Student needs for change in the university revolve around a number of complex issues requiring a complete re-examination of the relevance of university education in a complex society. Ultimately, the basic solutions to this problem will result from effective dialogue between all segments of the university. Owing to the physical size of the campus, the numbers of students and faculty and the self-imposed parochialism of specialists, inter-communication between different segments of this community are effectively inhibited.

It is tragic, therefore, that one large resource for increased communication which is now available and free, lies wasted. Except for a few privileged students UBC buildings are virtually deserted for more than half of each school day and every weekend. The opening up of such space would not only help to reduce the serious shortage of study room but would also create a campus where activities are not dictated by a commitment to a seven-hour day. I believe however, that the release of classroom space in the evenings will result in the rapid establishment of sects within each region owing to familiarity, habit and convenience, unless considerable effort is made to prevent such regionalism.

I submit that the communication crisis may be greatly overcome by building a pub on campus. Such a structure is uniquely suited to ameliorate existing frustrations. Although such a building would create a privileged class on campus, faculty would not be offended since all of them would be allowed in, and underage students could be pacified by the knowledge that all of them, regardless of sex, average or faculty, would become eligible.

At present, the distance of the Fraser Arms and Cecil Hotels from campus presents a formidable barrier to all but a hardcore. Moreover, the presence in these bars of a large alien population and a stifling atmosphere intimidates most from tablehopping. In a campus pub, the presence of friends at different tables and the warmth of camaraderie engendered by beer would soon result in new friendships and active discussion. Students might even have the temerity to speak to a professor, and a professor, the magnanimity of inviting students to have one on him. The passions of commitment to reactionary or radical ideals would be tempered by the effects of alcohol. When one ponders the implications of a campus pub, its importance becomes obvious and paramount—management, waitressing and bouncing could be learned by students running the establishment; the tremendous profits could be used to finance academic activities on campus; fraternities would lose their roles as social and booze centers, etc.

It is my firm belief that a campus pub could be a critical vehicle for resolving numerous university problems. I would strongly urge that all students and faculty who are firmly committed to bettering education place this need at the top of their priority list. Until such time as Victoria grants a licence, I suggest the facilities of the Faculty Club and Graduate Students Center could be used for such a purpose in the evenings.

WHAT THIS CAMPUS NEEDS . . .

is a new *UBC Reports* feature designed to provide a forum for the discussion of ideas or things which are now missing from the UBC campus. Contributions are invited from faculty members, students, alumni or other interested readers All you have to do is complete the sentence "What this campus needs is . . .," and then make a case for it in an essay not exceeding 1,000 words. Dr. David Suzuki, associate professor of zoology at UBC, is the first contributor. A specialist in the study of genetics, Dr. Suzuki was born in Vancouver and educated at Amherst College, where he received his bachelor of arts degree, and the University of Chicago, where he was awarded his doctor of philosophy degree. Dr. Suzuki, widely-known at UBC for his unorthodox teaching methods, has been a member of the faculty since 1963.

David Suzuki's article.

Stanley Park and holding it for ransom. The result was a donation of $1,200 to the Children's Hospital.

Slates, Slates, Slates: Slates at the AMS originally meant rounds. In the annual elections, the Executive (or in the really early years the whole Council) would be elected in two or three rounds: for instance, the president and a couple of other executives in the "first slate," with other executives being elected in the second slate.

During the sixties, though, the term slate came to mean a political grouping or party. In 1960–61, a group called New Blood on Council unsuccessfully ran a set of candidates. This year a group called the Reform Union did the same thing, but they too were unsuccessful. It would take a while for this new sort of slate to catch on, but when it did …

AMS EXECUTIVE
1968–1969

PRESIDENT *Dave Zirnhelt*

TREASURER *Donn Aven*

VICE-PRESIDENT *Carey Linde*

INTERNAL AFFAIRS OFFICER
Ruth Dworkin/David Gibson

EXTERNAL AFFAIRS OFFICER
Tobin Robbins

COORDINATOR OF ACTIVITIES
Jill Cameron/Rod Ramage

SECRETARY *Sally Coleman/ Isobel Semple*

UBYSSEY EDITOR *Al Birnie*

1969 TO 1970

Is the Revolution Over? Stan Persky thought so, announcing that the campus had entered a "post-coital" period. Everyone's wearing long hair and sideburns, he said, but what difference does it make? Still, there were a few things.

Amchitka Protest: Thousands of students blocked the border to protest the American nuclear test on Amchitka Island, in Alaska.

The *Ubyssey* rallied the troops for "Operation Borderclose" and warned about the possible consequences of the nuclear test.

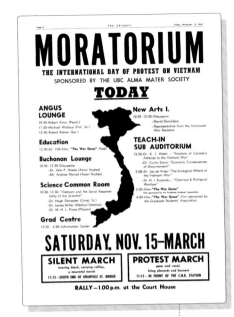

Promotional page for the anti-war moratorium.

Vietnam War Moratorium: UBC students also joined the North America–wide protest against the war in Vietnam. There was a huge march in Washington D.C., and thousands marched in Vancouver too, and yet the spirit didn't quite seem there anymore. The *Ubyssey* lamented the low turnout at a pre-march teach-in.

But There Are Lots of Left-wing Groups: Yes—yes, there were. Maoists, Trotskyists, anarchists, even the old Industrial Workers of the World back from the grave talking about Joe Hill and 1910. But this is a sign of weakness, said a political science prof: all this splintering.

And Maybe We're All Tired of Politics: Why is the AMS using our fees to block the border or to support a strike at Simon Fraser or to run a candidate in the provincial election? Maybe it's time to rein it in. Abolish it even. Or at least make it voluntary. Voluntary unionism. A death knell for the AMS, said AMS president Fraser Hodge. Left-wing leader Carey Linde thought this might even be a good thing, leading to a more activist union, but mostly the push for voluntarism was a move from the other end of the spectrum —and not one that won much support. Students voted two to one against the idea in a February referendum. Still, a retreat from politics was in the air.

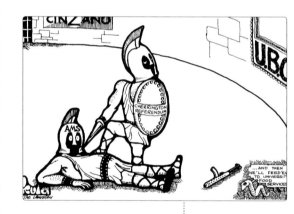

Despite the cartoonist's suggestion, it was the AMS that triumphed in the arena against the referendum, not the other way around.

Or Maybe We Want a Different Type of Politics: Let's talk about the Americanization of the campus. Why are so many profs from the United States? Why do we have to listen to sociology profs cite examples from

New Haven instead of Moose Jaw? It was Canadian nationalism, anti-American left-wing variety, arriving courtesy of economist Mel Watkins and poet Robin Mathews.

And Feminism: Feminism truly arrived this year. The Women's Liberation Movement. A Vancouver Women's Caucus. Talk of equal pay for equal work. Abortion rights. Birth control. Stop discriminating. Stop treating us like objects. The *Ubyssey* did an about turn, right in the middle of the year, moving from displaying cheesecake to saying that sort of thing was demeaning and, when called on it, merging its Help Wanted—Male and Help Wanted—Female ad sections.

And Maybe We Should Talk about Tenure: There was a fuss about two English instructors being denied tenure. Teaching versus research. Long articles in the *Ubyssey*. A motion passed by Council. The English department head saying this is not for students to decide. The new UBC president, Walter Gage, saying maybe think again. There's just too much democracy here, said the English department head.

We've Already Been Doing Evaluations: Following the lead of the students, who had begun producing "anti-calendars" evaluating professors, the University Senate said maybe there should be some official evaluations, which could aid in promotion and tenure decisions. Aha! (Though the students' evaluations

Speak Easy announced itself.

were perhaps more intended to help other students choose courses.)

And Services: In line with the shift in the political climate, the focus began to move to services this year. There were still people denouncing American imperialism and calling for restructuring of the University (or for "course unions," groups of students within departments who would push for democratization and other changes, most notably in Anthrosoc, the Anthropology-Sociology department).

But a push began to actually deliver things to the students. Even the self-proclaimed revolutionary group, the Black Cross, focused on setting up a food co-op to deliver cheaper food. This was thought to be in violation of the lease for the SUB, but in subsequent years plenty of food outlets would open (though not without some discussion about the legalities and even some friction between the University and the AMS).

More Services: A group gathered to look into day care facilities for student parents. The Speak Easy peer

counselling service got underway, originally provided by an unaffiliated group of students in social work, but even then receiving AMS funding and a room in the SUB, and eventually becoming an AMS service (as Speakeasy). A similar

Speakeasy in its early days.

service but focusing on legal matters was started by law students as Legal Aid. Far ahead of its time, the AMS began talking about providing a mental health program. And Shinerama, the national campaign to combat cystic fibrosis, made its first appearance on campus.

Pollution: The environmental movement, still in its early days, made an appearance, with a group springing up to warn against threats to water, air, and soil. AMS president Fraser Hodge said pollution was one of the things the AMS should concern itself with, and Stan Persky, now a student senator, called on the Senate to investigate what the University was doing about it, but his motion was ruled out of order.

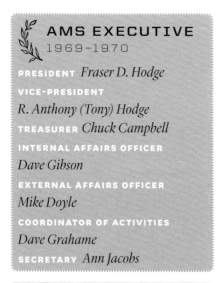

AMS EXECUTIVE
1969-1970

PRESIDENT *Fraser D. Hodge*

VICE-PRESIDENT
R. Anthony (Tony) Hodge

TREASURER *Chuck Campbell*

INTERNAL AFFAIRS OFFICER
Dave Gibson

EXTERNAL AFFAIRS OFFICER
Mike Doyle

COORDINATOR OF ACTIVITIES
Dave Grahame

SECRETARY *Ann Jacobs*

UBYSSEY EDITOR *Michael Finlay*

Shinerama arrived on campus.

1970 TO 1971

The Battle of Jericho: And lo the people of Jericho did refuse to move from their hostel until the army and the police force did forcibly remove them, pushing them out of the Jericho army base and onto Fourth Avenue, from whence they journeyed to the Student Union Building at UBC campus, where the students had said, "O ye homeless ones in need of shelter, you can rest here"— but then on second thought had said, No, sorry, you can't.

But the people of Jericho, jobless youth with nowhere to go, did come anyway and occupied the SUB for sixteen hours, staying overnight until the AMS Executive could find alternative lodging for them, while regular students grumbled that this was too much and the *Ubyssey* said it was not enough: it was time to stand up to the police state and oppression…

And that was the high point of militancy and activism for the year, a carryover from the sixties perhaps, and occurring the same weekend in October that the FLQ crisis erupted in Quebec and Prime Minister Pierre Trudeau invoked the War Measures Act, prompting protests at UBC, but not too much, despite the best efforts of the *Ubyssey*.

John Turner speaking.

John Turner Tries to Speak: Some protests did arise again in the spring, when Justice Minister John Turner returned to his alma mater, where he had been an AMS executive decades before. Protesters objecting to the War Measures Act shouted him down.

The *Ubyssey* depicted the Jericho hostel issue as a class struggle.

Protesters objecting to John Turner speaking.

Human Government: If activists had mixed results against evictions and the War Measures Act, they found more success at the ballot box, electing a new slate to all the positions on the AMS executive. Steve Garrod's Human Government group swept all before them, though not before the AMS had to rerun the presidential election because of irregularities. Garrod pledged democratization of the University and a reduction of American influence. He also promised a referendum in October to let the student body pass judgement on his program, a promise he would live to regret.

President-elect Steve Garrod.

Cyclists on the march.

Shades of Stan Persky: The Human Government slate drew inspiration from Stan Persky, UBC's leading radical in the sixties, who had called for student government (indeed all government) to be more "human." Persky himself was still around, serving as a student senator and getting himself turned away from a Senate meeting when he showed up dressed as an old man in a wheelchair.

Engineers Gone Wild: The Engineers reached new heights (or lows) this year, kidnapping a *Ubyssey* columnist and putting him through a mock crucifixion, kidnapping the Ombudsman and covering him in honey and feathers, trashing the Commerce students' lounge and stealing their beer, vandalizing the Commerce students' chariot, and causing the injury of a Forestry participant in the annual chariot race. Some even accused them of plotting to attack the SUB during the Jericho occupation to oust the occupiers, but that may have simply been their reputation at work. They did get into a fight with Maoists distributing literature in the SUB, and altogether their antics were so extreme that one group of Engineers, unhappy to be associated with such things, started a petition to withdraw from the Engineering Undergraduate Society.

Council, Who Needs Council? The AMS hired an outside consultant to make recommendations about structure, and one of their suggestions was that Council be abolished to allow the Executive to function without impediment.

The Executive didn't follow that recommendation, but did try to reduce the size of Council and of the Executive (which had grown to seven members, or eight, depending on who was counting). However, the two general meetings called to vote on constitutional changes both failed to meet quorum, so restructuring would have to wait for another day.

Meanwhile the *Ubyssey* complained that the AMS was wasting its time on such matters and should instead be focusing on housing, unemployment, and the nature of the university.

New Forms of Activism: If the AMS and students at large seemed uninterested in the *Ubyssey*'s agenda, new causes had arisen that would capture more support in subsequent decades. Feminism had already arrived the year before, and this year there was talk of starting a Women's Studies program. There was also the interesting situation of left-wing labour leader Michel Chartrand being called out for dismissiveness towards women: it was the old activism giving way to the new.

Also this year saw a cyclists' protest: about four hundred of them disrupted traffic on University Boulevard to demonstrate in favour of bike paths. This protest even seemed to lead somewhere: within a month there was talk of improving cycling facilities on campus.

1971 TO 1972

Now You See 'Em, Now You Don't: The AMS Executive, that is. For the first and only time in AMS history, the whole AMS executive, all seven of them, resigned this year after losing a vote of confidence in a referendum of the student body. We will take our program to the students, President Steve Garrod had promised, and if they vote against it, we will step down. And they did. Very noble, perhaps foolish.

Their program was a bit controversial, focused on radical politics, notably a protest against the American nuclear test in Amchitka, Alaska (yes, another one). Their opponents asked why money was being spent to block the American border while at the same time cuts were brought in for intramural sports. Club representatives said their interests were being neglected.

The radical *Ubyssey* strongly supported the Executive, asking, "Are clubs and intramural sports the first priorities for students? Do students want to return to government run by a bunch of aspiring Liberal hotshots?" Apparently, the answer was yes, and the Human Government slate got replaced by a more moderate group, the Students' Coalition, led by law student Grant Burnyeat.

Grant Burnyeat: the moderate replacement president.

Women's Studies: Before leaving office, one of the radical Executive's most ambitious projects was a course in Women's Studies, a program not yet offered at that time by the University. Anne Petrie, later a noted Canadian broadcaster, coordinated the course, with 650 people showing up in the SUB ballroom for the first lecture.

And in Other Progressive News: The Gay Liberation Front held a meeting in the SUB, saying, "We are the last struggle to be recognized." They eventually became a club (the Gay People's Alliance), and later turned into the AMS resource group known as Pride.

The AMS, under the human government executive, organized an "Indian Week" to celebrate Indigenous culture, a culture that had been crushed by "the Industrial Revolution, mercantilism, imperialism—in short . . . by our capitalist system," said the *Ubyssey* (they talked that way then).

There was even talk this year of starting an organic food store, though that would have to wait for a few decades. AMS Council did succeed in convincing the University to return to washable plates and cutlery in the SUB cafeteria: an early example of environmental sustainability.

Sports: It was a bit ironic that this would be the year of an Executive that seemed against sports, because it was quite a successful year for UBC athletes. Both the men's and the women's basketball teams won championships, and in the summer before the year began UBC student Debbie Brill won gold in the high jump at the Pan Am Games. She had done the same at the Commonwealth Games the year before.

Let's Talk about Classes: This was something the *Ubyssey* did in these days, running reports on what was going on in the classroom for everything from geophysics (an article by Vaughn Palmer, later a fixture in Vancouver journalism) to music appreciation.

Both the AMS and the *Ubyssey* continued to take a heightened interest in academic matters in this period, getting involved in tenure

TOP Better things to do? Lunching at the library, 1970.

BOTTOM At the "tuning fork" beside the Music building, 1971.

controversies in various departments, the most notable one this year being the denial of tenure to two junior professors in the department of Anthropology and Sociology (Anthrosoc as it was known). Perhaps the thinking was that if the students won't come to us, then we'll go to them. Which brings us to the notion of . . .

Positive Apathy: A term coined by the *Ubyssey* in response to poor turnout at the AMS annual general meeting. Or really in response to Grant Burnyeat's shrugging response to the turnout: "[It's because of] students having better things to do," he said, and maybe they did.

The Engineers (Again): After several months in which they were unusually quiet, the Engineering students got in trouble for a newsletter at the end of the year containing jokes about the Holocaust which many found offensive. AMS Council censured them, UBC president Walter Gage said he was ashamed, several instructors boycotted the Engineering building, and the University established a fact-finding committee.

On the other hand, the Engineers were in the news for positive reasons this year too: some of them built a model car to be entered into an international competition.

AMS EXECUTIVE
1971-1972

PRESIDENT *Steve Garrod/Grant Burnyeat*
VICE-PRESIDENT *Robert McDiarmid/Derek Swain*
TREASURER *David Mole/David S. Dick*
INTERNAL AFFAIRS OFFICER
Robert Smith/ Barbara Coward/Michael Robinson
EXTERNAL AFFAIRS OFFICER
Sharon Boylan/Gillies Malnarick/Adrian Belshaw
SECRETARY *Evert Hoogers/Hilary Powell*
COORDINATOR OF ACTIVITIES
Sue Kennedy/Rick Murray

UBYSSEY EDITOR *Leslie Plommer*

1972 TO 1973

Naked Came the Artsmen: Well, actually they didn't, though Arts Undergraduate Society president Brian Loomes had said they should to protest the lack of student representation. Also to eroticize the University. Show up to the next Arts faculty council meeting unclothed, he said. This made the *Ubyssey* shake its editorial head, though mostly they agreed with Loomes: on what he was advocating, just not his methods. And what a relief for them: they'd been lamenting the death of activism, and here it was alive again.

Politics or Services? This was the issue of the year. AMS politicians divided into two camps, those devoting themselves to student programs and services (a permanent pub in the basement, an indoor swimming pool, maybe AMS-run food services) and those saying the students' job was to fight the system, win more representation, run the university. Those old sixties times again.

And Speaking of the Old Sixties: Who emerged yet again but that "relic" from 1967, as the *Ubyssey* described him: Stan Persky. Supporting the Arts students, sitting on Student Council as a grad student representative, and finally running and winning a seat on the AMS Executive. Yes, finally, the end of the struggle. Or was it just the beginning?

But oh, Stan, You Got Some 'Splaining to Do: Persky prompted Council to come out in favour of an illegal strike at Denny's restaurant, which prompted Denny's to threaten legal action against the AMS. Uh oh. Council hurriedly rescinded its motion.

And What Did the Students Really Want? While a couple of hundred invaded an Arts faculty meeting, others wrote letters to the paper saying they were here to study, not demonstrate. And though the elections put radicals Brian Loomes and Stan Persky into power, the

RIGHT Some students thought the idea was to study (Main Library, 1986).

BELOW Students outside the SUB in the seventies. What did they really want from their Student Union Building?

Brian Loomes, AUS then AMS president. Clothed.

students amused themselves by electing several moderates as well. Persky warned that if the moderates got their way and continued to build the AMS up as a service organization or a business, in the end the AMS would turn the Student Union Building into a shopping mall with space rented out to conventions and a theatre, a pub, restaurants, a parking lot, and a hotel.

Well, the hotel never came to pass, but most of the rest describes what indeed the AMS brought into being over the next few decades.

Cycling and Recycling: Cyclists proliferated, but this did produce a bit of a backlash from some who complained that they weren't following the rules of the road. As to recycling, AMS pressure had got the University to abandon disposable dishes, but they seemed to be sneaking back this year under the guise of providing for students seeking take-out. The *Ubyssey* snorted at this excuse, saying that next the University would be saying the dish ran away with the spoons.

More Activism: The University sprung a rent increase on married students in the Acadia Park residence, prompting protests, which led the University to backtrack and offer a compromise. Not good enough, said the radicals, but in fact the University seemed to be giving way on several fronts, also offering concessions on student representation and raising the possibility of allowing the public to attend meetings of the Board of Governors. And then there was . . .

Women's Studies: After two years of an AMS-run non-credit program, the UBC Senate approved a for credit program in Women's Studies. This amidst a backdrop of protest about the situation of women on campus. The AMS funded a report on the status of women, which pointed to various forms of discrimination, including lower pay for similar work. And Council censured the Engineers for their Lady Godiva ride. Feminism was here to stay.

Speaking of the Engineers: They had the tables turned on them when some SFU students made off with their prize-winning energy efficient car (dubbed the Wally Wagon, after UBC president Walter Gage). Not enjoying being on this side of a prank, the Engineers threatened legal action, but eventually backed off.

More Legal Action: The AMS threatened some when the University didn't keep the SUB as clean as the AMS expected. And there were more disputes over who could be charged which fee. And then there was the slander case over the things some DJs said about some AMS executives. What's wrong with a little slander, said the *Ubyssey*, but later said they were joking. The DJs lost their jobs (really, volunteer positions at CYVR, the original name of the campus radio station).

And in Other News: The AMS joined a new student federation, the National Union of Students (NUS), which promised to be less political than the old Canadian Union of Students. The University talked about taking over the running of Intramurals (from the students). And the students voted in favour of a $5 fee to build an indoor aquatic centre.

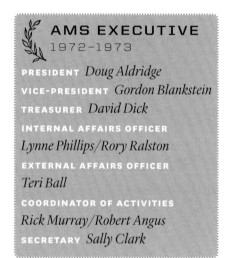

Engineering students push their Wally Wagon with UBC president Walter Gage inside.

1973 TO 1974

Protesters prevent work from going ahead at Wreck Beach. The work was meant to stop erosion that threatened the location of the future Museum of Anthropology, then called the Museum of Man.

Two Roads Diverged: And the AMS tried to take both of them. Costs were escalating, the AMS was short of money. What was to be done? It was more than a short-term thing, the *Ubyssey* suggested. There were two possible paths for the future: either continue to expand, developing projects like the Pit and the Pool, moving into food services and other business ventures to increase revenue. Or cut back on commitments by decentralizing: letting the clubs and undergraduate societies go their own way.

The *Ubyssey* pushed for the second course, as did the Engineers (a strange alliance). The Engineers even put a slate together whose whole focus was on decentralization. It came second in the annual Executive elections, ahead of three left-wing slates. But the winner in the election was . . .

The Students' Coalition, who already controlled the Executive.

This was the group dedicated to expanding the AMS. They were the ones who had pushed for the Pool and the Pit, and who talked about getting into food services. This was indeed the direction the AMS moved in, expanding its operations, initiating services and businesses, enlarging the size of its budget.

But at the same time the AMS did try to devolve some power and responsibility to the undergraduate societies and the clubs. And yet the central AMS administration would grow and costs would rise.

Looking Inward: Whether shrinking or expanding, the focus this year was on things AMS, within the society, or at least within the University. There was still some talk of external issues, from Chilean refugees to the marvels of China, and of social issues such as abortion. And there was a continuing debate about student representation, especially within the Faculty of Arts. But there were no mass protests, no marching on the Faculty Club. It's a conservative campus, said winning presidential candidate Gordon Blankstein. And the outgoing president, Brian Loomes, a lonely radical among Student Coalition executives, said the radical struggle did not attract "mass attention or support." Those days were gone.

Save Our Beach: The biggest protest of the year was only tangentially connected to the students. It had to do with plans to put down sand and gravel along the campus beaches, including Wreck Beach, an area already known as a refuge for lovers of nature and nude sun-bathing. Plans to begin the work, which was meant to prevent erosion of the cliffs at the edge of campus, were frustrated by members of the Wreck Beach Preservation Committee, who feared the work would ruin the beach. The *Ubyssey* and AMS Council endorsed the protest, but it wasn't the same as the protests of old.

More Peepers Than Streakers: The only other mass gathering (unless one counts the large turnouts for the Beach Boys and Cheech and Chong) took place when streaking came to town. Thousands of students turned up to watch 150 Engineers run naked through and around the SUB—but perhaps it was a sign of the times that there were more onlookers than participants.

Stan, We Hardly Knew Ye: Well, that's not quite true. The campus got to know Stan Persky quite well: he was the leading figure of the sixties generation. But this year after being elected to the Executive, finally, he suddenly resigned to take a leave from UBC, leaving a gap perhaps to be filled by Svend Robinson, the future NDP MP, who became the voice of the left at UBC as a student senator and a member of Council. He was also talked about as a potential member of the Board of Governors. Even though there were still no student seats on the Board,

there were rumours that the NDP government might fill a vacancy with Svend—but that was not the way he ended up on the Board.

Svend Robinson, new voice of the left.

Food: The AMS had been talking about taking over the SUB Cafeteria, but that never happened. On the other hand, when the SUB barber left (an indirect victim of the growth of men's hair) the AMS filled the vacancy with an independent food outlet that became a fixture on campus for the next four decades: the Delly.

The Delly opened on February 25, 1974.

This Campus Ain't Big Enough for the Two of Us: So said the *Ubyssey* when the *Georgia Straight* came calling. We're an alternative newspaper too, said the *Straight*. Go away, said the *Ubyssey*; you're stealing our advertisers. Freedom of the press meets commercial interests. The case went to Student Court and almost to real courts before the *Ubyssey* and the AMS backed down and let the *Straight* be distributed on campus.

Smokers' Rights: The *Ubyssey* also took an odd position on smoking this year: standing up for the right of students to smoke in classrooms. This brought a rejoinder from a professor who said he didn't want pollution in the air while he lectured. Second-hand smoke was just becoming a thing, so there was no immediate result, but two years later the University Senate banned smoking in classrooms, and it was the beginning of the end for cigarettes. In the meantime, however, the *Ubyssey* was still running cigarette ads.

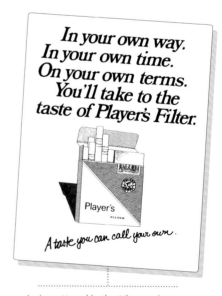
A cigarette ad in the *Ubyssey* in 1973.

The *Ubyssey* also incurred criticism for its joke articles and letters, and for its strong stand against a new University fee meant to pay for the use of recreation facilities. But on the whole the paper, co-edited this year by Vaughn Palmer, adopted a moderate tone, refusing to endorse any of the left-wing slates in that year's election. The paper could not, however, bring itself to endorse the service-oriented Students' Coalition nor the Engineers' slate, so instead it told readers to enter write-in votes for Ugandan dictator Idi Amin. Always kidding around.

The Pit.

Idi Amin: not really eligible.

Engineering: The Engineers' chariot race had become so violent that this year it was abandoned, but the result was a low turnout at the women's Teacup football game, which was usually paired with the charioteering. You need something "really gross" to attract people, said the Engineers, and the race would return.

Computing: Also rejected this year was a computer for the AMS. Computers, who needs them? But the AMS would eventually succumb.

Drinking: Now possible in the SUB's very own permanent pub, the Pit, which opened in November 1973. After five years of floating around the SUB as a sort of itinerant beer garden, the students' pub finally had a place of its own. Still no draft beer, though; just bottles. And only students and guests could enter.

Blissing Out: Rennie Davis, one of the radical protesters at the Chicago Democratic Convention in 1968, came to town with the Guru Maharaj Ji, preaching mystical salvation as the path to world peace. Cosmic fascism, the *Ubyssey* called it, and a sign of the decline of the Left. Peace, brothers.

AMS EXECUTIVE
1973–1974

PRESIDENT *Brian Loomes*
VICE-PRESIDENT *Gordon Blankstein*
TREASURER *John Wilson*
INTERNAL AFFAIRS OFFICER
Diane Latta/Doug Brock
EXTERNAL AFFAIRS OFFICER
Bonnie Long
COORDINATOR OF ACTIVITIES
Joanne Lindsay
SECRETARY *Stan Persky/ George Mapson*

UBYSSEY EDITOR *Vaughn Palmer/ Michael Sasges (co-editors)*

163

1974 TO 1975

Let Them Eat Elsewhere: So said UBC Food Services after complaints about the price and quality of their offerings. Students can walk to the Village, they said, or shop at the new Delly in the SUB basement. But when the *Ubyssey* was able to show that prices were rising much faster on campus than off, even the Board of Governors got involved and said something should be done. And something was: UBC's cafeteria in the SUB began offering selections similar to McDonald's, prompting McDonald's to say: If you want our style of food, why not invite us onto campus? But that would not happen for some years yet.

Let Them Go Swimming: Who wants a new pool, said some? And why should the students be the ones to pay for it? Let's think about this again. Let's have another referendum. No, said the Engineers, storming the Council meeting discussing this. And they took the leader of the anti-pool forces away for an impromptu swim. Undeterred, and with the strength of a referendum petition behind them, the anti-pool forces were able to force a new vote, but supporters of the pool had the last laugh: students turned out in droves to say go ahead; we want our indoor pool and are happy to pay for it. And so, eventually, it came to pass.

Despite opposition, construction of the Aquatic Centre eventually went ahead.

UBC's cafeteria in the SUB, 1979.

Let Them Live Elsewhere: Maybe in a hotel downtown. That was one suggestion floated by the University to cope with the campus housing shortage. There was even support from some students for the idea of the University buying hotels to transform into residences, but it didn't come to anything.

There was less support for University plans to increase the rates in campus residences (again), and a lot of confusion over whether residences fell under the Landlord and Tenant Act, and whether that would be a good or bad idea.

Let Them Throw Beer Bottles: Or don't. The landlord-tenant discussion came up because the University immediately evicted students who tossed beer bottles over a residence balcony during a party. The University shouldn't be able to act like that, some said. There would be a hearing and a thirty-day waiting period under the Landlord and Tenant Act. But some students feared they'd be worse off under the Act. The idea would remain a point of contention over the ensuing decades.

But I'm the President: And so he was (Gordon, or Gordie, Blankstein,

that is), but he could get little respect. The *Ubyssey* mocked him all year long, and the Engineers took him for one of their swims and then hoisted him up in a mock crucifixion. But on one issue even the *Ubyssey* praised him: for his role in stopping the dreaded . . .

Library Processing Centre: The library needed extra space and proposed to build next door to the SUB. No, said President Blankstein, our lease forbids that. But the library seemed intent. Council passed a motion objecting and sent off a letter. Individual councillors staged a protest. Legal action was mooted. And the library backed down: the Library Processing Centre went elsewhere.

Has Anyone Seen My Picasso? The AMS Art Collection was hit by theft, absent-mindedness, or at least bad record keeping. Eighteen paintings were missing, said one official. No, just eight, said another. Make a catalogue, said the *Ubyssey*. Keep track of these things. Get some security. The situation would eventually improve: a catalogue of the collection came

Help yourself.

out in 1988; security measures were introduced. But for a while things seemed quite disorganized.

Heads, You Win: And she did. Jennifer Fuller won election by a coin toss when she and her opponent tied in the race to become the Internal Affairs Officer. There had been talk of rerunning the election, but a coin toss it was.

You Can't Be Our Ombudsperson: Long before the University, the AMS created the position of ombudsperson, which in its early years was an elected position. An elected position for students, one might add. This year, though, it was almost as if the University wanted to get involved: William White, the bursar, one of the highest-ranking administration officials, was on the ballot. More than that, he finished second in a field of four, even surpassing the incumbent—and this despite not campaigning at all, for the very good reason that he didn't know he was running.

It was all a joke, of course. Not by the bursar, but by the Engineers, who had submitted phony nomination papers on White's behalf without his knowledge. Student Court threw out the whole election as invalid.

And in Other News: The University introduced an English Composition Test, which 40 percent of the students promptly failed. The new Universities Act took effect, and there were now two student seats on the Board of Governors, one of which was filled by Svend Robinson. The Varsity Outdoors Club worried that the AMS wanted to take over its cabin in Whistler; the AMS said it wanted to open the cabin to all AMS members: more on this later. The AMS opened a lounge called Lethe, rejecting the name Pendulum for it, though there would eventually be a Pendulum food outlet right next to the Pit in the SUB basement; it even sported a picture of Edgar Allan Poe (there's a literature joke in there). And . . .

Not with a Bang: Whimpering out, the decade that began with psyche-delia and mass protests ended in a year without protests or demonstrations, and with only dozens turning out to vote for the Senate seats their radical forebears had fought for. The *Ubyssey* sighed, beginning a long tradition of nostalgia for the sixties. And to add insult to injury, NDP premier Dave Barrett showed up on campus to reproach students with being a privileged elite out of tune with the working masses. Perhaps the answer would be to shake up the AMS: at least, that's what newly elected President Jake van der Kamp promised, and the following year would indeed see some radical restructuring.

AMS EXECUTIVE
1974-1975

PRESIDENT *Gordon Blankstein*
VICE-PRESIDENT *Doug Brock/ Robbie Smith*
TREASURER *George Mapson/ Pemme Muir Cunliffe/Dave Theessen*
INTERNAL AFFAIRS OFFICER *Joan Mitchell*
EXTERNAL AFFAIRS OFFICER *Gary Moore*
COORDINATOR OF ACTIVITIES *Lynn Orstad/Ron Dumont*
SECRETARY *Duncan Thomson*

UBYSSEY EDITOR *Lesley Krueger*

1975-1985

Students storm the wall:
a new tradition for the eighties.

Eugene Changey, the Son of God. The *Ubyssey* printed his words religiously. Not that they believed them. One can be sure that their motives were primarily to mock. But why bother? Changey complained that most editors refused to publish what he wrote. Why was the *Ubyssey* different? Perhaps it was that they were believers in a non-religious ideology and saw Changey's unintentional parodies of the Christ story as a means of attacking Christianity, a rival belief system.

Whatever the case, rival belief systems seemed to be on display in this decade. If the sixties had broken fifties conformism and devotion to pep rallies and beauty queens, with an unquestioned Christianity beneath it, what was there left to believe in during the seventies and eighties?

There was still Christianity, of course, though its practitioners seemed almost a tad desperate, bringing magicians and bunny rabbits and promises of dynamic sex along with them to set people right. There were progressives and radicals, still worshipping at the shrine of the sixties, that increasingly distant time of blissful revolution. And there were the promoters of a renewed school spirit, reviving the Arts '20 relay and inventing a new tradition in Storm the Wall.

There were the Restructurers, who sought nirvana in revising the AMS constitution—only to see it revised back again. And there were the business promoters and the providers of services, who thought a student society should either be making money or helping its members, or doing one to help pay for the other.

And there were the pranksters still, but they were a bit of a dying breed, with their Lady Godivas and their Volkswagens (well, not so much the Volkswagens; they would survive several more decades, being a sanitized sort of stunt, unlike the transgressive and aggressive kidnappings and the displays of naked women).

The University had grown and the student body had splintered. Of course, there had long been divisions between faculties and years, but now, perhaps like all of society, UBC's students had lost their old certainties and were searching for new ones. Or they were busy, as always, studying and partying and listening to the music of the day while their leaders argued over which way to go.

1975 TO 1976

Give Me an I, Give Me a C . . . It's ICBC, the insurance corporation, raising rates up to 300 percent for young male drivers. Students were upset. There was a rally in downtown Vancouver and a cavalcade of cars in Victoria. Also a protest on campus. Just like old times. AMS Council called for students to strike, to boycott classes for one day, just before the February mid-term break.

Strike: Well, it wasn't much of a strike. Sure, said some students, we'll take a day off—and go skiing. Skiing? Yes, the energy quickly drained out of the protests. It wasn't like old times after all, despite the attempts of the *Ubyssey* and the radical AMS Executive to stir up old-time fervour.

Some students mistook the slopes for the picket lines.

A Real Strike: Okay, but a couple of months previous UBC saw a real strike. The library and clerical workers went out for more pay. Pay equity was talked about (the strikers were mostly women and earning less than male workers on campus). Support this strike, said the Left.

But the students did not. They crossed picket lines, shouted at picketers, threw things at them, even drove at them in their cars. Svend Robinson was so disgusted that he quit as a member of the Board of Governors. The *Ubyssey* shook its head at these non-radicals, but students this year were more into skiing. They didn't even show up to vote in their undergraduate society elections, which were more important this year because of the radical restructuring of the AMS. But only 54 Science students (out of 3,667) and only 206 Arts students (out of 6,500) voted. Oh, apathy, thy name is UBC.

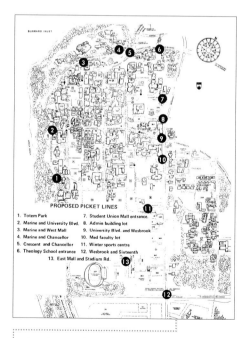

The *Ubyssey* showed where the picket lines were, and the students crossed them.

Protesting ICBC increases.

AMS Restructuring: The AMS ventured into strange, uncharted waters, abolishing Council and campus-wide elections to create a new body, the Student Representative Assembly (SRA), which included the student representatives elected to the Board of Governors and the Senate, combined with representatives from the undergraduate societies. This group would choose a president, who would be more of a chairperson than a leader. And the SRA was to shift focus away from internal AMS concerns and look to the issues discussed at Board and Senate: that's where the real power is, said the proponents of the new.

And there would also be a new administrative body, the Student Administrative Commission (SAC) to look after day-to-day AMS business. Would the SRA even have anything to do? Would it be able to do anything, with seventeen student senators expanding its ranks? Time would tell.

Sexual Assaults: Not for the first or last time, sexual assaults became a concern on campus. In earlier years they were not always taken seriously, though there was talk even then of maybe introducing a system of escorts, anticipating the creation of Safewalk at the end of the century. This year there was talk of improving lighting and increasing patrols, also of establishing a rape crisis centre, but that too would have to wait for several decades.

Lady Godiva: The Engineers' Lady Godiva ride came in for criticism again this year, including from the new UBC president, Doug Kenny, who also criticized the Engineers for their week of vandalism and "hooliganism," including pieing. He may have had a personal stake in this, having been victimized by a pie in the face full of shaving cream.

No Democracy or Insurance: Pat McGeer, the UBC athlete from years before who went on to become a professor of medicine and then a Liberal politician, shifted to the Social Credit party and became both Minister of Education and the minister responsible for ICBC, making himself a target in both capacities. No democracy at universities, he said, adding that students didn't belong on the Board of Governors. And as for increases in car insurance, he said those who couldn't afford insurance should just sell their cars and take transit. Students were appalled. Take transit, they said? Horrors. Not an acceptable option in those days, though there were new bus routes being talked of to go to campus and also talk of new-style trolley buses. But the real enthusiasm was for building multi-storey parking lots, or parkades.

Moe Sihota, later an NDP cabinet member and a talk show host, made his appearance on campus as the AMS ombudsperson and then the AMS External Affairs Officer. He also edited the revived Student Handbook, called *Insight* in his day.

Housing: Always an issue. Here the *Ubyssey* depicts the choices available. (Warning: some exaggeration may be involved.)

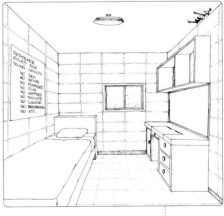

TOP A room in a private house.
BOTTOM A room in residence.

171

The poplar trees had to go to make way for the pool.

A Tale of Two Knolls (and Nineteen Trees): In the period around 2007 the campus knoll became a flashpoint of contention between the forces of development and those wanting to preserve their grassy refuge next to the Old SUB. But that was the second knoll. The first one was also near the SUB, but it had to go to make way for the new indoor pool, or Aquatic Centre, the construction of which was finally underway. This also meant the destruction of nineteen poplar trees that had adorned the first knoll.

Vendors: They also disappeared, at least temporarily. The SUB main concourse for some time had been a place for people selling crafts to set up shop. But the AMS said their presence was hurting sales in the AMS used bookstore (which sold crafts as well as books), and people

said it was a fire hazard, and besides, why should non-students occupy student space for free? Free? Yes, it seems the vendors weren't paying for the space, though they said they would be willing to. The AMS told them to leave, and they eventually did, but in years to come vendors would regularly appear in the concourse, though only after arrangements were made to turn them into paying clients.

Let's Settle the Middle East Dispute: Moshe Dayan came to town. Spoke in the SUB Ballroom. Fistfights broke out between pro-Palestinian and pro-Israeli supporters. Dayan, the former Israeli general, called for peace. His opponents tried to shout him down. Nothing was settled.

Quorum: A more successful meeting was the AMS AGM, which met quorum thanks to a rock band (Trooper) and some giveaways. It was the last AGM to meet quorum for close to 40 years.

More Music: Frank Zappa played heavy metal to a packed audience at the War Memorial Gym, where two years before the Beach Boys had entertained crowds with a somewhat different brand of music making.

1976 TO 1977

The Final Trek: Or the Trek to the Final Frontier. *Star Trek*. That's what students cared about. Not protesting or marching or making revolution. Listening to Gene Roddenberry talk about their favourite television series. Thousands came out for it to War Memorial Gym, many more than protested about the latest fee hike.

Where no Trek has gone before: Thousands attended a *Star Trek* convention on campus.

This Year's Fee Hike: But there was a fee hike this year, actually the first in a while, thanks to the lack of funding from the provincial government. And Council (sorry, the SRA) spent $10,000 to organize a rally against it, and got twelve hundred students to march across campus, with some being allowed into a Board of Governors meeting to state their case. The Board raised fees anyway.

And Then? Then the SRA became fiscally prudent and wouldn't spend money on the province-wide rally ten days later, prompting criticism from activists, saying there was no leadership at the AMS, which of course was only natural: the radical restructuring of the year before had reduced the AMS president to a mere figurehead, a creature of the SRA—and then people complained there was no leadership.

Conflict: What there was instead was internal conflict: the SRA and SAC (the other new body created by the restructuring) clashed. Should we pay a lot of money for Germaine Greer to speak? Should we stop the *Ubyssey* from boycotting CBC ads? And what about the Women's Office? Should we let them continue in the SUB?

Women: They'd had an office, but SAC decided that since they weren't a club, they couldn't keep it. Become a club, SAC said. "Women's liberation is not a club," was the reply. Eventually, after appeals to the SRA and protests among the students, the old Women's Office was transformed into a Women's Committee, which was eventually given an office again, so the Women's Office was back, offering a drop-in space, providing information and advocating.

Women's Athletics: Women advocated very well this year, for instance winning a $2 increase in funding for their athletic program. Every other AMS fee proposal went down to defeat by referendum, but the women got an extra $2 for sports: still only $2.80 per student as opposed to the $4.20 for men's athletics, but it was perhaps the momentum that mattered. "It's a great step forward for women's athletics on campus," said one of the organizers of the women's athletic program.

Demographics: Speaking of momentum, for the first time (perhaps excepting wartime) the intake of women into first year exceeded the intake of men. Eventually, the total number of women students would far exceed the number of men.

Cycling: Bicycles were a growing alternative to automobiles. Some people talked of public transit, but buses were seen as uncomfortable, slow, and expensive: cycling was the way to go. But cycling could only take you so far: the bike path along University Boulevard stopped three blocks short of campus, though one administrator said, No, no, it only seems to stop: look, there are all those back lanes cyclists can turn onto to get to their classes.

But the cyclists preferred to keep going along University Boulevard, riding on sidewalks or otherwise ignoring the traffic rules, so the University put up speed-bump-like curbs (booby traps, the cyclists called them) and had the police hand out tickets. There was much displeasure (and a few accidents).

You can't get there from here: cyclists had to stop three blocks from campus.

No More Pit? Well, at least for several weeks. The AMS feared being shut down for liquor violations, so how do you avoid having the government shut you down? You shut down yourself. We never recommended that, said an inspector. Students complained. The AMS worked on changing how it served beer: no more jugs, just glasses. Also reduced hours and seating capacity, but more staff. And when the Pit reopened there did seem to be a calmer atmosphere.

Buildings: The indoor pool finally got its funding complete (thanks to gov-

ernment grants), and the Engineers found a new home: the Cheeze, the old dairy lab to which they were exiled because the faculty didn't want them in the new Engineering building for fear of vandalism. So it was their bad reputation that gave the Engineers a new home.

The Engineers' Cheeze.

Here's an Idea: A student senator in the midst of talk of fee hikes said, Instead of raising them across the board, why not just do it for foreign students and students from other provinces? Appalling, said everyone from the SRA to the *Ubyssey* to the Senate. Even the University's new VP for student and faculty affairs (Erich Vogt) said the idea was ridiculous. And yet it would eventually come to pass (not for students from out of province, but for international students).

Differential Fees: Not for international students this year, but when the fee increase came in it was more for students in certain faculties (medicine, law, engineering, commerce).

More Internal Conflict: VOC versus AMS, decided (maybe) by Student Court, which ruled that though the AMS owned all club assets, includ-

ing the Whistler Lodge, since the lodge had been built by the Varsity Outdoors Club, the AMS did have a fiduciary duty to compensate them for taking it over. No, no, said the SRA, we can't hear you. There was talk of going to real court. There were discussions. Eventually, the AMS agreed to pay the VOC to put up some other cabins, which was more or less what Student Court and the VOC had proposed in the first place.

Do Fascists Have a Right to Speak? A South African politician came to campus and radicals denouncing apartheid disrupted his talk. Even the *Ubyssey* was appalled: even fascists have a right to speak, they said (not that the speaker was even a fascist). But later in the year they defended the law librarian who got in trouble for trying to stop the speech. Others disagreed: if even fascists have a right to speak, you can't defend someone who tries to stop them from speaking (though true, he shouldn't be fired perhaps: and he wasn't, just reprimanded). Ah, the perils of free speech at a university.

And in the End: It was a standstill year, said one of the *Ubyssey* editors. Students were wrapped up in their own lives rather than wanting to devote themselves to large causes. What they got the most upset about was the Pit closure. And more were going into commerce and engineering: not the best soil for making revolution.

So though at one point the *Ubyssey* tried to rally the students with

The *Ubyssey*'s unsuccessful call to arms.

In the library.

The revolution was over, said the *Ubyssey*'s cartoonist Bob Krieger, who went on to a long career as a cartoonist for Vancouver's *Province* newspaper.

a poster reminiscent of Maoist China, the students were not really interested; they were too busy attending classes and studying in the library.

Political Futures: Herb Dhaliwal, later a federal cabinet minister, became a member of the AMS Executive, working alongside Moe Sihota, who would become a long-time political associate.

In class.

1977 TO 1978

UBC's Lady Godiva in 1980.

What's Going on Here? These are strange times, said the *Ubyssey*. Indeed. UBC's president seemed more ready to fight government cuts than was Student Council, which dissolved its anti-cuts committee. Joe Clark, the leader of the federal Conservative party, came to campus and got a pie in his face for his trouble. Stan Persky came back, trying unsuccessfully to become UBC's chancellor. The Campus Crusade for Christ paraded around campus dressed as bunny rabbits. The Speaker's Chair from the legislature in Victoria somehow travelled all the way to the UBC Student Union Building, where the Engineers tried to present it to a visiting politician. And the biggest controversy was over a ride named after a medieval lady.

Lady Godiva: Yes, when they weren't stealing ceremonial chairs, the Engineers hosted their annual parade of a naked woman riding a horse, during Engineering Week, which this year coincided with Women's Week, hosted by the very active Women's Committee. There were pickets, a confrontation, and condemnation from UBC president Kenny (yes, leading the way again, and this from a president activists feared would be too conservative). And condemnation from other campus representatives, weeks of letter writing to the *Ubyssey*, in which students debated the meaning of sexism and exploitation, or joked about the exploitation of "unclad quadrupeds" (i.e., the horse). All capped off by the Agriculture students organizing a Lord Godiva parade of a naked man on a horse (the Engineers' student president in this case).

Racism: Besides sexism, racism prompted debate after a residence newsletter containing anti-Asian "jokes" appeared. Just kidding around, said the editor; some of my best friends are Asian. Not acceptable, said Chinese letter writers (and others). The president of the Chinese Students Association said it was good that Chinese students were finally speaking up about this sort of thing.

Speaking Up (and More): Also on the issue of racism, in this case South African apartheid, AMS Council voted to remove its money (well, some of its money) from the Bank of Montreal because of the bank's investments in South Africa. Later in the year there was also a campaign to get the University's Board of Governors to speak out against investments in Chile.

The Chinese Students Association.

Welcome, said the bank. Not so welcome, said the students unhappy with its investments in South Africa.

SRA, SRA: But mostly AMS Council (still called the SRA) did little this year, at least in the eyes of the *Ubyssey*, which questioned the whole restructuring from two years before. The focus of student leadership seemed to have shifted away from Student Council, and now this was thought to be a bad thing, though it had been the whole point of the restructuring.

Student Leadership Conference: The focus shifted a bit to a revival from earlier times, a conference at Camp Elphinstone just like old times before the radicalism of the sixties killed it. Students, faculty, and administrators got together to discuss the future of the University. Even the editor of the radical *Ubyssey* was there; and even more surprisingly he pronounced it a useful exercise, looking forward to more of them.

AMS Council, aka the SRA, in 1978.

Undergraduate Societies: The focus also shifted to the Arts Undergraduate Society and the Science Undergraduate Society, both of which were seeking independent fee levies to carry on activities, including the revival of anti-calendars, those published compilations of student opinions of professors. In the sixties these had been too extreme and controversial; now there was an attempt to bring them back.

Elections: What would election season be like without a controversy? The Engineers (they were busy this year) were accused of irregularities in getting one of their own re-elected to the Board of Governors. The SRA investigated and referred the issue to the Senate. The Senate referred it to a committee. The committee came back to Senate. In the end the results stood, though the *Ubyssey* thought it was all very fishy, and thought the SRA should have asserted itself more.

Moe Sihota: Though the time was past for Stan Persky, Moe Sihota continued to make his mark on campus politics, raising issues like cutbacks and teaching quality, and getting into trouble for allegations he made about racism and for talking too much to the press about what went on at the Board

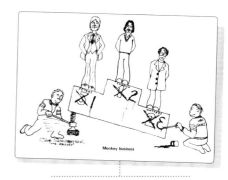

Monkey business

There was monkey business in the election, said the *Ubyssey*, suggesting that Engineer Basil Peters did not really win.

of Governors. But then his term on the Board ended and he was gone.

All Gone: The sixties were gone too, as the *Ubyssey* kept lamenting. Students joined the Dance Club instead of political groups, or played pinball. Students are protesting elsewhere, the paper said, but at UBC things were somnolent.

Others protest while UBC students snooze, or so thought the *Ubyssey*.

🏛 **AMS EXECUTIVE**
1977–1978

PRESIDENT *John DeMarco*

SECRETARY/TREASURER
Arnold Hedstrom

DIRECTOR OF FINANCE
Shanon-Dale Hart

DIRECTOR OF SERVICES *Dave Jiles*

EXTERNAL AFFAIRS OFFICER
Paul Sandhu

UBYSSEY EDITOR *Chris Gainor*

1978 TO 1979

Punk was going to come to UBC,
but then it didn't.

Shop at Imaginus for the
posters you want.

Disco versus Punk: People loved their music in the seventies, or hated it, which comes to the same thing. Some were blasting the latest disco sounds in their residence rooms, prompting at least one letter writer and the *Ubyssey* itself to complain. When the *Ubyssey* waded into musical waters, it tended more towards the punk end of the spectrum, organizing a concert which was to have been headlined by the punk band D.O.A. However, the RCMP expressed concerns about liquor and possible violence, and the AMS ended up cancelling the whole thing, much to some students' dismay.

Life Goes On: Meanwhile concerts featuring Burton Cummings and the Atlanta Rhythm Section went off without a hitch at the War Memorial Gym, and students went to tapings of the CBC radio program, *Dr. Bundolo and His Pandemonium Medicine Show,*

in the SUB Auditorium. They also drove their Volkswagens to record stores to get new needles for their turntables or bought posters for their walls at the Imaginus sale in the SUB Art Gallery.

State of the art stereo
systems in 1978.

Studying Too: In the new Sedgewick Library, buried underground across from the old Main Library. Sedgewick had started out as a section of Main, then became independent in the seventies, only to be swallowed up in the nineties by the new Walter C. Koerner Library. Fame is fleeting.

Sedgewick Library, where UBC undergraduates studied in the seventies and later.

Music and Studying: They could even listen to music in the library, at the Wilson Recordings Collection in Sedgewick.

Listening to music in the library.

or mono prevention, all emanating from the Central Committee of the Revolutionary Trutchkeyites, who would often meet at Trutch House, whatever that was (just a house on Trutch Street?), or sometimes in the SUB Cafeteria. Party on, comrades.

Amnesty International display in the SUB.

RCMP anti-theft ad. Theft was up this year until the RCMP launched an awareness campaign.

And of Course Clubs: From the new Toastmasters, where students could master the arts of public speaking, to Amnesty International, where they could take part in writing letters protesting the incarceration of prisoners of conscience, to skydivers and hang gliders, ethnic clubs and academic ones, not to mention joke ones like …

The Revolutionary Trutchkeyites: Every week or so in the *Ubyssey*'s 'Tween Classes column, amid announcements for the Debating Society and the Club Français, there would be cryptic references to Fellini and spaghetti, or sock searching,

And Other Everyday Stuff: Registration and exam writing in the Armouries, that the Second World War–era building that would survive into the nineties. Speed reading with Evelyn Wood. Using the card catalogues in the library (no computers yet), walking by the half-finished Asian Centre, registering for jobs at the new Canada Employment Centre at Brock Hall, lamenting the death of Keith Moon, going to see *Heaven Can Wait* or *Animal House*, or perhaps a Kurosawa retrospective. Learning how to scuba dive with the Aquatic Society (Aquasoc), learning not to leave valuables unattended, skating at the Thunderbird Winter Sports Centre, swimming at the finally opened Aquatic Centre, or log-rolling in the outdoor pool.

'Tween Classes let students know what club events were going on. The Revolutionary Trutchkeyites are the third item.

The Aquatic Centre opened in September.

And the Leaders? Yes, where were the leaders this year? Squabbling among themselves about the AMS constitution, gearing up to fight another tuition fee increase, arguing some more about Lady Godiva, and trying to get the membership to pay more for AMS activities.

Fee Referendums: The students had to go through two of these this year. First in the fall, one that failed. Then in the spring, one that passed thanks to the clever notion of announcing that half of the proposed increase would be earmarked solely for the support of Intramurals, thus beginning a long tradition of dedicated fees. Nestor Korchinsky, the face of Intramurals for years at UBC, was pleased.

Nestor Korchinsky, director of intramural sports, 1970–2003.

ABOVE LEFT Using the card catalogue in the Main Library.

ABOVE RIGHT Log-rolling as part of Forestry Week.

Transit: One interesting innovation this year was the student bus pass. It wasn't as successful as expected, perhaps because it brought only modest savings, nothing like the U-Pass decades later, but it survived its original year when some were saying it wouldn't.

Other Innovations: This year saw the beginnings of the general student co-op program, something that had begun as a program for women only, to encourage them to enter non-traditional occupations like engi-

1980 TO 1981

Don't run alone: That's what a member of the Medicine team in the Arts '20 relay learned this year: he ended up being abducted in the middle of the race while in the lead. And who did it? The Enginee . . . ? No, no, it was pirates. Well, six men wearing Pittsburgh Pirates uniforms. The Medicine team was knocked out of contention, and the winners were . . . the Engineers.

Big Plans: A year of planning grandiosely. The University talked of connecting Main and Sedgewick

The Arts '20 relay race in the eighties. Watch out for pirates.

Libraries (that never happened) and of building a new bookstore (that did). The AMS Executive talked of renovating the SUB, creating new offices and a lounge, a darkroom for Photosoc (the photography club), maybe some new shops, an underground mall. Also perhaps a second SUB in the part of campus near the Agriculture and Forestry students—but those students objected: Hey, you didn't ask us. And the general student population, when asked in a referendum about using the old SUB fee to do these new projects, said No, thanks.

What Should We Do with Your $15? The Student Union Building was finally paid for this year, thanks to the portion of the annual AMS fee set aside for that purpose. So what should we do with that money now, said the Executive? Their first plan was to use it for the SUB renovations. When the students said no to that, the Executive said, Okay, we'll just hold onto it for whatever new building plans we come up with in the future. No way, said the students, give us our money back. And while you're at it, how about reducing beer prices in the Pit?

No, no, said the incoming AMS president, we can't have the students deciding beer prices: do you expect us to run our businesses by referendum? But the students did get their $15 back.

So What Should We All Be Doing? As the eighties began, everyone seemed to be at loose ends. The *Ubyssey* ran a cartoon saying there were no issues anymore. But in fact in second term things began happening again. Tuition fees and student aid problems began to galvanize the population. There was even a rally and a march. Was activism coming back?

There's nothing to cartoon about, said the *Ubyssey* cartoonist early in the year.

185

And Here's an Issue, Maybe Two: An Environmental Interest Group formed on campus and talked about pollution and the need to reduce our reliance on fossil fuels: not because fossil fuels might be causing climate change but because they were non-renewable resources that we might run out of if we weren't careful.

And the group brought Ralph Nader to campus. The American consumer advocate encouraged students to form a Public Interest Research Group (PIRG) to look into corporate corruption, freedom of information, the environment, and related issues. At first there seemed quite a bit of interest in the idea, but when put to referendum, it failed too.

And More: It was the International Year of the Disabled, and the *Ubyssey* ran features. Someone noted the lack of wheelchair access in the SUB. UBC wheelchair athlete Rick Hansen, who went on to win much attention a few years later with his Man in Motion World Tour, started along that path with a "Rickathon" race around campus to raise money and awareness.

But Here's Something That Really Matters: Why aren't there raisins in the cinnamon buns anymore, said a plaintive letter-writer. UBC's cinnamon buns were highly celebrated.

ABOVE But are there raisins?

RIGHT One of the burgeoning number of dance clubs.

And There's Always Kurt: Kurt Preinsperg was back, writing articles on religion, pornography, and sexual harassment, with predictable results.

And Even Stan: Oh, no, Stan Persky? Yes, running yet again for the Chancellor's position, also with predictable results. J.V. Clyne won re-election.

And Joe: Federal Conservative leader Joe Clark was back, asking, Is that guy with the pie around? (He'd got a pie in his face on his previous UBC visit.)

And in the End: John Lennon died, something sadly noted in the *Ubyssey*. Tennessee Williams, the Dalai Lama, and Timothy Leary visited campus. But students mostly kept their heads down. Students don't want to be activists, said one letter-writer early in the year. Tell us about dances and campus events. We just want to learn to get along in our society, not change it. And yet . . .

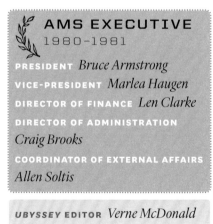

Rick Hansen receiving an honorary degree in 1987.

1981 TO 1982

And Now for Something Completely Different: Monty Python's Graham Chapman came to campus to sign copies of his autobiography. He talked, he signed, he gave an interview. Later he showed silly film clips and talked some more. Over eight hundred went to see the film clips, which though panned by the *Ubyssey* were probably a lot more fun than the rest of the news this year, which was mostly about . . .

Cuts, Increases, Finger-Pointing: Funding was down, because of the provincial government, or no, the federal government. Or it was because an arbitrator gave faculty too big a salary increase. And the University was planning to cut, cut, cut, striking a retrenchment committee, which met in private. Why are there no students on the committee, students asked? And the faculty was unhappy, and the TAs, who threatened a strike. And of course the *Ubyssey* was unhappy, and said the AMS wasn't unhappy enough.

The University announced tuition increases, and there was a rally downtown, drawing a thousand people, but only three hundred were UBC students. Former NDP Premier Dave Barrett came to campus and told students to wake up, but they must have been too busy practising silly walks. Surprisingly, the *Ubyssey* ran a cartoon that seemed to blame faculty for the fee increases.

The *Ubyssey* blames the profs.

But later the paper would editorialize on the need to create alliances, and would criticize AMS president Marlea Haugen for suggesting that the University find a way to break tenure to get rid of expensive professors.

More Pranked Against than Pranking: The Engineers found their cairn with a giant E on it defaced by students from other faculties. This became a longstanding tradition, which meant the Engineers would have to painstakingly repaint the E.

TOP The Engineers' cairn.
MIDDLE The Engineers' cairn "redecorated."
BOTTOM Repainting the cairn.

Not to Be Outdone: You can't keep a good Engineer down, though. Spreading the good news of Engineering to the downtown intersection of Pacific and Burrard in the middle of the night, some Engineering students left a giant E blocking the way. Arrests were made.

And More from the Engineers: This year their *Red Rag* publication so crossed the bounds of propriety that UBC president Kenny ordered their building padlocked, and publication ceased.

Speaking of Publications: Two new ones sprung up at the end of the year, a summer *Ubyssey* and a *Conventioneer*, the latter aimed at non-students holding conventions on campus during the summer. The two papers, though both published by the AMS, did not get along, but eventually merged. Meanwhile, tired of AMS control, the *Ubyssey* sought independence via referendum. However, it failed. Independence would have to wait for another decade.

Not a Good Year for Referendums: An AMS referendum to raise fees to pay for SUB renovations failed. So did a second attempt by the Public Interest Research Group (PIRG) to get funding. Money was tight all around this year, which may explain it, though the students seemed to have money to spend on the latest craze: video games. Pac-Man arrived in the SUB Games Room, and new AMS General Manager Charles Redden announced his determination to find new sources of revenue to fund AMS services.

Video games in the SUB Games Room. Most of the clientele was younger.

Thieves Like Us: That is, they liked the UBC campus, including the newly popular video games area, which was hit four times for $3,000. Bike thefts remained another popular target, and this year thieves diversified, stealing an Arts '20 banner, the Speakeasy sign, and a ballot box.

Elections: Well, they tried to steal a ballot box, but that theft was foiled, the vote results stood, and Dave Frank, the popular Science president, became president of the AMS. Meanwhile slates were looking for a revival, but the new activist slate went down to defeat this year, just as the joke Platypus slate had the year before. Slates would have to wait for another time.

Do You Believe in . . . ? The Campus Crusade for Christ was back, this time with a magic show. Other evangelical Christian groups also made noise, so much so that complaints came in to the *Ubyssey*. And then there were the Marxist-Leninists and the Trotskyists, slagging each other, and also criticizing the *Ubyssey* when it ran an interview with the leader of the Ku Klux Klan: the KKK were another group trying to find a foothold on campus.

Kurt: Yes, Kurt Preinsperg, giving all others a run for their money in terms of provoking outrage. He wrote an article saying food aid to foreign countries should be linked to birth control. Readers were not amused.

Hoax of the Year: A *Ubyssey* article saying a computer malfunction had destroyed thousands of student records. It wasn't true. The registrar was not amused.

(AOSC). There would be implications in this for the AMS and the travel agency (Travelcuts) formerly run by AOSC.

And in Other News: An occupation of the Museum of Anthropology demanded that Indigenous rights be added to the constitution, and succeeded! CiTR, the student radio station, began broadcasting on FM so that listeners could hear it far beyond campus. The SUB cafeteria was remodelled and renamed SUBway (not to be confused with the sandwich chain, which did show up in the SUB some years later).

The graduate students staked a claim to the Graduate Student Centre, in the process creating the Graduate Students Society, which eventually took over from the old Graduate Students Association.

A new student federation was formed: the CFS (Canadian Federation of Students), by amalgamating the old National Union of Students (NUS) with the Association of Student Councils

1982 TO 1983

As Almighty God, I Greet You: So began letter after letter published in the *Ubyssey* over more than a dozen years, all emanating from Eugene Changey in Maple Heights, Ohio, who claimed to be the Son and Voice of God. He called on people to abandon their disagreements and seek Divine guidance (from him). But this year he announced, or God announced through him, that he was approaching retirement. He continued to send out missives for a few more years, but then the word from God stopped.

And Disagreements Continued: There was Ando vs. Pinkney, a Student Court case about a disputed election, and conflict between the AMS and the Film Society, and then conflict within the Film Society, and then conflict within the new Graduate Students Society. But mostly there was a general uneasiness over . . .

Cutbacks: The perennial issue. UBC was scrambling to make do with less again, and there were cuts at the library, classrooms were overcrowded, and to top it off financial aid was in short supply. The government delayed releasing student grants, then mused that maybe non-repayable grants were not a good way to hand out money: maybe they should be done away with in favour of repayable loans. This turned out to be more than just musing, as did the recommendation at a Social Credit party convention that international students pay higher fees. Wait till next year.

Students went around in circles trying to get aid.

Cruising, Pornography, and STDs: There was some protest on and off campus about plans to test cruise missiles in Canada. There was more protest against the sale of *Playboy* and *Penthouse* in the campus bookstore and against the selling of pornography by Red Hot Video elsewhere in the Lower Mainland. But the biggest fuss of the year came in reaction to another hoax article in the *Ubyssey*, in which it was announced that herpes had been found in the swimming pool. Letter-writers excoriated the paper for irresponsibility.

The *Ubyssey* promoted opposition to the cruise missile.

On a Brighter Note: The AMS leadership, notably President Dave Frank, somehow convinced the students to vote to double their fees. This in the midst of cutbacks, poor job prospects, and uncertain financial aid. In previous years, the students had voted down fee increases of $2 and $3. Maybe the problem was that the AMS wasn't thinking big enough. Give us $20, said President Frank, and we'll use it for Intramurals, services, and a large-scale building program, day care, and student housing. Yes, said the students overwhelmingly in one of the biggest turnouts ever before the U-Pass referendums of the next century.

Services: The AMS started a JobLink program to help students find jobs, and a volunteer service started on campus, which would eventually find a home within the AMS.

René Lévesque offers referendum advice to the AMS president, but really he didn't need any help at all.

More Fuss: Letter-writers and others also got exercised when a fraternity pledge got drunk in the Pit and did lewd things with an inflatable doll. And there was also much discussion about whether homosexuality went against the teachings of Christianity. Bible passages were cited, but no one turned to Eugene Changey for guidance.

New This Year: An AMS security team in the SUB. A national football championship (their first) for the UBC Thunderbirds. A new University president, George Pedersen, and a new or newly repurposed house for him. UBC decided to spend $500,000 to renovate the old president's house on campus, which hadn't been used since the time of Kenneth Hare. The *Ubyssey* was outraged. Give him a room in Totem (the student residence) if he wants to live close to the students, the newspaper said.

And in Other News: The Queen paid a visit, asbestos had to be removed from the Pit, and a new bus route was established to campus (the No. 25 on King Edward Avenue), and the Chinese restaurant in the Old Auditorium got a new name: Yum Yums.

ABOVE The *Ubyssey* joked about asbestos and beer.

LEFT The *Ubyssey* explored students' views on spending money to refurbish the president's house.

HOUSE SURVEY

What is your opinion on spending $500,000 to renovate the UBC presidential house?
- ☐ Good idea
- ☐ No way!
- ☐ Don't care
- ☐ Only if I can go for tea
- ☐ _____

Tear out and drop in ballot boxes marked "Ubyssey House Survey" in SUB, in Sedgewick and outside the bookstore.

1983 TO 1984

The Cuts! The Cuts! Restraint, restraint, said the newly re-elected Social Credit government, cutting back spending and taking away people's rights. Solidarity, solidarity, said the people, forming coalitions, marching in rallies, going out on strike. We will join you, said the AMS of UBC, worried about funding cuts and the tuition increases that might follow.

And they did follow: tuition went up 33 percent, and for good measure the government jumped in and cut student financial aid by 83 percent and abolished all grants, leaving students free to accumulate debt. And if you were a foreign student, good luck. For the first time in its history UBC began charging more to international students.

And Just to Confuse Things: The office workers at the AMS went on strike for the first time in their history right in the middle of the Solidarity walkouts, and kept on picketing even when the Solidarity walkouts ended, confusing the students, who wondered why there were still strikers trying to keep them from entering the SUB.

No Good Deed: And there were complaints that the AMS was becoming too much of a business, making too much money from such things as the Pit Pub and the Games Room. We're supposed to be a non-profit society, said a presidential candidate, and when general manager Charles Redden was given a raise for his good work, the *Ubyssey* complained bitterly and published his salary for all to see.

Politics: That's what the *Ubyssey* wanted the AMS to spend more time on: the Solidarity movement, of course, and also the campaign against military research. Some students petitioned successfully for a referendum calling for an end to such research, but it failed for lack of quorum. The *Ubyssey* took comfort in the fact that at least the majority of those who turned out to vote supported the anti-military side, but in general it sighed about apathy and wished there was more politics and less business on campus.

The Other Solidarity: The provincial Solidarity campaign took its name from the Polish movement of the day, and to bring things full circle, another Solidarity group sprang up on campus to protest the bringing to UBC of a Polish professor known for his connections to the pro-Soviet military government. Led by Bill Tieleman, a longtime *Ubyssey* staff member and later a Vancouver political analyst, Campus Solidarity picketed outside the visiting professor's classroom, prompting debate about free speech and academic freedom.

TAs Stay Away: Away from picketing that is. Bucking the trend this year, the TA union voted not to go on strike.

Fun and Games? The Engineers did their best to be non-serious, hoisting a Volkswagen on top of a lamp post, but they were increasingly coming under attack for some of their other antics, notably their Lady Godiva ride and the content of some of their publications.

And In Other News: Trolley buses were promised for campus, after first being suggested some years before, but students suffered another blow when they learned that their

The *Ubyssey* imagines dire results from the cuts to student aid.

"Oh God, please let them increase student aid SOON!"

No complaints about stunts like this, but the Engineers again came under attack for sexism this year.

discounted bus fares were going to vanish.

Areas of the SUB had to be closed temporarily (again) for asbestos removal.

James Hollis set some sort of record by being elected to the Executive for the fourth year in a row, three of them as Director of Finance.

Lisa Hebert, later to be a CBC personality, was the executive mentioned most in the *Ubyssey*, perhaps because her activist approach was closest to theirs—and when her term ended, she became a *Ubyssey* writer.

Speaking of *Ubyssey* writers, John Turner returned to his newsroom roots at UBC for a friendly visit during his campaign to become leader of the Liberal Party (and thus Prime Minister). He received a much warmer reception than in 1971 when he came under attack for his association with the War Measures Act.

AMS EXECUTIVE
1983-1984

PRESIDENT
Mitchell A. (Mitch) Hetman
VICE-PRESIDENT *Renee Comesotti*
DIRECTOR OF FINANCE *James Hollis*
DIRECTOR OF ADMINISTRATION
Alan Pinkney
COORDINATOR OF EXTERNAL AFFAIRS
Lisa Hebert

UBYSSEY EDITOR *Editorial collective*

1984 TO 1985

Pasta! Hot Dogs! Photocopying! All available in the SUB now, courtesy of the AMS, which began opening more and more new businesses: Tortellini's, Snack Attack, a photocopying business. And there was money for day care and bursaries and a set of courses on resumé writing and applying to graduate school: Briefing for the Real World. The AMS was doing its best to serve its members. There was even another attempt at a used bookstore and a lottery for free tuition, with proceeds going to bursaries.

But . . . The big issue was still the cuts. UBC was short of money. There was talk of another tuition increase and an even bigger increase for international students. There was a controversial new athletics fee. But it didn't seem this would be enough. There would have to be program cuts, even layoffs. The faculty began to get nervous. They called for a new Trek and dragged the students along for it, a march from campus to downtown: perhaps 2,500 showed up, but the effect was minimal. What would happen?

Bye Bye, George: What happened was that, to the surprise of most, UBC president George Pedersen resigned, saying he could no longer run a university under these conditions. The result was a new president who would find a different approach to dealing with the University's financial difficulties, an approach that would ease the pressures, though at perhaps too great a price. That was in the future, though. In the meantime, the students suffered through overcrowded classes, shorter library hours, and the worry that programs they signed up for might not even last long enough for them to get their degrees in them.

The *Ubyssey* cartoonist worried that UBC had lost its captain. (The cartoonist at this time, known then as Yaku, went on to a respected career as the author and artist Michael Nicoll Yahgulanaas.)

Other Worries: It was enough to make a student want to drown their sorrows in a pint—but suddenly that wasn't so easy anymore. The administration decided to forbid weeknight

The AMS went into the fast food business with a new pasta place.

partying in the residences, and the RCMP made it harder to get liquor licences. At least let us drink on Wednesdays, said the students at Gage Residence in a thousand-strong petition, and they did get their Wednesday beer nights back.

And Still More Worries: Billy Graham, the world famous preacher, packed War Memorial Gym to talk about disarmament, of all things. He was just back from the USSR, the West's Cold War adversary. Who knew that the Cold War would be over in half a decade? In 1984–85 people were scared about nuclear annihilation and, as if the blast and radiation weren't enough, now there was a new fear: nuclear winter, global cooling. It could wipe out all the earth's species, said Helen Caldicott, an anti-war activist who also packed the War Memorial Gym.

What was the answer? God, said Billy Graham. Suicide, said the UBC Peace and Disarmament Club: let's

DR. BILLY GRAHAM
SPEAKS ON
Peace in a Nuclear Age
Is peace possible
in the midst of a turbulent world?

UNIVERSITY OF BRITISH COLUMBIA
WAR MEMORIAL GYM
Friday, October 12, 1984
12:30 p.m.

Billy Graham provided answers to soothe troubled souls.

stock up on cyanide so we can go quickly. (They later explained that they didn't really mean it; they were just trying to raise awareness. Still.)

Life Goes On: Of course. Students studied, worrying over the regular things like exams, and walked around with their calculators, bought cookies from a new cookie store in the SUB (Duke's), played video games and pool, went to movies at the first Cineplex in Vancouver, and even watched production companies film TV shows on campus: obscure ones at first, but in 1986 a Perry Mason movie and later, episodes of *MacGyver* and the *X-Files*.

LEFT Some were worried about a nuclear apocalypse.
RIGHT Students enjoyed the new cookie store in the SUB.

And they complained about spitting on the walkways and the lack of left-handed desks or the piles of smelly garbage that for some reason were accumulating on campus (was that the cuts too?). And they survived a bus strike and a four-minute AGM, and practised for the LSAT, the MCAT, and the GMAT.

195

Duke's Cookies.

dent to support two refugee students from places such as Ethiopia and Uganda.

CiTR: And the campus radio station convinced AMS Council to give it the money needed for a high-powered transmitter.

GSC: And the Graduate Student Centre was taken over by the administration, much to the consternation of the Graduate Students Society. An agreement was eventually worked out, but in the end the grad students somehow had an extra $12 fee to pay.

AMS EXECUTIVE
1984–1985

PRESIDENT *Margaret Copping*

VICE-PRESIDENT *Doug Low*

DIRECTOR OF FINANCE *James Hollis*

DIRECTOR OF ADMINISTRATION *Glenna Chestnutt*

COORDINATOR OF EXTERNAL AFFAIRS *Nancy Bradshaw*

UBYSSEY EDITOR *Editorial collective*

Calculated Genius

BA-55
- Operates in three modes: financial, cash flow and statistical.
- Tilt-top styling makes the big 8-digit LCD display even easier to read.
- Constant Memory™ feature allows the calculator to retain stored data even when the power is switched off.
- 32-step programmability and 5 constant memories.
- APD™ Automatic Power Down.
- Comes with handy problem-solving guidebook and quick reference booklet.

TI-66 Programmable
- More than 170 built-in scientific, engineering, and statistical functions.
- Over 500 merged program steps.
- Up to 10 user flags are available, as well as 6 levels of subroutines.
- Up to 9 sets of parentheses allow up to 8 pending operations.
- Convenient horizontal design includes a large, easy-to-read, 10-digit liquid crystal display.

TEXAS INSTRUMENTS
Creating useful products and services for you.

Calculators were the mobile device of choice in these days, and one of the most popular brands was Texas Instruments, a company belonging to Cecil Green, a major UBC benefactor who this year was awarded the AMS's Great Trekker award.

CFS: And they said no, overwhelmingly, to the Canadian Federation of Students, which wanted $7.50 per student for the privilege of joining a lobby group that some saw as socialist and others saw as focused on the wrong jurisdiction (federal instead of provincial), and which would drown UBC's voice in a sea of small colleges. The referendum vote was 85 percent against.

WUSC: On the other hand, the World University Service of Canada won their referendum for 50 cents a stu-

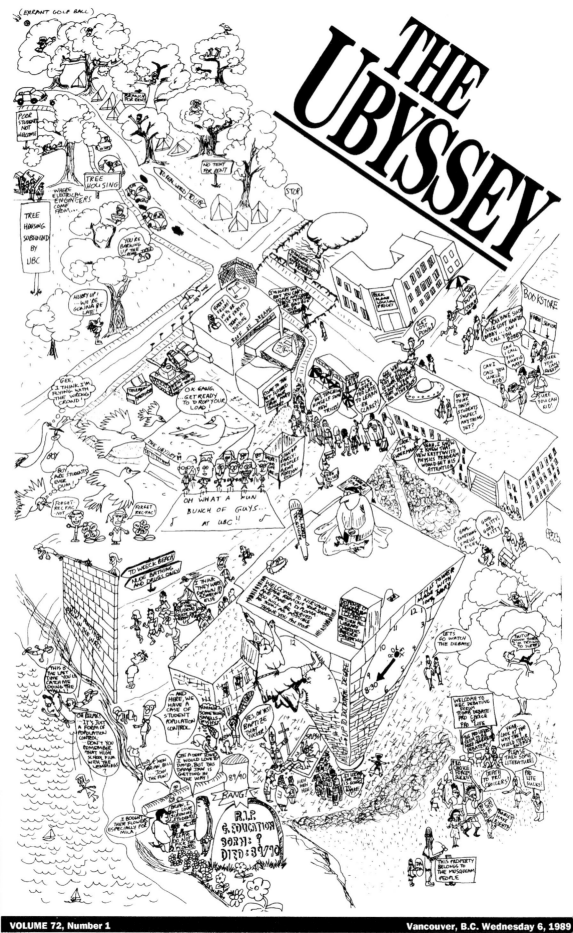

1985-1995

BUILDINGS, BUILDINGS, BUILDINGS, BUILDINGS, SOME ECO-RADICALISM, AND PIZZA

With the advent of UBC president Strangway, buildings were going up everywhere, it seemed, some of them provoking protest. Some students were not keen on condos coming to campus or in general the focus on bricks and mortar. And there were protests against tuition increases, of course, and as the eighties turned into the nineties a spurt of what almost seemed like sixties-era radicalism, with an especially ecological twist: down with styrofoam, long live recycling. The Student Environment Centre formed, along with something that would later be known as the Social Justice Centre. And there were Anti-Discrimination campaigns and a devotion to respecting the First Nations (the University even put up a First Nations House of Learning), and Lady Godiva was finally put to rest and Women's Studies became a major . . .

And yet it was all seemingly a surface spray; the bulk of the student population did not mobilize and occupy the Faculty Club (though there was talk of that), and perhaps the signature moment of the decade was the fuss within the AMS over the romantic musings of its president, Kurt Preinsperg.

Or was it the defeat of the proposal to spend AMS fees on a recreational facility? Or the AMS decision to replace the popular Duke's Cookies outlet with the AMS-run Blue Chip Cookies? Food seemed a big deal in this decade, as the AMS moved beyond its pasta place and its hot dog stand to open a pizza place called Pie R Squared, causing strains with an administration which thought it should have a pizza monopoly on campus. *O tempora, o pizza.*

Or was it the shutting down of the *Ubyssey*? Or the beginning of the concert extravaganza that was Arts County Fair? Or the expansion of AMS services (Safewalk, Rentsline, Tutoring, etc.)? Or was it the struggle between the AMS and the University over who should control the SUB and the Aquatic Centre, or the beginnings of the even larger struggle over the look of the whole campus?

1985 TO 1986

Anti-apartheid protesters urge the Board of Governors to divest.

The World Knocks at UBC's Door: A space shuttle blew up, and later a nuclear reactor. Reagan and Gorbachev held a summit. People still worried about nuclear winter. There was a fishy scandal in Canada. But the issue that roused the most interest at UBC was probably . . .

Apartheid in South Africa: Opposition to apartheid increased worldwide this year, especially on university campuses. In the United States there was a National Action Day against apartheid. At McGill student protests got the University to divest itself of its South African holdings.

At UBC results were more modest. Council debated whether to ban products associated with South Africa (Rothmans cigarettes, Carling O'Keefe beer), but contented itself with putting up signs to let students know about the South African connection.

Activists mounted a protest at the Board of Governors urging total divestment, but the Board demurred, though said it would pursue a policy of selective divestment. The *Ubyssey* bemoaned the lack of turnout at the protest and said UBC had become a backwater as far as activism went.

New Man at the Helm: David Strangway became UBC's tenth president and tried to signal his connection to the students by sitting down for a beer with them. Mostly, though, he turned his attention to the University's financial situation and after talking at first about government funding, he focused more on outside sources of revenue. This would lead eventually to the World

President Strangway talks to the student press.

of Opportunity fundraising campaign and the creation of the UBC Real Estate Corporation (later UBC Properties Trust), which brought condos to campus.

Student Finances: Another tuition fee increase hit this year, though it was not as big as the year before. Bus fares went up too, and the AMS tried to help by raising money for student bursaries. There was also talk of starting a campus food bank, but that would not come to pass for another two decades. The government did help out by introducing a loan remission program, and there were always jobs at Expo: Expo 86 arrived, and was popular with students both as a source of employment and a place to visit; ticket sales were brisk in the Student Union Building.

But despite all this there was talk of some students graduating with as much as $25,000 in debt from their student loans.

Lady Godiva: Yes, that old thing. The debate raged again. The Engineers seemed to back down by cancelling the ride and holding a mock funeral procession instead, but then created outrage by hiring a stripper to perform in Hebb Theatre. The University talked about holding back the fees intended for the Engineering Undergraduate Society, which prompted protest from the AMS.

The Old Order Changeth (Slowly): Personal computers arrived: ads promised 130K of memory! The AMS opened a word processing centre (for those who didn't yet have their own computer), but at the same time the *Ubyssey* was still running ads for typewriter rentals, and one letter-writer warned against revealing one's typing skills: it would doom you to clerical work.

An ad in the *Ubyssey*. Still typing after all these years.

And the SUB Slowly Changeth: Adding new club offices, but causing kerfuffles when the long-standing Dance Club was forced to

The Copy Centre moved into the old bowling alley and became CopyRight.

move. And replacing the bowling alley with an expanded photocopying service, later to be known as CopyRight (it wasn't a paperless university yet).

So What Were the Ordinary Students up To? They weren't bowling, but they did a lot of skiing. Dancing, of course, and hanging out at "bzzr gardens" (a new euphemism, replacing "bear gardens"). Or they went to the Pit to cheer on the Blue Jays: first time Vancouver people ever cheered for Toronto, someone was heard to say. Or they shopped at one of the many booths in the SUB main concourse. There were so many booths that some complained the SUB was becoming a shopping mall, but others just shopped.

TOP Skiing.

BOTTOM Shopping.

What Else Were They up To? Well, some were pulling the fire alarms for a joke (or to get into the Pit more easily): or no, said the AMS, it's high school students coming to the SUB Games Room; they're the ones. Or they went to hear talks by visiting literati from Margaret Atwood to William Golding. Or they listened to Brother Jed and Sister Cindy harangue onlookers about sin. Or they gave blood (but not as much as usual because of the AIDS scare). Or they complained to the AMS ombudsperson about supplemental exams and fee disputes.

Sister Cindy at UBC.

Or they "decorated" the AMS president's office with newspapers and graffiti (a longstanding tradition when a new president took over). Or they went to see a cleanshaven Jerry Rubin tell them that the route to liberation was not through occupying the Faculty Club but through making money.

ABBIE HOFFMAN
vs JERRY RUBIN
"The Debate of the Decade"
SAT. FEB. 8th
ORPHEUM
Networking 7 pm
Great Debate 8 pm
Yippie vs Yuppie
Questions 9-11 pm
RESERVE YOUR TICKETS NOW
All VTC/CBO outlets, Eaton's, Woodward's, Mall Info Centres, AMS UBC or charge by phone 280-4444; Common Ground, Healthy Gourmet, Banyen & Duthie Books

The return of Jerry Rubin.

Or they called the TRIUMF Centre (UBC's atomic research lab) in a panic after the *Ubyssey* ran a joke cartoon about a near nuclear explosion at a campus meson facility. Or they argued in the letters pages about the controversial gay love issue in the paper. Or they waited overnight in the SUB bookings line-up to get a room for their club. Or they simply joined a club at Clubs Days, like, for instance,

the Pre-Dental Society. Or maybe the Medieval Society.

But what few of them did was vote in the AMS elections. Indeed, a pre-election cookie poll showed the most sales for the cookie candidate named A. Pathy.

The comic strip that panicked UBC, and a follow-up cartoon.

ABOVE The Pre-Dental Club recruiting members. **BELOW** The Medieval Society putting on a display in 1985.

And Then There's Kurt: Yes, Kurt Preinsperg writing letters to the *Ubyssey*, including one about the problems Baby Boomers were having getting jobs because the previous generation was still in place. Baby Boomers would hear more about this in later decades, but from the other side of the generational fence.

AMS EXECUTIVE
1985-1986
PRESIDENT *Glenna Chestnutt*
VICE-PRESIDENT *Jonathan Mercer*
DIRECTOR OF FINANCE *Jamie Collins*
DIRECTOR OF ADMINISTRATION
Simon Seshadri
COORDINATOR OF EXTERNAL AFFAIRS
Duncan Stewart

UBYSSEY EDITOR *Editorial collective*

A clothed Godiva.

1986 TO 1987

The Constant Gardener: Bill Vander Zalm, the owner of Fantasy Gardens, became premier, causing the *Ubyssey* to grumble that now there'd be no more culture, just horticulture. But by the end of the year the paper was singing the new premier's praises for restoring funding, especially for student aid. Happy days were here again?

UBC president Strangway also welcomed the funding but was still exploring fundraising options, and there was talk of getting into the market housing business. Stick to lobbying the government, the *Ubyssey* warned.

Premier Vander Zalm visiting the campus.

Athletics: The University was already talking of increasing its new $32 athletics fee, and the AMS complained that students didn't know where this new money was going, let alone have a say in where it would be going. The AMS had threatened to sue when the new fee came in, saying it violated an agreement, but backed off in return for seats on a new University Athletics Council (UAC). But the UAC hardly met, and student leaders felt frustrated. But on a brighter note the football Thunderbirds won the national championship and the Vanier Cup for the second time.

Apartheid: More frustration for the leadership, at least the activist wing of it, on this file. Council again declined to ban products alleged to be connected to South Africa, but did call a referendum on the issue—which was soundly defeated. Yes, the students voted in favour of apartheid! Well, not really. There was dispute over whether the beer from Carling O'Keefe was really South African. And besides, said one commentator, students like their beer. Apartheid would die in South Africa anyway.

Godiva: Lady Godiva would die soon too, but not quite yet. The Engineers staged a sanitized version of the ride, with a clothed Godiva, winning praise even from the director of the Women's Students Office.

Tamer in that direction, the Engineers managed to affront on another, with homophobic remarks in one of their publications, and it was a difficult year in some ways for gays on campus. The offices of the Gays and Lesbians of UBC were vandalized more than once, and Gay Pride Week was mocked by a Hetero Week, put on by one of the fraternities, with the slogan, Born to Breed.

Meanwhile, Kurt Preinsperg wrote letters about discovering his feminine side. Stan Persky ran yet again for chancellor (he lost, of course). Students stormed the wall and also took part in the Intramural Centipede Race. And they listened to cassette tapes on their Walkmans or watched videotapes on their VCRs or chatted in Sedgewick Library.

There's too much noise, said some about the chatting: "Sedgewick is a library, not a social centre." Monitors were introduced, and presumably all talking stopped.

And some went scuba diving, and others went for the hot lunch at Hillel House, and still others volunteered to show visitors around during UBC's first Open House in eight years.

TOP The Centipede Race.

BOTTOM You could buy your Walkman at the bookstore.

The Dangers of Fun: Sex was dangerous now that AIDS had arrived. Condoms made a comeback in dispensers in the SUB washrooms and also in free giveaways.

Fun in the form of rock concerts was also causing danger, or damage, to the War Memorial Gym, or at least so said the Athletics department. And the AMS was reluctant to hold the concerts in the SUB Ballroom, so where was a poor student to go to get his (or her) ears blasted?

TOP Chariot race in 1980.

BOTTOM The Teacup game in 1978.

The Teacup football game and the Chariot Race were still going on, but one letter-writer complained of the dangers of being hit with excrement during the racing.

So maybe the best thing was just to stick to studying. The *Ubyssey* had advice on this: if there's two hours to go before your exam and you don't

know whether to cram or nap, the answer is that it's too late for either.

Good-bye Bus Stop: The Bus Stop Cafe with its motherly waitresses and coffee and omelets, not to mention its winding counters, announced its imminent demise. Students lamented and started a petition, but the decades old institution would vanish to give way to an expansion of the Commerce building. Students would have to be content with Chinese food at Yum Yums in the Old Auditorium, which would last for several more years.

And in Other Frustrations: Line-ups were worse than ever. There were even line-ups at the parking lot after the University introduced an unpopular gate system. There were line-ups still at registration, though not for much longer because Telereg was on the way.

And students were lining up at the bookstore, which was short on textbooks. It was enough to make some people . . .

Protest! This year's feature protest was against American naval ships arriving in Vancouver harbour. Greenpeace organized a Peace Flotilla to greet them. Council considered a motion condemning nuclear-armed ships, but voted No: Not our jurisdiction, said AMS president Simon Seshadri.

Some protested the plan to give an honorary degree to Vancouver businessman Jimmy Pattison, and faced with the uproar, Pattison declined the honour. A letter-writer objected to the *Ubyssey* running ads for a business selling term papers. Red-faced, the *Ubyssey* announced that it would no longer do this. But it kept running tobacco ads even after another letter-writer complained about those.

And in Other News: The AMS contemplated hiring part-time student staff to assist the Executive. A club was formed to work for easier access for students with disabilities, and the AMS planned ramps for the SUB and a mini-elevator to the SUB Auditorium. There was talk of an express line to UBC along Broadway, the University cracked down on smoking, and the *Ubyssey*, which seventy years before had denounced him as disgusting, now dismissed Oscar Wilde as banal. Wrong both times perhaps.

play the game.

education,

Psst, wanna buy a used term paper?

1987 TO 1988

K.D. Lang performing for UBC students.

It's a Barbecue! The fourth annual AMS barbecue (though really, weren't there barbecues before?). In any case, someone decided to start counting from 1984, and eventually (though not yet), this would become known as the Welcome Back Barbecue, held at the beginning of September every year, with drinking and bands and, when the AMS was lucky, sunshine.

With K.D. Lang: Perhaps the most famous performer ever to show up at the barbecue.

And Condoms! To publicize the fight against AIDS, the AMS dressed up a truck as a Trojan Horse and tossed condoms from it (Trojan condoms, of course). The year before, as AIDS concerns mounted, there had been talk of starting discreet condom delivery services because AIDS was, though dangerous, you know, embarrassing. But attitudes were changing quickly, and now condoms were, quite literally, out in the open.

And Bylaw Amendments: Taking advantage of the crowds, the AMS leadership declared the gathering a Special General Meeting and had the attendees raise their glasses in favour

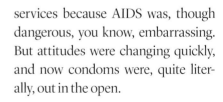

Huge crowds show up for the fourth annual AMS barbecue in September 1987.

by first donating them to a political party. The self-described starving student disagreed with Kurt's attack on tenure and also expressed dismay that the AMS did not follow through with its food bank proposal.

Meanwhile, Kurt was mostly focused on fee waivers for the children of university professors, a perk won by the faculty in their latest bargaining with the administration. He won the support of the *Ubyssey* and AMS Council in this crusade against faculty "privilege," and he also found time to attack the use of make-up and the attitude of "lookism."

But not everyone was pleased with Kurt's constant appearance in the *Ubyssey*. "Please! Find someone to take that typewriter away from Kurt Preinsperg" was the headline on a letter in January (were students still using typewriters?), and another letter-writer complained that Kurt's missives were well in excess of the *Ubyssey*'s published word limit.

Double Dragon: When not writing letters to the *Ubyssey*, students were occupying their free time playing video games in the SUB Games Room, but there were objections to one particular game (Double Dragon) which depicted violence against women, and it was removed, though not before some debate in Council and in the letters pages.

Cruising and Logging: Letter writers also debated the cruise missile (again), but an even bigger topic was clearcut logging and the use of

of some changes to the AMS constitution. The *Ubyssey* later grumbled that this seemed very irregular, but it was mostly housekeeping, so whatever.

Blair T. Longley: Kurt Preinsperg had a rival in the letters pages of the *Ubyssey* this year. Blair T. Longley, unsuccessful candidate in past AMS elections, registered agent for the Rhinoceros Party, and later to become leader of the

The great Trojan Horse condom giveaway.

Canadian Marijuana Party, occupied the paper's pages with a call for legalizing marijuana. The year before he had made the news by advocating for a lowering of the voting age in BC to eighteen (it was still nineteen until 1992), and he was later to develop an elaborate plan for deducting tuition fees from income the Stein Valley forest, especially after David Suzuki came to campus and argued with Forestry students. Economics or the environment? That was the question.

Fun and Games? The Law students held a tricycle race, the frosh in Totem Park residence partied—but perhaps too much: some had to be taken to hospital for alcohol poisoning, and there was talk that some of the drinking was forced, part of a hazing ritual. Was hazing coming back? And then there was an incident downtown with Totem Park students getting in trouble for tossing eggs. And the Forestry students for some reason destroyed the Engineers' cairn. Ah, youth.

Money, Money: Everyone was interested in money. The AMS Executive asked for a raise, the University administration created the UBC Real Estate Corporation and began planning what became the Hampton Place condo development, and the AMS held a tuition lottery again, which this year resulted in the AMS president winning one of the prizes. No, no, said Council, that's not right, and wouldn't let her keep her winnings.

Buildings, Buildings: Besides condos, UBC president Strangway was interested in putting up other buildings on campus: a new library, a concert hall. And indeed within a decade the Walter C. Koerner Library rose up, as did the Chan Centre for the Performing Arts.

And Who Decides What Our Money Should Be Spent On? There was fuss this year over AMS funding for the Gays and Lesbians organization. Largely, this was a debate over homosexuality (another topic for the *Ubyssey* letter writers), but at least one student raised the issue of letting the students decide where their AMS fees should go. Individually. That is, each student would indicate when paying fees which services they were okay with the AMS supporting. This would most likely have been a logistical nightmare; in any case, the suggestion was not taken up.

Telereg: In an attempt to end the nightmare of registration (the line-ups, the waiting, the running across campus) the University introduced registration by phone. Not cellphone (who had those yet?), but using the latest in landline technology: touch-tone telephones. Students could just punch in their course preferences and presto! they were registered. This was all just a transitional way station en route to online registration, but it did spell the end of signing up for courses in person.

And in Other News: Trolley buses were coming to campus, but a new parking garage was also going up (the North Parkade). Athletics tried to revive the Victoria Invasion with a basketball game across the water, and the UBC Thunderbirds lost one-sidedly in the Vanier Cup (to McGill). Tuition went up again, but so did student aid, UBC introduced a policy on sexual harassment, and there was the beginning of debate on campus about free trade, but more on that next year.

The Law students' trike race.

AMS EXECUTIVE
1987-1988

PRESIDENT *Rebecca Nevraumont*
VICE-PRESIDENT *Jody Woodland*
DIRECTOR OF FINANCE *Don Isaak*
DIRECTOR OF ADMINISTRATION *Tim Bird*
COORDINATOR OF EXTERNAL AFFAIRS *Caroline Rigg*

UBYSSEY EDITOR *Editorial collective*

1988 TO 1989

Those Were the Days: It was a time of floppy disks and VCRs, Ben Johnson and testing for steroids, and of course free trade. Students could listen to politicians and professors tell them that if the free trade deal proposed by Brian Mulroney's Conservative government came into force, it would be the end of Canada as we know it.

Floppy disks were where it was at.

Global Warming: Students could also hear talks about global warming, the greenhouse effect, and carbon diox-

ide. Suddenly the biggest threat was not nuclear war (and nuclear winter) or even acid rain and the destruction of the ozone layer; it was the spectre of climate change.

But Let's Stick to the Local Scene: There was RecFac, the ambitious plan for a new recreational facility on the edge of MacInnes Field. Students voted to pay $30 each to build it, despite the opposition of those who said there were other priorities, and why should the students have to pay? And also: it was unfair because AMS Council was so strongly in favour of it.

But it would have gone ahead if only the University hadn't decided to raise tuition by 10 percent. Wait a minute, said the students: we're going to help you build a University building and you're still going to raise our tuition? No way! And so there was a second referendum, or at least it was agreed to hold one in September 1989.

Speaking of referendums, there was an attempt to hold one about the cookie store. The AMS was planning to take over Duke's so that cookie revenue could go towards bursaries and student services instead of private profits, but there were campaigns to save Duke's cookies, though it turned out these weren't entirely student-run campaigns and the referendum petition to save the old store was found to be invalid because of non-student signatures.

Not to worry, said the Duke's supporters, we'll get another petition. And when that one turned out to be invalid too, a third. But by that time it was too late. Duke's was gone, and AMS Blue Chip Cookies took its place. The AMS can't make cookies, Duke's supporters said, but in fact Blue Chip became quite popular.

And Speaking of Tuition Increases: Some students became very angry about them. Students Opposed to Tuition Fee Hikes, led by Vanessa

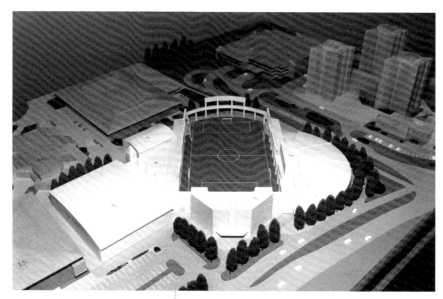

The recreational facility that was going to be.

Students protest the tuition increase.

Geary (later to become Coordinator of External Affairs), organized a protest, and then another. The AMS even lent its support, though at first it suggested a letter-writing campaign. There was even talk of occupying the Faculty Club. Just like 1968. But it all rather fizzled out, and the fee increase went through, and the *Ubyssey* grumbled that students weren't what they used to be.

Money, Money, Money: That's the problem, said the Board of Governors, we're short of money. That's why we have to raise tuition. But if you prefer, we could try raising it from the busi-

ness community (no, no, said the *Ubyssey*, we'll turn into an "education corporation") or by selling real estate (no, we don't much like that either, said some, though other students were willing to let that go ahead).

Accessibility: That's what's threatened by fee hikes, said the students, while at the same time the University was restricting enrolment by ceasing to accept everyone who met the minimum requirements.

And another sort of accessibility was also in the news: make the campus, including the Pit and the rest of the SUB, wheelchair accessible. Ramps, lifts, electric doors: these were all on the way.

And in Other News: There was fuss when UBC said it wouldn't help host the Gay Games for fear of seeming to be identified with a political cause or homosexuality. But then it changed its mind.

A student went missing, and was never found. Money was raised for day care. MUSSOC came back with a revue of its big musical numbers from the previous seventy-three years. And the *Ubyssey* revived Page Friday.

Emerson Dobroskay: never found.

Causing Offence: The Engineers with their publications and another Lady Godiva Ride (but this was the last one). Filmsoc for offering free admission to *A Fish Called Wanda* for anyone eating a live fish. A downtown nightclub for allegedly discriminating against Chinese students from UBC.

Catching Up with the Times: There was talk of doing away with UBC's idiosyncratic marking system (out of 150 instead of 100) and its system of units instead of credits.

And Finally, a Pop Quiz: Who said, "Swaying to the booming rhythms you can soak up the free-floating eroticism of the Pit while sliding into a pleasant stupor, your human complexity safely submerged in a sensuous feast of sounds and sights"? Stan Persky? Kim Campbell? K.D. Lang? No, no, you know, that constant letter-writer and now a student representative on the Board of Governors. Yes, of course, Kurt Preinsperg.

AMS EXECUTIVE
1988-1989

PRESIDENT *Tim Bird*
VICE-PRESIDENT *Carolyn Egan*
DIRECTOR OF FINANCE *Mike Fahy/ Karl Kottmeier*
DIRECTOR OF ADMINISTRATION *Leanne Jacobs*
COORDINATOR OF EXTERNAL AFFAIRS *Lisa Eckman*

UBYSSEY EDITOR *Editorial collective*

1989 TO 1990

The Job of a University Is Not to Sell Real Estate: Or so said AMS executive Vanessa Geary when the first UBC condo project (Hampton Place) got under way, but it was only the beginning. All UBC president Strangway is interested in is "endless building projects," complained the *Ubyssey*, and it wasn't just condos, but a new concert hall, an extension to the Commerce building, plans for a new library, and of course the . . .

Student Recreation Centre (formerly known as RecFac): The students held another referendum and after much gnashing of teeth and disputes over quorum, and even a summoning of the long dormant Student Court, it was decided that no, the students were not willing to pay $30 each to build it via an AMS fee. All this meant in the long run was that the University imposed its own $40 fee and built a scaled down version of the original facility, but it

was perhaps a sign of restiveness in the population.

Activism: The students seemed to be reviving from their political slumber this year. Perhaps it was the influence of world events, from Tiananmen Square to the Montreal Massacre of female engineers. The latter did indeed have an almost direct influence at UBC, killing off the Godiva Ride for good, with the Engineering Undergraduate Society declaring that such things (parades of naked women) were no longer "socially appropriate." And then they went and spoiled it all by publishing an offensive edition of their *nEUSlettre*, which was generally condemned for being racist, sexist, and homophobic.

But Activism: Yes, there was the newly formed Student Environment Centre launching a war against styrofoam and promoting car pools. At the very end of the year there was the formation of the Global Development Centre, later to be known as the Social Justice Centre. And in between Council banned Rothmans cigarettes to protest apartheid, Students for a Free South Africa protested against UBC interactions with Shell (also because of apartheid), there were plans to put up a Goddess of Democracy to honour those who fell in Tiananmen

Square, the letters page of the *Ubyssey* saw a long-running series of letters denouncing animal research, Council declared its support for the Vancouver Gay Games, and there was continued opposition to . . .

Tuition Hikes: The hike this year was actually quite modest: 4.75%, the inflation rate at the time, but perhaps that was because of the campaign the AMS had launched against it before

the exact amount was announced. There was a task force and a banner or carpet-style petition that got displayed in the SUB and then unrolled in front of the Old Administration Building. Just like old times, almost. (But no Treks.)

But a Trek Celebration: This being the year leading up to the University's seventy-fifth anniversary, celebrations were afoot, including the re-creation of the iconic U-B-C photo from the time of the Great Trek. However, some protesters decided that they would update things by creating the image of a dollar sign hovering over the giant U-B-C.

Protesters try to organize themselves into the shape of a dollar sign atop the celebratory recreation of the U-B-C formation.

And in Other News: The AMS created a First Year Students Program and an emergency loan program. Students were able to win the creation of the Fast Trax discount program for students on transit: not as good as the U-Pass would be, but it did help those travelling long distances through the multiple zones of Vancouver's complicated transit system. So it wasn't just protest; there were services, or protests mixed with services. There was the new discount program for people bringing their own mugs, for instance. And a drive to help the Vancouver Food Bank.

Dark Matter: There was the case of Karl Kottmeier, the AMS director of finance who resigned in disgrace over financial irregulari-

ties. This prompted much political talk too, though some of it pushed against activism: Don't do anything, pleaded one letter-writer to the *Ubyssey*, seeking to give advice to the newly elected AMS president Kurt Preinsperg—wait, Kurt Preinsperg became AMS president? Kurt Preinsperg, the writer of controversial letters to the *Ubyssey*? The very one.

Ordinary Life: But of course most students were busy cramming for exams or playing late night ball hockey at the Osborne Gym, taking part in the new Day of the Longboat races, or playing Ultimate Frisbee. And there was still Storming the Wall, complaining about leaves in the Buchanan courtyard, wondering what happened to the wandering minstrel playing Jethro

Tull tunes, trying not to inhale secondhand smoke in the cafeterias, buying library discards at the bookstore or, in a more celebratory vein, handing out awards to deserving faculty and staff at the annual Just Desserts presentation, begun by the AMS back in 1984.

And Slates: Slates rose from the dead, as a Progressive group swept the election of Arts representatives to Council.

What's in a Name? "Alma Mater Society," the name itself, provoked discussion. AMS president Mike Lee worried that because it literally meant "nurturing mother" students would expect the AMS to coddle them. And one letter writer thought it sexist: why mater and not pater?

Oh, Dear: Spare a thought for the suffering student who lost a purse, a briefcase, a lunch bag, and even an eraser to thieves in the Main Library stacks (the PQ section), the Sedgewick study area, and even a Buchanan washroom.

Get with the Program: And then there was the student who complained that they had no place to carry a mug to avoid using disposable styrofoam. Don't be silly, someone responded; we all have backpacks.

So a year of mugs, backpacks, and recriminations.

AMS EXECUTIVE
1989–1990

PRESIDENT *Mike Lee*
VICE-PRESIDENT *Sarah Mair*
DIRECTOR OF FINANCE
Karl Kottmeier/Mark Brown
DIRECTOR OF ADMINISTRATION
Andrew Hicks
COORDINATOR OF EXTERNAL AFFAIRS
Vanessa Geary

UBYSSEY EDITOR *Joe Altwasser and others*

The Buchanan Building courtyard. It looks fine now, but wait till the leaves start falling.

213

1990 TO 1991

President Kurt: From letter writer to AMS president, the Kurt Preinsperg story. And if only he'd stopped writing once he made it to president . . . But no, it was after all part of his platform to improve male-female relations on campus, and so he dashed off a list of 31 hints to help young men get off to a good start with the woman of their choice. And he sent it to the *Province* newspaper, whose romance columnist was happy to publish it.

Oh, dear. Condemnation was quick in coming. He was being sexist and treating women as objects. He was misusing his position as president. He was making a laughingstock of the presidency: Kurt Landers, someone called him. Someone even started a petition to have him removed from office (but this came to nothing). Later a UBC film student made a mockumentary about Kurt and his list, called *Rules for Romance*.

Kurt Preinsperg, AMS president and, according to the *Ubyssey***,** the High Priest of Love.

But, but, but, said Kurt, I just want people to get along better. Oh, well.

People Not Getting Along: Kurt was actually not the only executive in danger of being removed from office. John Lipscomb, the director of finance, encountered a lot of hostility over such things as his involvement with the Global Development Centre. His own fellow executive, Jason Brett, the coordinator of external affairs, even wrote a letter to the *Ubyssey* saying Lipscomb wasn't doing his job. I am doing my job, replied Lipscomb, also in the *Ubyssey*. Other people wrote in to say, What's going on? Stop all this infighting.

But it didn't stop, not right away. Jason Brett started a petition to have John Lipscomb removed from office. It's political, Lipscomb said; people don't like my involvement in environmentalism (which was not yet a mainstream movement).

Even odder than all this, Lipscomb began running classified ads in the *Ubyssey* inviting students to help him transform the AMS into more of a grassroots organization

addressing environmental issues or, alternatively, to dissolve the AMS altogether and let the University's Board of Governors take over. What?

One letter writer harked back to the forced resignation of the previous year's director of finance and suggested it was time students took to the streets against their leadership. But they didn't.

ABOVE John Lipscomb, director of finance.

BELOW Jason Brett, coordinator of external affairs.

Taking to the Streets (Not): The students didn't seem much interested in this sort of thing this year. After what seemed to be a revival of activism the year before, this year the students stayed home (or in the library) when called on to rally: only three hundred showed up to protest the latest tuition hike and less than one hundred answered the call to quiz UBC president Strangway at a tuition forum. Maybe the call should have gone to their "mummies and daddies," said one commentator: after all, they're footing the bill.

Progressive Leadership? And yet the students' leaders, when they weren't attacking each other, did bring in some progressive measures. Concerned about women's safety on campus, Council initiated the Walk Home program, later to become Safewalk, an institution on campus for the next twenty-five years. Student senators succeeded in getting the Senate to review the teaching evaluation system. Senate even agreed to look into putting students on tenure and promotion committees. Council created an anti-discrimination program and appointed a non-voting First Nations Councillor. ("I'm pretty much for it," said one Council member. "We're on their land.") And there was an awareness campaign about drug and alcohol abuse and an Environment Week, in which the Student Environment Centre tried to convince students that environmentalism was not some "hippy dippy" thing, and eventually it wasn't.

Not Progressive Enough? None of this was enough to satisfy the *Ubyssey*, of course, and it got especially irritated with Council when it refused to pass a motion condemning the First Gulf War (the war to repel Saddam Hussein's invasion of Kuwait). Instead, Council voted to create two committees, one pro and one con. Take a stand, dammit, said the *Ubyssey*.

The *Ubyssey* was not shy about taking a stand, denouncing the war and taking other radical positions during the year on such things as illegal squatting in uninhabited buildings, getting on buses without paying your fare, denouncing President Strangway, and so forth. In March they put out their annual women's (or "womyn's") issue in which they called for a ban on hiring men at UBC. The Science students' paper, the *432*, responded by putting out a satirical "myn's issue."

So What Were the Regular Students Up To? They weren't rioting in the streets. Instead, they were checking bulletin boards for their exam schedules or worrying about flashers in the Main stacks or looking forward to the new sound system Filmsoc was promising for the SUB Auditorium. Or they were trying out the new Fireside Lounge in the Graduate Student Centre or enjoying beer and board games at International House (despite rumblings from the Administration about shutting International House down and combining it with the Graduate Centre). Or going to the lunchtime barbecue outside the SUB.

Some of them were grumbling about the lack of cable television and phone lines in Gage residence (no cellphones yet) and others were getting to experience new courses, for instance in International Relations, one of the fastest growing programs on campus, or in real estate, a new program in the Faculty of Commerce. The University also announced this year that its women's studies courses would now constitute a major, and the *Ubyssey* wrote of a course in the English department exploring gay subtexts in classic literature.

Another English course focused on Canadian unity this year, in the wake of the failure of the Meech Lake Accord. The instructor said her students did not have optimistic views of the future of French–English connections in the country, and a PoliSci professor said his students were tending less and less to identify as Canadians but spoke more of their various multicultural backgrounds.

The AMS began a Walk Home program, later known as Safewalk.

The AMS outdoor barbecue next to the SUB.

And What Were the Engineers Up To? Chastened after the *nEUSlettre* incident from the year before, the Engineers were putting on workshops on rights and freedoms and also finding out that they would now be required to take a course entitled Society and the Engineer, dealing with ecology, ethics, gender, and race. Some worried that Engineering spirit would be crushed, but the Engineers still went on a few limited rampages, stealing anti-war placards and trashing an Artsmobile during the Homecoming Parade. This provoked much criticism, though the Engineers had for years been trashing the Forestry students' mascot car (named Omar) without anyone thinking much of it.

Artsmobile trashed by Engineers.

Homecoming, You Say: Yes, a special celebration this year to mark the University's seventy-fifth anniversary, drawing 200,000 visitors, including twenty-seven participants in the 1922 Great Trek and Pierre Berton, who was awarded the AMS Great Trekker Award.

TOP Pierre Berton receives the Great Trekker Award from AMS president Kurt Preinsperg.

BOTTOM UBC letter people help celebrate UBC's seventy-fifth anniversary celebration at Open House.

Slates: Back for real this year, in part because of the shenanigans in the Executive. The disunity prompted a group of students to put forward a "Unity" slate in the hopes of electing an Executive that could work together, and this slate did indeed sweep the election. But the most interesting slate (there were three suddenly competing) was . . .

The Radical Beer Faction: A joke slate that survived for the next dozen years (until slates were abolished) running on a platform of, well, beer. This year they were a bit tentative about it, giving half-serious answers to reporters' questions, but at their peak they developed the technique of saying that the solution to whatever problem they were asked about was beer, beer, and more beer. Truly radical beer.

And they did surprisingly well this first year, finishing second to the Unity slate in three races, ahead of the Progressive slate. Throughout the years they often came close to winning, but never quite did—so the students never found out what would have happened if Radical Beer types had taken over.

Beer and Politics: More on this theme. In the fall at the Welcome Back Barbecue the AMS leadership decided it would be a good idea to copy the example of 1987 and hold a Special General Meeting during the festivities in order to make some bylaw changes. This had been accepted in 1987, but this time there were objections. Student Court was called on and ruled that the whole meeting was invalid because no attempt had been made to restrict voting to AMS members. Anyone attending the barbecue could have voted, and that could have included any number of non-students. So back to the drawing board.

And in Other News: The automatic parking gates at B-lot disappeared, the students at the Vancouver School of Theology (a UBC affiliate) voted to

join the AMS, students had to put up with several bomb scares, especially in the Buchanan building, UBC's phone system switched to an 822 prefix (from 228), Green College and the Belkin Art Gallery were on the way, the Student Health Centre said students weren't exercising enough or eating properly, several male residents of the Cariboo House residence (part of Place Vanier) were suspended for sending obscene and threatening messages to female residents, and the Goddess of Democracy statue appeared, despite pressure from the Chinese consulate.

AMS EXECUTIVE
1990-1991

PRESIDENT *Kurt Preinsperg*
VICE-PRESIDENT *Johanna Wickie*
DIRECTOR OF FINANCE *John Lipscomb*
DIRECTOR OF ADMINISTRATION
Roma Gopaul-Singh
COORDINATOR OF EXTERNAL AFFAIRS
Jason Brett

UBYSSEY EDITOR *Rebecca Bishop and others*

The Goddess of Democracy was installed between the SUB and the Aquatic Centre in June 1991, to mark the second anniversary of the Tiananmen massacre. It was later moved to the north side of the SUB.

1991 TO 1992

The University said no, but the AMS opened its pizza place anyway.

Boom! Pizza: Who would have thought that a pizza slice could be so explosive? We're going to open a pizza place, said the AMS. In the SUB next to where the University sells pizza slices. No, you don't, said the University. And so there was struggle and negotiations and even a pizza delivery to the UBC president. And the pizza place, cleverly called Pie R Squared, did open even though the University would not approve renovations, and it did well, and the University ground its teeth and eventually got the AMS to pay for something called the . . .

IPF, or Innovative Projects Fund. An innocuous sounding entity for a worthy cause (funding innovative projects for campus), but the money was to come from the AMS as extra payment for maintenance costs for AMS commercial outlets in the SUB. No more $1 a year rent: if you're going to use the SUB to make money, then you're going to give some of it to us. So said the University.

And on Another Front: There was struggle prompted by the University's attempt to renegotiate the agreement on the Aquatic Centre so that the AMS would no longer have equal power on the Centre's management committee. But all this was done quietly behind the scenes. It didn't lead to anything as public as a . . .

Strike! No, but there was a strike at the end of the year, by the CUPE union locals on campus, whose mostly female members were seeking pay equity. Classes continued, but students were to be allowed to honour picket lines—or were they? It was very confusing. And the AMS was accused of strike-breaking for keeping the SUB open, and the *Ubyssey* stopped publishing as an act of labour solidarity, leading to the emergence of a new student newspaper called the . . .

Campus Times: They were called strikebreakers too, though they protested that they actually supported the strike, just wanted to provide campus news to the students in the absence of the regular student newspaper. And even when the *Ubyssey* returned, the *Campus Times* continued with very much the same raison d'etre, for while the *Ubyssey* focused on struggles against oppression around the country (and even the world), the new paper tried to stick closer to home, covering Student Council and the constituencies, notably the . . .

Engineers: The Engineers were still dealing with the aftermath of the *nEUSlettre* incident from two years before. They were supposed to pay a fine imposed by Student Court, but had no money to pay a fine because the University had imposed its own penalty by refusing to collect fees for them. The case went back to Student Court and to Council, and a special committee was set up that included Engineers and representatives of groups their paper had insulted (women, Indigenous people, and gays).

Some had thought all this would kill Engineer spirit, but in second term the Engineers pulled off one of their pranks: stealing the Rose Bowl football trophy from the University of Washington. Not everyone was amused, however. Why don't they stick to hoisting Volkswagens? asked the *Ubyssey*.

And What Was the *Ubyssey* Sticking To? Mostly advancing progressive causes, running special issues on women, what it's like to be gay and come out, First Nations, and the environment.

Less politically, they advised students to do something beyond their studies: join a club, drink coffee and chat in the SUB Conversation Pit, eat a ginger snap (no, sorry, those were gone). They also ran items revealing how UBC was seen at the end of the twentieth century. It's a big place, said one student (more than thirty thousand students now): so big it makes you feel small. And the buildings are rundown, and there's these annoying green worms hanging down from the trees—but the climate is nice, at least compared to prairie winters.

And What Were the Students Doing? Going to Laffs at Lunch in the SUB for some comic relief or drinking beer in the Pit on Wednesday Pit Nights or, if more serious, reading books for the blind at the Crane Library, or hunting for summer jobs. Starbucks, tree planting, emptying trailers. I'm going back to Vernon to live with my Mom, said one: it's a way to save some money.

Students help create talking books at Crane Library.

And Some Were Writing Letters: About racism and reverse racism, the correct spelling of "women" (wimmin, womyn?), whether Engineers were being picked on, the true nature of the Reform Party, the bad guys in Yugoslavia, and of course the Middle East. Not to mention a whole new issue: "goofism." After someone in the racism discussion called someone else a goof, a whole slew of letters arrived defining and elaborating on the nature of goofism. Goofs need to be defended, said one, and another commended the *Ubyssey* for hiring so many of them.

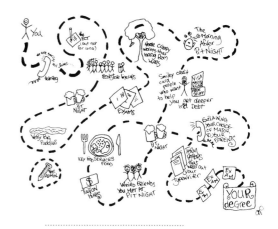

The *Ubyssey*'s conception of life on campus, including typewriters (still), and lots of Pit Nights.

Shoe on the Other Foot Department: Meanwhile the Engineers were complaining about reverse sexism in a T-shirt being sold in the Bookstore.

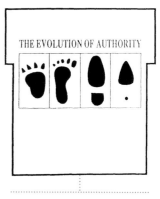

Is this sexism?

And in the Classroom? Well, the *Ubyssey* noted that new theories like deconstruction were appearing, and the granddaddy of UBC courses, English 100, disappeared, along with the dreaded English Composition Test, to be replaced by a smorgasbord of first year offerings and a new screening exam called the Language Proficiency Index (or LPI).

219

The very popular Arts County Fair in 2000.

And the University kept introducing innovative programs, especially programs with an international flavour, such as the Ritsumeikan exchange with Japan, for which a Ritsumeikan House went up on campus.

Hitchhikers' Guides: Geographically, the *Ubyssey* helpfully explained that south was for Engineers and Foresters, middle was for Science, and to the north was Arts. Then there were the "polarities of power": the Greeks (frats and sororities), the Engineers, and the Activists. But these three, noted the *Ubyssey*, accounted for only 10 percent of the student population. The other 90 percent? Well, it seems they had no power.

Poor Kurt: Yes, whatever happened to Kurt Preinsperg? Gone from the presidency and also gone from the letter pages of the *Ubyssey*—except for an announcement by the *Ubyssey* editors saying, Kurt Preinsperg, your letter is too long: please shorten it and resubmit. But he never did, or if he did, it never appeared: how the mighty, etc., etc.

Boom! Music: The year went out with a bang. The last day of classes and Arts County Fair appeared: a big concert and beer-drinking party in Thunderbird Stadium, hosted by the Arts Undergraduate Society and featuring bands like Spirit of the West and Barenaked Ladies. Attended by fifteen thousand students (and others). Year One of Sixteen.

220

AMS EXECUTIVE
1991-1992

PRESIDENT *Jason Brett*
VICE-PRESIDENT *Shawn Tagseth*
DIRECTOR OF FINANCE *Ranjit Bharaj*
DIRECTOR OF ADMINISTRATION
Martin Ertl
COORDINATOR OF EXTERNAL AFFAIRS
Kelly Guggisberg

UBYSSEY EDITOR *Paul Dayson and others*

1992 TO 1993

A Testy, Testy Year: The AMS was still fighting the University over businesses and, of course, money. The students were protesting tuition hikes. The *Ubyssey* reached new heights in provoking outrage. Vandals were smashing things. There were sexual assaults and fears of sexual assaults, and the minister of advanced education even insulted the UBC president. Can't we all just get along?

Perhaps What We Need Is an Ombudsperson: But there was even discontent there. Two AMS ombudspersons resigned this year, the second in circumstances full of tension after an in-camera Council meeting, which ended in voting to keep him on (but he quit anyway).

Oppressed Llamas in Zimbabwe: That's the sort of thing the *Ubyssey* is interested in, said Jason Saunderson of the Young Conservatives. Let's shut this paper down.

But instead AMS Council moved against the moderate paper, the *Campus Times,* saying it was run by non-students, which was technically true (their two editors had just graduated). We can't have an outside paper competing with our *Ubyssey,* said the AMS Director of Finance. Shades of the *Georgia Straight* circa 1974. But the *Ubyssey* tested the patience of the AMS too. First over bus fares …

It's Only Illegal if You're Caught: So said *Ubyssey* editor Frances Foran when asked by BCTV to defend the paper's editorial advocating cheating the bus company. Sneak on the back door. Pay with pennies (yes, there were still pennies then) and don't put in enough. Carry around invalid transit tickets. Oh, there are all sorts of ways to fight the system. And the law is on your side, because it's not illegal if you don't … well, you know.

But Wait, There's More: How about a sex issue, complete with graphic images and a revenge fantasy about sexually mutilating a man and leaving him to die? That will provoke discussion.

Well, it provoked something. It was really the beginning of the end for the *Ubyssey* as an AMS paper.

Meanwhile: The University's VP-students was saying the University would never enter into another contract with the AMS. The administration said the AMS just wasn't being fair: selling pizza in the SUB. That's what the University was meant to do.

K.D. Srivastava, the VP-students: no more contracts for you!

And truly Stan Persky would have shaken his head at how the AMS had moved into business. Selling pizza, cookies, beers, and burgers. Why isn't the student society leading protests?

But They Were: When the University announced an 18 percent tuition hike, the AMS organized a petition and a postcard campaign and even a march on a meeting of the Board of Governors, which actually backed down and lowered the hike to 11.9 percent, only to see the government lower it even further, to 10. But that meant …

Cutbacks: President Strangway announced a hiring freeze. Library cutbacks had already been announced. Would courses have to go? Was this 1983 all over again?

Is It the End of Civilization? There were vandals in the parking lot and in the library, smashing cars and mutilating books. Someone destroyed expensive equipment in the Chemistry building, someone else caused damage at the offices of the Science

221

ABOVE Students protesting the proposed fee hikes.

BELOW The *Campus Times* presented their view of tuition increases.

Undergraduate Society (but perhaps that was just the Engineers), and there was also damage done at the site of the Longhouse, the First Nations centre the University was putting up.

And Even When You Try to Do Good: There used to be an inspiring giant sequoia tree outside the Main Library. It would get decorated with Christmas lights every year. It looked beautiful. But if only students wouldn't lean their bicycles against it and generally crowd around. Oh, here's an idea: let's put a concrete barrier around it. That'll save it. What's that, you say? Installing the barrier meant severing some of the tree's roots? Well, that's okay, it has lots of roots, doesn't it? Oh, well.

Let's Get Away from It All: We could go hiking on the North Shore mountains. Or skiing. Or even snowboarding. Snowboarding: that's the latest thing. Snowboarders even asked to join the Ski Club. Oh, dear.

That provoked more tension (but eventually we got the Ski and Board Club).

Never Mind Skiing: Let's concentrate on our studies. That's what we're here for, right? But make sure to check the exam schedules: another phony set went up this year, and the *Ubyssey* published a nightmare before Christmas editorial about missing your exam, being behind on your term papers, worrying over Christmas cards and a dying pet gerbil, and through it all subsisting on coffee and dill-pickle chips. The life of a student.

Coffee? Did someone say coffee? UBC students bought two million cups this year, according to one set of statistics. And there was new coffee coming in: not just your regular cream and sugar, but cappuccinos and espressos and lattes. The revolution would be well caffeinated. But it did mean a lot of . . .

Stress: UBC Student Health reported high levels of it, and was offering seminars on how to deal with it. But perhaps the best thing would be to go to the jazz festival the AMS put on this year and then go around humming Ella Fitzgerald songs. Or join the UBC Symphony Orchestra and play Beethoven and Tchaikovsky. Or sit in on SUB Sonic Thursdays at the Pit. Or the bands at Live @ Lunch.

Don't try dealing drugs in the Pit, though: someone got busted for that this year.

The old sequoia tree that once graced the front of the Main Library.

Romance: Maybe that's the thing to deal with stress. A *Campus Times* writer decided to go looking for it. Try the Bookstore, someone said, but there was no romance in the Bookstore. The couches in Sedgewick, then: and there was some there, but mostly the people in Sedgewick Library were, you know, studying. Then the SUB. Of course. Why, she heard there'd even been a marriage proposal in the SUB Conversation Pit. Or how about the other Pit, the pub: but no, that was just "one big wiggle arena" of people dancing under strobe lighting. But she did see a couple driving away on a bicycle built for two. Sweet.

And in the End: The year ended, students finished their exams and went looking for summer jobs, though they were scarce this year, and Bill Clinton and Boris Yeltsin came to campus (why can't everyone get along like those two?), and the students at Regent College voted to join the AMS, and Student Senator Orvin Lau, who had pushed the previous year for a review of the teaching evaluation system, pushed this year for Senate and the Board of Governors to investigate classroom conditions. Some classrooms are so cold you can see your breath, said a reporter in the *Campus Times*.

And then there was Derek Miller, student rep on the Board of Governors, full-time paid researcher for the AMS (the AMS was professionalizing more and more), and columnist for the *Campus Times*, who also wrote for the *432* (the

Science students paper), where he regaled readers with tales of Dik Miller, Private Eye.

ABOVE Orvin Lau, student senator and later student rep on the Board of Governors.

BELOW Jack of all trades Derek Miller.

But Before We Go: The AMS produced a film called *A Perpetual State of Consent* to warn against date rape. The University opened its Writing Centre, where students needing remedial help could go for a term before enrolling in first-year English. The University also tried to replace the old Bus Stop Cafe with a restaurant called Trekkers, but it didn't last. There were demonstrations of Bhangra dancing from India, a Great Trekker Award for John Turner, a new coat check system in the Pit to allow clubs to make some money, and the wave of the future was either the Internet or

CD-ROMs (well, we all know how that turned out).

And it rained and rained (or for a change of pace, snowed) and students blew off their anxieties on the last day of classes by going to the second edition of Arts County Fair. Not, though, before getting a chance to vote in AMS elections for the Famous Dead People's Slate of JFK, Groucho Marx, and Salvador Dali. Radical Beer, eat your heart out.

AMS EXECUTIVE
1992–1993

PRESIDENT *Martin Ertl*
VICE-PRESIDENT *Carole Forsythe*
DIRECTOR OF FINANCE *Bill Dobie*
DIRECTOR OF ADMINISTRATION *Caireen Hanert*
COORDINATOR OF EXTERNAL AFFAIRS *Marya McVicar*

UBYSSEY EDITOR *Frances Foran and others*
CAMPUS TIMES EDITOR *Aaron Drake*

Speaking of Acronyms: The AMS launched CORP this year, or the Committee for Organizational Review and Planning, an ambitious attempt to restructure the Society and bring its leadership into better contact with the membership (a constant AMS concern).

And in Other News: Automatic library fines of $1 a day for overdue books became a thing (before, you only got charged if there was a hold on the book). The Faculty Club went bankrupt (what would Jerry Rubin say?), the old Armouries came down, Sedgewick was about to be swallowed up by the new Koerner Library, and the AMS and all other student societies dodged a bullet over the ...

Writing an exam in the Armouries in 1991.

the AMS became alarmed because it, too, charged mandatory fees to all UBC students. The case went to the courts, the AMS was granted intervenor status, and in the end it was all dismissed because the commissioner had exceeded his jurisdiction.

And a Few More Things: More parkades were going up (the West Parkade is a great place to skateboard, someone commented), there was an early attempt to rein in slates in AMS elections (it failed), and Michael Hughes, who had made his mark in the tuition protests the year before, got elected as a student representative on the Board of Governors, where he would serve for three consecutive years, matching the record of Don Holubitsky a decade before.

Don Holubitsky, long-time representative on AMS Council and the Board of Governors in the eighties.

Help us figure things out, said the AMS.

Feldhaus Case, in which a student at Simon Fraser University convinced a commission overseeing societies to invalidate the student society's bylaws there because they imposed mandatory fees. The commissioner making the judgment said mandatory fees were a violation of the Charter of Rights, and

Michael Hughes, long-time representative on AMS Council and the Board of Governors in the nineties.

🌿 **AMS EXECUTIVE**
1993-1994

PRESIDENT *Bill Dobie*

VICE-PRESIDENT *Janice Boyle*

DIRECTOR OF FINANCE *Dean Leung*

DIRECTOR OF ADMINISTRATION
Roger Watts

COORDINATOR OF EXTERNAL AFFAIRS
Carole Forsythe

UBYSSEY EDITOR *Douglas Ferris*

CAMPUS TIMES EDITOR *Tim Carter*

1994 TO 1995

David Borins, who would go on to become AMS president two years later.

Students protesting the Axworthy cuts at the Vancouver Art Gallery.

The Year There Was No *Ubyssey*: For the first time since 1917–18 no *Ubyssey* was published. The AMS had finally had enough and tried to impose its own editor on its unruly newspaper, but its two choices both declined the job, and so there was . . . nothing. Well, the *Campus Times* tried to fill the void, and the administration paper, *UBC Reports*, tried to include more student-oriented material, but there was no sex issue, no advice on how to cheat the bus company, hardly anything offensive.

But Fear Not: The *Ubyssey* would return. Spearheaded by the Freedom of Expression Action Coalition, led by David Borins among others, there was a referendum to set up the paper on an independent basis, an arrangement satisfactory to both the paper and the AMS.

Action Now: Out of the *Ubyssey* campaign came a left-of-centre slate, Action Now, which took four of the five Executive positions in the January elections, ending what the *Campus Times* called the Dobie Dynasty, Bill Dobie having been president for two consecutive years, the only student in AMS history ever to do such a thing. (The only other AMS president to serve twice was Bruce Armstrong fifteen years before, but his terms were not consecutive, and one was not a full term.)

Funding Cuts: The big issue of the year across the country was a controversial plan by federal minister Lloyd Axworthy to transform the way the federal government funded higher education. There was talk of drastically reducing the money sent to support universities, while introducing a new Income Contingent Loan Repayment plan. Thanks, said the students: you'll increase our tuition and as a bonus increase our debt. But the planned cuts got postponed.

What's an Education for Anyway? The Axworthy proposal prompted much soul-searching among administrators and students. The University produced a report to demonstrate that universities have a positive impact on the economy and are not a drain on society. The AMS said the same and added that besides, there were non-economic benefits to producing well-rounded, educated citizens with critical minds.

Oh, come on, said a columnist in the *Campus Times*, everyone knows that the real point of post-secondary education is to serve as a recruitment centre for middle managers. That's what your BA will get you: a nice job in a bank.

If Only: But will it do even that? One recent graduate lamented that all she could get with her bachelor's degree was work serving food in a cafeteria. I should have spent less time reading Plato's *Republic* and more learning how to use Excel spreadsheets, she said.

But no, no, no, said people at a conference on Beyond the BA. There is hope. Polish your resumé, prepare for your job interviews. We can show you how.

But that's life after being a student. While still a student in 1994–95, you might have been doing the following:

Eating in Pacific Spirit Place (the new name for the SUB Cafeteria, aka SUBway). Or, if you were a Forestry student, tossing axes and taking part in other logger sports. Or, at Totem Park residence, playing a Mission Impossible game shooting other students with plastic darts (until the RCMP stepped in and said enough of that). Or listening to author Mordecai Richler answer a question on Canadian identity (not something I've paid much attention to, actually, he said) or hearing the NDP's Svend Robinson say no, socialism is not dead.

And More: You might have gone to the free Spirit of the West concert at the War Memorial Gym, hosted by the AMS in the hopes that enough students would show up to constitute a quorate General Meeting at which a new set of bylaws could be approved. But it didn't work.

And Why Were There New Bylaws? Because the Committee for Organizational Review and Planning

Even a free concert couldn't lure the three thousand students needed for quorum for a general meeting. About twelve hundred showed up.

(CORP) had issued its report with ninety-seven-plus recommendations for structural changes in the AMS to better enable it to connect with its members. Many of these entailed bylaw changes, and when the bylaw package failed the AMS scrambled to bring in what changes they could, which in fact was rather a lot. After CORP, Council would be chaired by a speaker rather than the president, the AMS got a mission statement (committing it to working to improve the "educational, social, and personal lives" of its members), and oh, by the way, the AMS Executive would now get real salaries instead of $200 honorariums.

And: There was juggling and roller-blading and wondering if O.J. Simpson would get convicted. And looking forward to an expanded Reading Break (a full week instead of two days). And complaining about life

in residence: the *Campus Times* ran a series of horror stories, and the AMS named a housing commissioner to work on the issues. And . . .

Singing: The University Singers went to Europe and won a major competition.

And Traffic: The University decided to change traffic patterns on campus to better allow the mixing of cars and pedestrians (not to mention cyclists and skateboarders), prompting complaints saying the changes would just make things worse.

A rollerblading demonstration outside the SUB.

Students juggling.

And Parking: B-Lot is so far away, and the new parkades are too expensive. What's a poor student to do? Take the bus, said some, but it still cost too much.

And Why Are the Buildings So Run Down? New buildings keep going up, but old ones are suffering from lack of maintenance. Why is that? Well, explained the University, we can get money from donors for new buildings, especially if we put their name on them, but not too many donors want to pay for new light bulbs.

And the Gallery Lounge was threatened with extinction (by a new design plan), but councillors objected, and the lounge lived on.

AMS EXECUTIVE
1994-1995

PRESIDENT *Bill Dobie*
VICE-PRESIDENT *Janice Boyle*
DIRECTOR OF FINANCE *Randy Romero*
DIRECTOR OF ADMINISTRATION
Tim Lo
COORDINATOR OF EXTERNAL AFFAIRS
Leah Costello

UBYSSEY EDITOR *No* Ubyssey *this year*
CAMPUS TIMES EDITOR *Tim Carter*

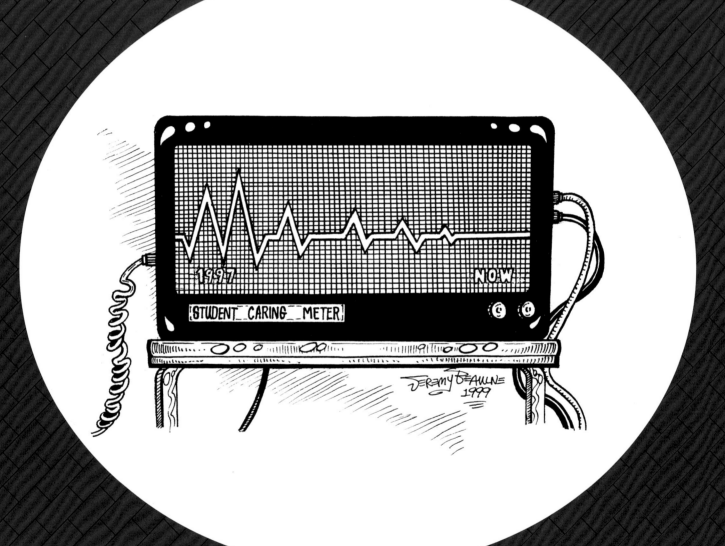

1995-2005

LOBBYING AND SERVICES

In 1999, on the eve of the new century, a *Ubyssey* cartoon lamented a drop in what it called caring, by which it meant activism. Certainly, the decade seemed to demonstrate a move away from sixties-style protests (and their early nineties echo) towards a different sort of student leadership. There were still protests, to be sure, but the emphasis shifted to lobbying and services. In response to tuition increases, student leaders didn't take to the streets, but instead visited the University's boardroom. And in general the AMS focused less on demonstrating against corporatization in favour of developing services for its constituents: from the U-Pass and a health and dental plan to extra-curricular courses and advice on personal budgeting.

As to corporatization, the decade began with the controversial Coke deal, which split the AMS leadership and eventually led to a resolution not to enter such things again. However, if the anti-Coke forces won that battle, they lost the war: the AMS began to solicit more and more sponsors, not for long-term exclusivity deals in the manner of Coke, but for time-limited one-time events and programs.

At the same time, perhaps to counter this acceptance of corporations, the AMS began moving strongly in the direction of progressive policies in other areas, notably sustainability and women's issues. An Impacts Committee, an organic food store, and fair trade coffee came in, and so did a Sexual Assault Support Centre. Moving with the times, the AMS combined progressive social policies with fiscal conservatism, while moving away from protests and activism.

1995 TO 1996

Would You Like Politics with That?

Food and drink were contentious issues this year. The AMS joined the University in a ten-year exclusivity agreement with Coca-Cola, prompting much protest from within and without the Society. Then McDonald's announced it was opening a branch on campus, in the University Village, leading to more protests. And there was even a fuss over a hot dog vendor, Mr. Tube Steak, which the University first invited to campus and then told to leave because of objections from its food service union.

The *Ubyssey*'s satirical take on the Coke deal.

More Politics: Controversy also arose over a report into alleged racism and sexism in the Political Science department. The McEwen Report found systemic and pervasive racism and sexism, and recommended shutting down admissions to the PoliSci graduate program, a recommendation followed by the University, at least temporarily, even though some said the findings were biased and unfair. Again there was division within the AMS, but AMS Council formally endorsed the report, as did the Graduate Students Society.

And Still More: There were still fears that federal funding cuts would lead to increases in tuition, prompting protests in the fall and the spring. "It's just like the sixties," said one demonstrator. In the end the NDP provincial government saved the day, at least for students, by introducing a tuition freeze which lasted for half a dozen years.

Rival Student Groups: The student protests were organized by the Canadian Federation of Students (CFS), the radical group created in the early 1980s. By this year there was also a second, more moderate student group on the scene, the Canadian Alliance of Student Associations (CASA). The AMS had been instrumental in the creation of CASA, but by the end of the year withdrew owing to alleged financial mismanagement. (The AMS would rejoin CASA in 1998, but would withdraw a second time in 2011.)

Honours, or the Past Is Always with Us: Evelyn Lett came back this year, aged ninety-nine, to help celebrate the creation of a childcare bursary fund the AMS initiated. The last surviving member of the very

Students protest against funding cuts and tuition increases. With a Coke truck looming in the background.

232

first Student Council came to the AMS Annual General Meeting and made a short speech. From a slightly later era, the late 1940s, Alfred Scow made an appearance to accept the year's Great Trekker Award, which honoured him for breaking ground for Indigenous people in the legal profession.

On a sadder note, the AMS Film Society lost a longtime member, Normand Bouchard, who died at the age of twenty-five. It renamed the SUB Auditorium in his honour, and it quickly became known as the Norm, anticipating the informality that led students a decade later to call the Irving K. Barber Learning Centre "the Irving" (or just "Irving").

The Norm Theatre

Athletics, We Hardly Knew Ye: The intercollegiate program was long gone from AMS control, and Intramurals had been slowly transferring to University control, but the opening of the Student Recreation Centre this year meant that Intramurals would leave the Student Union Building, almost completely ending the AMS connection (though not AMS funding).

Speaking of funding, the AMS ended its longstanding contribution of $7 per student to the intercollegiate program this year and redistributed the funds to its newly established Student Resource Groups and an external lobbying fund. Part of the money was also set aside to increase the contribution to the intramural program, so the funding connection to sports remained partially intact.

Apathy (Yawn): Yes, that old bugbear was still around. The *Ubyssey* had great fun with an AMS event meant to allow students to say what they wanted from their student society, to which virtually no one showed up (which was just as well, because the sound system didn't work).

However, the students at large had the last laugh by turning out in unusually high numbers for the January elections and referendum (perhaps because they wanted to support the Evelyn Lett Childcare Bursary Fund, or perhaps because they hoped to win the tuition lottery that the AMS held at the same time as the vote).

The AMS Executive ran an extended campaign to support the childcare bursary, using a much admired photo of young children:

The photo that helped win a childcare referendum.

Arrivals and Departures: The *Ubyssey* was back after its one-year hiatus and was somehow friendlier to the AMS and less mutinous now that it was independent. Telereg, the telephone registration system, was on its way out. Everyone had loved it when it first came in, but now it seemed to be a source of frustration, and would be replaced by online registration.

A set of emergency Blue Phones on campus was in the works after complaints from the students about safety and a safety audit conducted by the AMS.

An emergency Blue Phone outside the SUB.

More as a defence of advances made than as a new development, CiTR joined an All Day All Gay protest against censorship of gay material on a Halifax student radio station.

Meanwhile plans were underway to replace UBC president Strangway, with students calling for a new direction and someone less focused on "bricks and mortar" (i.e., the physical development of the campus)—something that did not end with the Strangway era, however.

Also, after years of sporadic publication of student evaluations of instructors, the AMS began issuing something new to help students choose their courses: the *Yardstick*.

There had been anti-calendars in Arts and Science before, but this was an attempt to encompass all faculties; it never quite fulfilled that goal, but it did give partial coverage for several years until it was suspended to make way for a promised fuller version issued by the University, which, however, did not come to pass.

The *Yardstick*: the AMS's guide to student evaluations.

AMS EXECUTIVE
1995-1996

PRESIDENT *Janice Boyle*
VICE-PRESIDENT *Namiko Kunimoto*
DIRECTOR OF ADMINISTRATION
Am Johal
DIRECTOR OF FINANCE *Tara Ivanochko*
COORDINATOR OF EXTERNAL AFFAIRS
David Borins

UBYSSEY EDITOR *Siobhán Roantree*

1996 TO 1997

Hell No, We Won't Go: What is this, the sixties? asked the *Ubyssey*, reporting on student occupations to protest fees. There were anti-fee protests across the country, and at UBC students occupied the office of President Strangway to protest a massive increase in fees for international students, along with an increase in ancillary fees (the University's way of getting around the provincial freeze on tuition fees).

The UBC sit-in ended after six days, with the fee increases still in place, but the following year some students would take a different, non-sixties approach, by taking the University to court—with dramatically different results.

Student Housing, Student Transit: Looking for funds somewhere, in the wake of government cutbacks and the tuition freeze, UBC began talking about allowing more market housing on campus. Student leaders pushed for student housing instead, and the AMS staged a "shantytown" protest to call attention to the lack of housing for students, both on and off campus.

Meanwhile the AMS also pushed for what became known as the U-Pass, a cheap monthly bus pass for students, something it would take a half-dozen years to implement, but which was extraordinarily successful, even too successful, when it finally came to pass. The resulting shift from cars to buses meant an overloading of public transit, which

The AMS shantytown protest: Carolyn Granholm of the AMS External Commission spends a night like a homeless person.

in 1996 was already overloaded despite the introduction of the 99 B-Line express bus to UBC.

A 99 B-Line arrives at the old bus loop.

Protesters outside the Administration building.

APEC Is Coming: The Asia-Pacific Economic Cooperation group of countries bordering the Pacific Ocean agreed to hold its annual meeting in Vancouver, with one session at UBC. Protests immediately took shape, focusing on the poor human rights records of some of the participants (China, Indonesia). Some protesters took to calling UBC's Goddess of Democracy statue, put up to honour China's Tiananmen protesters, the Goddess of Hypocrisy and inserted a gag in her mouth. And all this months before the conference actually opened. More would follow.

In With the New, Out With the . . . The AMS introduced a new Asian food outlet in the SUB. The Moon, with its menu of Chinese food, would cater to the increasingly large Asian student population, said AMS director of administration Jennie Chen.

Meanwhile, the rise of AMS food outlets helped contribute to the struggles of the University-run main cafeteria in the SUB. The University made plans to shut it down and replace it with franchised food outlets (Subway, A&W, Starbucks).

Not quite shut down, but losing some of its lustre was the War Memorial Gym, the great post-war achievement of UBC students, which was losing its central place in athletics to such facilities as the new Student Recreation Centre and was also losing its role as the site of graduation ceremonies: these were now to take place at the new Chan Centre.

The Chan Centre: the new site of grad ceremonies.

Everything Old Is New Again: It was announced that UBC would introduce male cheerleaders as if this was some unheard of thing, which it had been for a while, but anyone who could remember the 1920s would have known that in the beginning all the cheerleaders were male.

Name Change, and Other Stuff: The Gays, Lesbians, and Bisexuals of UBC (GLBUBC) became Pride. The AMS president, Ryan Davies, got in trouble for supporting a technology fee (which students later voted down). An AMS Councillor pushed for an end to smoking in the Gallery Lounge, because the clouds of smoke there billowed into the main SUB concourse.

AMS EXECUTIVE
1996–1997

PRESIDENT *David Borins*

VICE-PRESIDENT *Lica Chui*

DIRECTOR OF ADMINISTRATION *Jennie Chen*

DIRECTOR OF FINANCE *Ryan Davies*

COORDINATOR OF EXTERNAL AFFAIRS *Allison Dunnet*

UBYSSEY EDITOR *Scott Hayward*

1997 TO 1998

Here's Pepper in Your Eye: And the world's leaders came to UBC to discuss free trade, and the students protested, and the police sprayed them with pepper spray. And Nardwuar the Human Serviette (from CiTR student radio) asked Jean Chrétien what he thought about it all, and the Prime Minister said pepper was just something he put on his plate. And the press went wild. Such was APEC (Asia-Pacific Economic Cooperation) in Vancouver in November 1997.

The Gagged Goddess: Even before November the students were protesting and for some reason vandalizing the Goddess of Democracy statue. At one point she was gagged with a label saying Coca-Cola, suggesting that the point was to attack what some saw as excessive corporatization of the campus. Not only was the Coke deal still in force, but there was talk of both the University and the

Police disperse protesters at the APEC summit.

AMS entering into other exclusivity deals. This sort of thing led to one graffiti artist putting up slogans on the new Koerner Library.

The new Walter C. Koerner Library. Graffiti free at this point.

China versus Tibet: Just to complicate things, a (verbal) side battle erupted when the graduate students hoisted a Tibetan flag on their building to protest Chinese rule in Tibet. Chinese students protested vigorously in the *Ubyssey*'s letter columns.

Keep Those Cards and Letters Coming In: The *Ubyssey* also provoked a flurry of letter-writing when it published allegations of sexism and racism against the Law faculty. One of the *Ubyssey*'s themes this year was the lot of women. The paper focused on Take Back the Night marches and the lack of bathrooms for women in the Buchanan Building (this lack was actually addressed this year).

One letter-writer complained that the paper was going overboard with tales of "feminist victimisation."

Feminist Triumphs? Meanwhile the AMS Executive achieved a high point of female power this year: four of the five executives were women. And in the presidential election for 1998–99, the two serious candidates were both women: Vivian Hoffman, the outgoing director of finance, bested the coordinator of external affairs, Shirin Foroutan, to become the new president.

Perhaps this simply reflected the fact that there were now more female students than male for the first time since the gone-to-soldier days of the First World War.

Executive Triumphs: This marked the eighth year in a row that an outgoing Executive member won the presidency, a streak that would continue for another five years. It was hard for non-executives to win the AMS presidency in this period, and when they did controversy seemed to follow: from Kurt Preinsperg in 1990 to Amina Rai (2004) to Blake Frederick and Bijan Ahmadian (2009, 2010).

Slate Triumphs: This was the heart of the slate era, in which candidates for the Executive banded together in rival groups and won the vast majority of positions. Only occasionally did an independent like David Borins, Lica Chui, or Scott Morishita get elected.

Football Triumphs: The Thunderbirds won their third Vanier Cup.

And Nature Triumphed: By raining, of course.

Shades of Duke's Cookies: The Thunderbird Shop, an outlet selling school supplies in the SUB, had been an AMS tenant for 25 years, but when its lease expired, the AMS did not renew it, saying that it could make more money running such a store itself. Students protested, even forcing a referendum, which, however, failed for lack of quorum, and

Director of Finance Vivian Hoffman (*top left*) faced off against Shirin Foroutan (*bottom left*), the coordinator of external affairs, in the race for the presidency.

the Thunderbird gave way to the new AMS convenience store, the Outpost.

Oops, Sorry about That: With the tuition freeze still in place, but no additional funding arriving from the government, UBC tried to increase funding by introducing "ancillary fees." Students sued, the court ruled in their favour, and UBC had to refund $1 million.

On the other hand, the judge ruled in favour of the University in its increase of international student fees (not covered by the freeze). Even though UBC had violated its own policies on raising fees, that didn't matter: such policies were not binding, said the court, prompting AMS vice-president Ruta Fluxgold to comment that it was now clear that if students wanted to ensure that the University followed its own policies they would have to get the University to sign a contract.

Kinder, Gentler Engineers: The president of the Engineering Undergraduate Society vowed that the Engineers would henceforth be less rowdy and boisterous. Less drinking, fewer dunkings in the library pool. But still stunts: this year they performed their signature stunt of hoisting a Volkswagen Beetle on high, in this case on top of Rogers Arena (then known as GM Place).

They also stole the Great Trekker trophy and returned it with a new inscription, honouring that greatest of Great Trekkers: James T. Kirk.

The Great Trekker award: honouring UBC graduates, but not starship captains.

Imagine: UBC held its first Imagine Day, a day-long orientation and welcoming session for first year students, in later years extended to all undergraduates. The AMS collaborated on this effort, eventually merging its old Orientations program with the University's, though it also developed a First Week program of concerts and other events to complement Imagine Day. And of course there was the Welcome Back Barbecue, which remained a September fixture for students.

AMS EXECUTIVE
1997–1998

PRESIDENT *Ryan Davies*
VICE-PRESIDENT *Ruta Fluxgold*
DIRECTOR OF ADMINISTRATION
Jennie Chen
DIRECTOR OF FINANCE *Vivian Hoffman*
COORDINATOR OF EXTERNAL AFFAIRS
Shirin Foroutan

UBYSSEY EDITOR *Joe Clark*

1998 TO 1999

A Productive Year: The *Ubyssey* couldn't see it, but the AMS actually achieved quite a lot this year. In the fall Council passed a policy on exam hardship, calling on the University not to require any student to have to take more than three exams in a twenty-four-hour period, and by March the University had agreed.

Earlier the AMS successfully lobbied against the elimination of the Fast Trax discount program for students on the Vancouver transit system. In February the AMS Bike Co-op opened a "Bike Kitchen" for campus bicycle repairs, which became an institution in the Student Union Building.

The *Ubyssey* mocked AMS plans to renovate the SUB Courtyard, but the renovations went ahead, opening up the full courtyard for student use, though as the *Ubyssey* noted, it was not a place to go in rainy weather.

The AMS, or at least two former AMS executives, also had a hand in the creation of UBC's Humanities 101 program. Allison Dunnet, the coordinator of external affairs in 1996–97, who had already helped found UBC's Imagine Day program, worked with Am Johal, director of administration in 1995–96, to convince UBC to follow an American model and offer free Arts courses to disadvantaged people in Vancouver's Downtown Eastside. The program was still going strong two decades later.

And one of the AMS's most successful programs was just getting off the ground at the end of this year: there was talk of holding a referendum to approve a health and dental plan.

ABOVE The *Ubyssey* suggested that the AMS was all sound and fury signifying nothing, but in fact a lot got done this year.

BELOW Allison Dunnet (*left*) and Am Johal (*right*), former AMS executives who made a difference on the Downtown Eastside.

A Contentious Year: It's true that it wasn't all sweetness and light this year. A senior AMS staff member left under a cloud, the executives didn't always get along, the AMS budget kept getting sent back for review by Council so that it didn't get approved until more than halfway through the fiscal year, and elections were a fiasco.

The University Senate stepped in concerning the elections and insisted on a rerunning of the vote for one of the student Board of Governors representatives. Meanwhile, the AMS ombudsperson, citing two dozen complaints and irregularities, called on Council to rerun the Executive elections as well. Council refused, prompting one defeated presidential candidate to seek to go to Student Court. However, the AMS, after unsuccessfully attempting to abolish Student Court a few years before, had not filled it for years, and had even removed the rules on it from its Code of Procedure.

The upshot was that Council instructed its Code and Policies Committee to look into the rules on elections and on the Court, the result of which was a complete overhaul of the Code of Procedure the following year.

CASA: The on again, off again romance with the Canadian Alliance of Student Associations was on again this year, as Ryan Marshall, the coordinator of external affairs, convinced Council to rejoin the organization that the AMS had helped found as an alternative to the more radical Canadian Federation of Students (CFS). This despite the opposition of AMS president Vivian Hoffman, who called for unity in the student movement and wanted the AMS not to join either association.

There was also opposition to the move among the general student body, who forced a referendum on the issue, which would have required the AMS to withdraw again, but which failed for lack of quorum. This time the AMS stayed in CASA for over a dozen years before withdrawing in 2011.

Apathy? What Apathy? Some saw the poor turnout for the CASA referendum (and also for the AMS elections) as a sign of student apathy, but others argued that the students weren't being apathetic; they were just active in different ways: for instance, by joining AMS clubs or helping out in the AMS services. The debate may have reflected a deeper tension between activists and those pushing for services and lobbying, something like the split between the CFS and CASA. With some notable exceptions over the next dozen years, the AMS would tend in the latter direction (towards services and lobbying rather than protesting).

Even when activism won support within the AMS this year, it was more as a joke than anything else: an article by the anti-consumerist group Culture Jammers in the AMS orientation guide, *Inside UBC*, prompted discussion at Council because of its use of offensive language. This led to a motion to support the

How the *Ubyssey* saw the elections.

Dave Tompkins, defender of profanity and general managers.

use of profanity, moved by Dave Tompkins, a long-time fixture on Council who would later serve for several years as speaker of Council, and who was also instrumental in getting General Manager Bernie Peets reinstated in 2004-5 when the Executive tried to remove him.

Just Like Old Times: There was talk of building a residence for nursing students at the Vancouver General Hospital, back where UBC had begun in its Fairview Shacks so many years before, but nothing came of it. The medical students, however, had already ensconced themselves in the area, with a Medical Students and Alumni Centre, which had opened in 1990.

And hazing was back: not on an AMS-wide scale, but among UBC's athletes, especially on the men's swim team, where rookies were apparently subjected to various forms of humiliation. There were articles, criticisms, apologies, and promises to reform.

Not Like Old Times at All: There was talk of increasing the number of international students at UBC, something that did indeed happen over the next fifteen years, so that from less than 3 percent of the student population, the number of international students rose to over 20 percent (over 30 percent among graduate students). This despite concerns that the increase in fees for foreign students would deter them. As numbers rose, the concern became more that only well-off foreign students could attend.

Governance: The increase in the non-student population on campus led to discussions of governance models. Should UBC join the City of Vancouver? Should it become its own municipality? Should it remain as an entity ruled by its Board of Governors with some oversight from Vancouver? A committee was established which somehow excluded students. It came to no conclusions and faded away, but the governance issue would continue to be raised over the years, especially in relation to decisions over development: who would decide about building condos, commercial properties, and the like?

Should the Students Pay for Everything? The Commerce Undergraduate Society (CUS) approved a whopping increase of $250 per student in their undergraduate society fee, largely to assist the Faculty of Commerce in bringing in improvements. This was in part a response to the tuition freeze, which was restricting the University's ability to increase its revenue but which did not restrict the students from increasing their own student fees.

The AMS itself had done this by agreeing to collect a new fee for bursaries and an increased fee for athletics after UBC discovered it couldn't do so itself because of the freeze. But there would begin to be some uneasiness among some student leaders, especially when a few years later the CUS introduced an even larger fee for its members to help the University renovate the Commerce building (the Henry Angus Building).

1999 TO 2000

Not on our campus, said the AMS, launching a campaign against discrimination. But what they really didn't want on campus was GAP, the Genocide Awareness Project, an abortion display brought to UBC by the AMS's own Lifeline Club, which made people uncomfortable (or angry) by comparing abortion to the Holocaust.

AMS Council passed a motion saying it did not endorse bringing the display to campus and seeking to ban it from the SUB. UBC tried to hinder it too, but in the end it came, provoking violence around the statue of the Goddess of Democracy, where its posters went up only to be ripped down by three students associated with the AMS (two were members of the AMS External Commission; one was a councillor).

The Lifeline Club brought a video of the proceedings to the next Council meeting and were sup-ported by President Ryan Marshall in denouncing the destruction of the display, but others on Council (notably Nathan Allen, the coordinator of external affairs) directed their fire at the display itself, saying it promoted hatred and harassment.

Council declined to send the issue to Student Court, so members of Lifeline sued in real court; the result was that the three students involved were found liable and had to pay damages, but the AMS itself was exonerated, with the judge ruling that there was no rights violation in keeping GAP materials out of the SUB.

The GAP display destroyed.

RTA, RTA: A new acronym captured headlines this year as students debated the merits of applying the Residential Tenancy Act to those living in student residences. In a rare move, AMS Council endorsed a candidate, Jon Chandler, in the Vancouver municipal elec-tions, even voting money for his campaign, which focused on the RTA issue. The AMS External Commission called for the RTA to apply to campus, and it also became the major issue in the AMS elections in January, when Nathan Allen's Action Now slate campaigned for it, while the opposition slate and students actually living in residence said, Not so fast; we're not so sure this is a good idea.

Action Now lost, and the RTA issue faded away, at least for a few years (it came back in 2014).

Everything in Moderation: The slate that defeated Action Now was the more moderate Students for Students, who swept all five Executive positions, a feat it repeated in the two following years, allowing it to set the AMS on a more moderate course focused on services, renovations, and lobbying. Oh, and lawsuits . . .

The old bus loop near the SUB. On the wall you can see a poster for Maryann Adamec, one of the leading members of Students for Students.

Travelcuts Is Ours! Or so said the AMS in joining a lawsuit against the Canadian Federation of Students (CFS) over who should benefit from its highly successful travel business. The business actually pre-dated the CFS, having once been run by a group of student societies that included the AMS. The AMS and three other student societies said they had been unfairly excluded when ownership transferred to the CFS.

The lawsuit dragged on for years, ending in a settlement in 2006.

Services, Services, and more Services: But the focus was on services this year. The AMS even held a referendum to establish a dedicated fee to support its services (primarily to support the Safewalk program; also to provide funding for CiTR, the campus radio station).

And Health Care: The same referendum also approved the Health and Dental Plan, which despite worries by the *Ubyssey* that it was being rushed through, forced on students, was too expensive, etc. etc., proved to be a huge success. Students almost immediately began using it, putting in so many

The *Ubyssey*'s view of the proposed health and dental plan, with AMS president Ryan Marshall appearing as an over-eager doctor.

The package of referendum questions, which even included an opinion poll on marijuana, prompted this humorous depiction in the *Ubyssey*.

claims that the insurance company sought to increase the premiums.

Thar She Blows: The SUB got a refurbished Courtyard, complete with a two-spray fountain, courtesy of the Class of 1999. And other renovations were in the works or already completed. There was a new lounge, the South Alcove, next to the cafeteria in the SUB, and plans were afoot to completely redo the SUB lower level. There was even talk of moving the Council Chambers down there, but that didn't happen. (The *Ubyssey* did get moved downstairs, into windowless rooms, which didn't particularly please them.) Michael Kingsmill, the longtime AMS designer, was busy.

The old SUB Courtyard, before the fountain.

Sustainability: The AMS began to get serious about sustainability this year, establishing an impacts committee to work on preserving "the well-being of the planet." Its first project was to get the AMS to introduce fair trade coffee at its outlets, focusing on providing proper payment to small coffee producers, but its focus shifted in later years to environmental matters.

No Smoking for You! Originally required to do so by a new provincial law, the AMS banned smoking in the Pit and the Gallery Lounge, and even when the law was temporarily suspended continued the ban, having discovered that the majority of its customers preferred a smoke-free environment.

Playfully alluding to Y2K fears about the year 2000, the AMS announces the end of an era: no more smoking in its drinking establishments.

And in Other News: To handle its burgeoning service side, the AMS created a new position, the Executive Coordinator of Student Services (ECSS), later to be called the Student Services Manager. It also renamed the members of the Executive, so that starting the next year they would all be vice-presidents.

An attempt to unionize food and beverage workers at Pie R Squared failed, but with a support workers strike looming, Council passed a motion calling on the University to guarantee students the right to respect picket lines.

To deal with excessive "spillage" at the Welcome Back Barbecue, Council passed a motion requiring everyone serving beer to be paid staff: no more volunteers handing out free drinks to their friends.

Another former AMS executive (Vivian Hoffman, president the year before) helped initiate a new UBC program: this time, student-directed seminars.

And Karen Sonik, the director of finance, got the budget done way earlier than usual— though still past the deadline, prompting a rethink that resulted in the introduction of preliminary budgets.

AMS EXECUTIVE
1999-2000

PRESIDENT *Ryan Marshall*
VICE-PRESIDENT *Maryann Adamec*
DIRECTOR OF ADMINISTRATION
Tina Chiao
DIRECTOR OF FINANCE *Karen Sonik*
COORDINATOR OF EXTERNAL AFFAIRS
Nathan Allen

UBYSSEY EDITOR *Bruce Arthur*

2000 TO 2001

Not Paris, Not 1968: So lamented the *Ubyssey*, complaining that instead of leading the students on the barricades, the AMS had lulled them into a "boredom-induced coma." But in its boring way, here's what the AMS achieved this year:

Mini School: The brain child of AMS president Maryann Adamec, Mini School was a program of non-academic courses from bartending to massage therapy. It was a big hit from the start and lasted a dozen years, discontinued mainly because it became a victim of its own success: students eventually created clubs to do what the courses had done.

First Week: With the University taking over the official side of Orientation, the AMS revived the notion of a First Week of fun activities, from concerts to games to movie nights, to complement the traditional Welcome Back Barbecue.

TOP A climbing wall at the First Week carnival in 2002.

BOTTOM Cotton candy at First Week.

The Space Programme: No, the AMS did not try to send up an astronaut, but its constituency organization in Arts launched a campaign to raise

244

fees to pay for dedicated student space in the Buchanan building, what eventually became the Meekison Arts Student Space (MASS), named after long ago Council member James Meekison, who donated $450,000 for it.

Science students, meanwhile, were not so well off. They were shunted from place to place in the Science buildings until a few years later they did the Arts students one better and built a freestanding building for themselves: the Abdul Ladha Science Student Centre.

And Other Boring Things: The AMS began planning for a new bagel store in the SUB (eventually to be called Bernoulli's). VP-Finance Mike Warner arranged workshops for students on budgeting and personal finance, and also arranged free tax preparation. Now that it could pay its volunteers, the Safewalk program expanded, escorting students across a campus that some saw as not being entirely safe. And the AMS tried yet another version of a used bookstore, SUBtitles.

Less Boring Things: Those who yearned for protest could still see some when the controversial anti-abortion display returned (twice), prompting rival demonstrations by Students for Life and Students for Choice (non-violent this time). And a UBC student, Kate Woznow, made headlines by unfurling a Free Tibet flag in Beijing, getting herself detained by the Chinese authorities for her efforts, but eventually mak-

ing it safely back to UBC, where she later served on AMS Council.

And Oh, Those Engineers: Engineering students outdid themselves this year. Not content with hoisting Volkswagens onto UBC and Vancouver landmarks, they journeyed to San Francisco to dangle a Beetle from the Golden Gate Bridge. The authorities were not amused.

A Barn Razing: The AMS restarted negotiations this year on transforming the old Horse Barn into a second SUB for students on South Campus. However, the University instead bulldozed the structure and transformed it into a community centre for non-student residents.

Who Is This Campus for, Anyway? And where did these non-student residents come from? Condos on campus. Starting with Hampton Place in 1989, but not ending there. There should be a University Town, some said, to make UBC a more vibrant place. High-rises, shopping outlets. A shopping mall, said the plan's detractors. The fight for the soul of the campus would continue through the decade.

And Can't We Have Fun? The authorities began cracking down on student beer gardens (still being advertised as "bzzr gardens" to get around provincial liquor laws). But even the word "bzzr" might have to go, said the University. And maybe no more POITS (the Commerce beer garden in the Henry Angus building, but it would stay).

The old barn.

Here was an issue students could go to the barricades for, not that they did actually, but a few years down the road they even voted to bring a microbrewery to campus. Malt does more than Milton can . . .

Or at Least a Sip of Water? Conspiracy theorists had a field day when it emerged that drinking fountains were being removed from some campus buildings. It's all a plot by Coke, they said. Probably not, but concerns lingered over the lack of water.

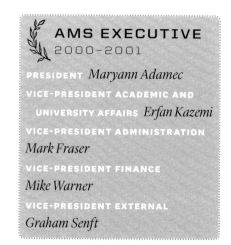

AMS EXECUTIVE
2000–2001

PRESIDENT *Maryann Adamec*

VICE-PRESIDENT ACADEMIC AND UNIVERSITY AFFAIRS *Erfan Kazemi*

VICE-PRESIDENT ADMINISTRATION *Mark Fraser*

VICE-PRESIDENT FINANCE *Mike Warner*

VICE-PRESIDENT EXTERNAL *Graham Senft*

UBYSSEY EDITOR *Daliah Merzaban*

245

2001 TO 2002

Even the *Ubyssey* declared itself speechless and ran a page of memorial candles.

And the Pall of 9/11 Hangs Over It All: At least it did for a while. The attack on the World Trade Center captured the attention of the campus. There was a memorial service led by UBC president Martha Piper. The AMS started a blood drive and raised donations for the Red Cross. And when the Americans responded by entering Afghanistan some students countered with protests and "die-ins." But eventually life moved on.

Bye-bye Freeze: The big news post-9/11 was the end of the tuition freeze, lifted by the new Liberal government of Gordon Campbell. UBC responded by saying it would raise tuition to match the national average. Why, said the AMS, wondering about the relevance of tuition levels in Ontario. Show us what you're going to spend the money on, and make sure some of it is on financial aid and other student services. The University did back down from its objective of matching the national average and began producing booklets showing where the money would go, but fees did rise significantly.

Protests! While the AMS leadership made presentations to the Board of Governors, some students decided more radical action was needed, marching on campus, occupying the Administration Building, and even invading the Executive corridor at the SUB to criticize newly elected AMS president Kristen Harvey. Harvey said the protesters, who were calling not just for a continuation of the freeze but for a reduction in tuition, did not represent majority opinion on campus. They certainly did not represent the majority view on AMS Council, which defeated a motion to support the reduce tuition campaign; some councillors said that the tuition freeze, coupled with government cutbacks, had jeopardized the quality of education at UBC and increases were needed.

Klahowya: Speaking of Kristen Harvey, her election meant that for the first time the AMS had an Indigenous president. It was a far cry from the days when UBC students appropriated Indigenous themes without being Indigenous themselves.

Kristen Harvey, the first Indigenous president of the AMS.

Would You Like to Live in a Lounge? UBC underestimated the number of students who would show up this year and had to scramble to turn lounge space in the residences into

The *Ubyssey* imagines students sleeping in the library because of the lack of residence space.

temporary sleeping quarters. There were also pressures on classroom sizes and a lack of textbooks.

First Coke, Then Volkswagen? An AMS councillor objected to the size of a Volkswagen promotion organized by the AMS on MacInnes Field. This just months after the *Ubyssey* finally succeeded with a Freedom of Information request in getting the details of the notorious Coke deal made public. Opinion within the AMS had certainly shifted away from long-term exclusivity deals like the one with Coke, but in response to the complaint about Volkswagen the consensus seemed to be that what was needed was clearer rules on corporate sponsorship: not an end to corporate sponsorship, just clearer rules.

And in Other News: AMS Council debated election slates: they're unfair to independents and outsiders, some

said. Council voted against banning them—this time—but their days were numbered.

Overshadowed by the general freeing of tuition fees, international fees (which had never been frozen) went up again. The AMS responded by creating an International Students Commissioner position to focus on the special issues facing international students.

The University opened a downtown campus, but it was mostly for Continuing Studies. It also introduced Turnitin software to check for plagiarism, causing some uneasiness among the students: AMS president Erfan Kazemi said it would be better to focus on educating students about what plagiarism is.

The AMS was made even more uneasy by Administration plans to impose academic penalties (e.g., withholding of transcripts) for unpaid parking fines, but an AMS

policy opposing the plan did not deter the University.

And the AMS Used Bookstore (SUBtitles) was struggling and there was talk of making it a purely online service.

AMS EXECUTIVE
2001-2002

PRESIDENT *Erfan Kazemi*

VICE-PRESIDENT ACADEMIC AND UNIVERSITY AFFAIRS *Evan Horie*

VICE-PRESIDENT ADMINISTRATION *Mark Fraser*

VICE-PRESIDENT FINANCE *Yvette Lu*

VICE-PRESIDENT EXTERNAL *Kristen Harvey*

UBYSSEY EDITOR *Duncan M. McHugh*

MacInnes Field in 1999.
Student Rec Centre in the background.

2002 TO 2003

Tara Learn, the moving force behind the U-Pass.

You Passed the U-Pass! Yes, indeed, by a two-to-one margin and with a huge turnout (over fifteen thousand voted), students approved the discount transit pass program. After four years of negotiations, students ended up with a $20 a month pass giving them unlimited access to buses, the SkyTrain, and the SeaBus. TransLink, the transit authority, predicted there could be a 30 percent increase in passengers. In fact, the increase was more than 50 percent; the program became incredibly popular, so much so that it put a strain on bus capacity. As AMS VP-external Tara Learn said in a bit of an understatement, "It seems . . . that it's something UBC students really like."

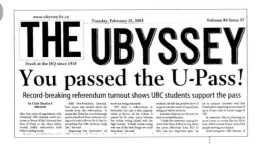

The *Ubyssey* let everyone know there would be a transit pass.

A Busy Year: Besides the U-Pass, there was a strike and the introduction of electronic voting and the opening of a Sexual Assault Support Centre . . .

Strike! UBC's teaching assistants went on strike in February. AMS Council first passed a motion saying that if picket lines went up, they would shut down the SUB in solidarity. But a week later, after much pushback, councillors thought better of the shutdown plan, in part because of the financial hit that would result: Council rescinded its original motion and instead voted to donate money to the union strike fund.

SASC: The AMS granted space in the SUB for WAVAW (Women Against Violence Against Women) to open a Sexual Assault Support Centre, then approved funding that would lead to a partnership with WAVAW to jointly operate the SASC. (In later years, the partnership ended, but the AMS continued running the centre as one of its own services.)

The Queen! Yes, the Queen visited campus, meeting with dignitaries, but also receiving a traditional red jacket from a delegation of Engineering students. Reportedly, on seeing a young woman in the delegation, the Queen said, "You're an Engineer?" Certainly, times had changed, at least a little: from being an almost exclusively male enclave, Engineering was now 20 percent female: still much too low a number, grumbled the *Ubyssey*.

The *Ubyssey*: But the *Ubyssey* grumbled less this year. It even praised the AMS on occasion, for instance for pressuring the Administration to be more accountable about tuition money. The AMS did push hard to get guarantees of financial support for students who might not be able to afford the latest 30 percent tuition increase and succeeded in getting the University to reverse its planned fee for deferred exams (exams a student might have to write because of a personal emergency).

And the *Ubyssey* ran a flattering article on the wide variety of student clubs the AMS administered, and ran a separate article enthusiastically featuring the AMS Bike Co-op (where students could go to repair their bikes).

Sushi Yes, Books We're Not So Sure: The AMS used bookstore (SUBtitles) closed up shop, or at least went online, making room for a hair salon (On the Fringe) and also for a planned sushi bar (eventually to be called The Honour Roll) in the SUB basement.

Online Voting: Buying secondhand books was not the only thing students could start doing online this year. For

The Engineers display the sweater they made for the Queen.

the first time the AMS conducted its elections electronically. Supporters said this would increase turnout. Detractors (notably the *Ubyssey*: so it didn't like everything the AMS did) said turnout would likely decrease. In the end, turnout remained much the same, and electronic voting became the AMS way, though not without a few hitches down the road.

Sponsorship: The AMS entered an agreement with Zoom Media to put advertising in the SUB's washrooms and then established a committee to look into sponsorship and fundraising more generally. VP-Academic Chris Lythgo mused that some might say the AMS was selling itself "to corporatization and the interests of corporate Canada," but he said there would be safeguards.

Tea and Voting: The Esteemed Afternoon Tea Society, one of the student clubs the *Ubyssey* spoke favourably of, decided to have some fun in the election, submitting nomination papers for all eighteen of its members to run for AMS president, rather cluttering up the ballot and leading to a change in the nomination rules.

University Town: That phrase became the watchword of certain members of the University administration, who pushed plans to transform UBC from a commuter campus to a "destination campus," which would mean putting up eighteen-storey highrises all around the SUB, among other things. The students were not amused. Nor were others.

Other News: The AMS began investigating a collaboration with the University to expand the coverage of teaching evaluations. Unfortunately, this meant the AMS gave up publishing its annual *Yardstick* of evaluations of professors in some departments in anticipation of a centralized online site for evaluations from all departments, but that site did not materialize.

Tired of having its meetings regularly go beyond midnight, Council established a committee to look into how to keep things shorter.

Chris Eaton, the elections administrator, livened up his report to Council by having his team sing "Hail UBC," the old 1930's-era fight song for the campus.

Amid reports of new restrictions on beer gardens, some AMS Councillors worried that UBC was trying to turn itself into a dry campus again.

AMS EXECUTIVE
2002-2003

PRESIDENT *Kristen Harvey*

VICE-PRESIDENT ACADEMIC AND UNIVERSITY AFFAIRS
Christopher Lythgo

VICE-PRESIDENT ADMINISTRATION
Oana Chirila

VICE-PRESIDENT FINANCE
Nick Seddon

VICE-PRESIDENT EXTERNAL
Tara Learn

UBYSSEY EDITOR *Various acting editors*

2003 TO 2004

Sex! On campus. I know: you're shocked. Students go to the Pit Pub hoping to find someone to have sex with. The *Ubyssey* broke the news on February 10, and it provoked a firestorm of controversy. Said the AMS Safety Committee, along with some AMS Executives and others: This sort of reporting seems to condone heterosexism and sexual assault, legitimizing what should be condemned. Somewhat abashed, the *Ubyssey* said it never meant . . . it doesn't support . . . it was just reporting . . . and yes it was outrageous what some students told the interviewer, but that wasn't us . . . really . . . Moral: sex is dangerous, and writing about it is even more dangerous.

Slates: Gone, done, finished forever, or at least for the rest of UBC's first hundred years. Councillor Spencer Keys convinced a Student Council full of slate members that slates were unfair: by allowing groups to com-

bine their resources for elections, it meant an independent could never get elected. And he would know, having gone down to defeat against the slate machines. But once slates were abolished . . . well, just wait.

Spencer Keys: slayer of slates.

But Before They Go: In the final election in which slates were allowed, the more radical of the two major ones swept all before it. The Student Progressive Action Network (SPAN) took all five Executive positions, and promptly undermined Council's trust in them by exceeding their mandate in negotiating a contract to allow Pacific Spirit Family & Counselling Services to have space in the SUB. A sign of things to come.

I've Seen Fire and I've Seen Rain: The AMS Archives got rained on because of a fire. An arsonist set copies of the CiTR publication, the *Discorder*, alight, setting off sprinklers which wouldn't shut off. The result: some very wet boxes, but luckily no important documents were lost.

Strapped for Cash: Still short of funding from the government and straining to serve a student population that went over the forty thousand mark for the first time (making it more than a hundred times bigger than the student population in 1915–16), UBC resorted to another tuition increase and also pushed forward with its University Town plan, meant to liven up the campus and, incidentally, bring in millions for UBC's coffers.

Students protested both approaches, saying there hadn't been enough consultation on the University Town plan, and high-rise condos next to the Student Union Building were a really bad idea. The University backed down on that one, but continued to make plans for commercial development in the campus core.

As to tuition, there were protests across the country, which the AMS gave only lukewarm support to. In fact, one group of UBC students, led by Joel McLaughlin of the UBC Young Conservatives, protested the protesters, saying some tuition increase was needed to preserve quality.

Okanagan, Here We Come: The government decreed that there would be a second UBC campus in Kelowna, created by taking parts

Near disaster in the archives.

UBC's new campus in the Okanagan.

of the old Okanagan University College (OUC) and merging them with UBC. Student leaders at OUC expressed outrage, saying they were being turned into a branch plant. The AMS in subsequent years would hold out a hand of friendship to the Okanagan students, though it would be a while before the gesture was reciprocated.

And in Other News: Safewalk ran into trouble with the union at Campus Security, which objected to Safewalkers driving vans. They didn't much like Safewalkers walking, either, saying it was patrolling, which was their job.

The AMS began exclusively selling fair trade coffee, not just to ensure fair compensation to coffee producers but to ensure a chemical-free, organic product. Sustainability rules!

Drink Responsibly: The AMS brought in rules to govern beer gardens.

Money for Science: Abdul Ladha, a UBC graduate, donated $750,000 for the planned new Science student social centre.

And Finally, Everything Old Is New Again: The Student Leadership Conference, last heard of in the 1950s and '60s (or perhaps the '80s), was brought back to life, and became a fixture over the next decade.

AMS EXECUTIVE
2003-2004

PRESIDENT *Oana Chirila*

VICE-PRESIDENT ACADEMIC AND UNIVERSITY AFFAIRS *Laura Best*

VICE-PRESIDENT ADMINISTRATION *Josh Bowman*

VICE-PRESIDENT FINANCE *Brian Duong*

VICE-PRESIDENT EXTERNAL *Sam Saini*

UBYSSEY EDITOR *Hywel Tuscano*

Safewalk: Just trying to help people be safe.

2004 TO 2005

The Times They Are A-Changin': Or not. The new AMS Executive certainly tried to make some changes, seeking to shift from negotiating to protesting (staging a Let Them Eat Cake demonstration against rising tuition fees) and also seeking to withdraw the AMS from a number of its associations. It cancelled SUDS, the annual gathering of student societies hosted by the AMS, sought to withdraw the AMS from CASA (the Canadian Alliance of Student Associations) and from an international body, Universitas-21, and discouraged the general manager from attending meetings with fellow general managers from elsewhere in the country.

Did Someone Mention the General Manager? The high (or low) point of the Executive's campaign to shake things up was its attempt to fire Bernie Peets, the AMS General Manager. On December 7, AMS staff arrived to discover that their boss had been unceremoniously removed from the Student Union Building and told his services were no longer needed.

This sparked quite a firestorm. Council, which had not been consulted, forced a pair of late night emergency sessions during the exam period, eventually deciding to reinstate the general manager. It then turned on the Executive, first asking the president to resign (she refused) and then attempting to remove her from office by vote (that failed). In the end it contented itself by censuring the whole Executive and ensuring that Bernie Peets returned to his position, leading to the interesting situation of the fired general manager returning to work with the Executive that had fired him.

The AMS Executive Photoshopped UBC president Martha Piper to look like Marie Antoinette to protest tuition increases.

ABOVE AMS president Amina Rai.

BELOW Bernie Peets.

"*Let them eat cake*"

Join the AMS at the SUB South Plaza
Wed, March 17   12:00-2:00pm
for FREE CAKE in honour of the

16% Tuition Increase Proposal

brought to you by your student society
www.ams.ubc.ca

But It Wasn't All Bad News: VP-External Holly Foxcroft piloted another U-Pass referendum to successful completion, setting a record for the number of voters: 20,705 cast ballots, 19,192 of them saying yes to continuing the U-Pass and extending it to the summer, numbers not to be exceeded until the 2013 U-Pass referendum.

There was still talk of apathy this year; hardly any students voted in Arts elections, and who knows how many paid attention to the war between Council and the Executive, but ask them if they want cheap bus fares, and they're all over it.

And on a Lighter Note: In one of the most successful joke candidacies ever, Darren Peets ran a campaign to get a fire hydrant elected to the University's Board of Governors, and fell only six votes short. Some members of the administration were actually amused, and the UBC president Martha Piper posed for a photo with Darren and his hydrant.

Darren (nephew of AMS general manager Bernie Peets, by the way)

Darren Peets and his fire hydrant.

was later elected in his own right to the Board of Governors and became a leading figure in opposing the University's plans to transform the campus into a "University Town."

And Then There's GAP: As a sort of harbinger of the Christmas war over the General Manager, a month earlier VP-Administration Lyle McMahon provoked Council by firing off a letter to the University deploring the fact that they were still allowing graphic anti-abortion displays (from the Genocide Awareness Project) onto campus.

After the 1999 abortion war, a sort of armistice had been brokered between Students for Choice and Students for Life, allowing both the displays and a counter-demonstration to take place a couple of times a year. This year VP McMahon argued that the presence of the display was causing psychological distress. Councillors saw McMahon's letter as asking for censorship, but were most disturbed by the fact that they had not been consulted.

Protest and counter-protest: the war over abortion.

Spencer to the Rescue: Finally, after months of conflict, new elections brought Spencer Keys to power. Yes, the same Spencer Keys who had engineered the abolition of slates. Keys ran on a platform of putting the AMS house in order, and won easily over a candidate endorsed by outgoing President Amina Rai.

Food! In times of stress, people turn to food. Student societies too. The year 2004–5 saw the opening of Sprouts, an organic food co-op. Also the opening of a Food Bank for students not able to make ends meet. And increasing concern about the fate of the UBC Farm, for which an annual FarmAde celebration was inaugurated (this was actually the second year of it).

International, Indigenous, African, and . . . Conservative? The Executive pushed, unsuccessfully, for the creation of special seats on Council for international and Indigenous students. More successfully, it campaigned for UBC to create an African Studies program. As a satirical response to these attempts, Council's token Conservative, Joel McLaughlin, proposed a motion to create a seat for conservative students. It failed.

Carried Away: Shocked by reports of the tsunami in Indonesia, Council voted to contribute $10,000 to relief efforts. Science representative Patricia Lau (later to be named Councillor of the Year) warned that this would use up three years' worth of the money in the donations fund, and what if something else came up? This did indeed lead to problems in subsequent years.

Don't Look Now: Influenced by supporters of the Wreck Beach Preservation Society, Council approved a policy supporting restrictions on the building of student residence towers on Marine Drive overlooking the clothing-optional beach. Opponents of the towers said they would violate privacy or be an eyesore, or both, but Council later decided that, since their main mandate was to represent students, including students needing housing, they would modify the policy to encourage the housing project to go forward.

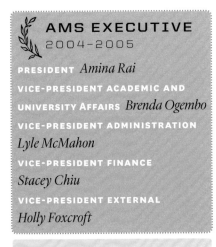

AMS EXECUTIVE
2004–2005

PRESIDENT *Amina Rai*

VICE-PRESIDENT ACADEMIC AND UNIVERSITY AFFAIRS *Brenda Ogembo*

VICE-PRESIDENT ADMINISTRATION *Lyle McMahon*

VICE-PRESIDENT FINANCE *Stacey Chiu*

VICE-PRESIDENT EXTERNAL *Holly Foxcroft*

UBYSSEY EDITOR *Jesse Marchand*

2005-2015

BEING PROFESSIONAL

The University will listen to students, said AMS VP-academic Kiran Mahal, who seemed to have a knack for getting them to do so. But other times the AMS felt that the University was just going through the motions in consulting them. Still, the trend this decade was for the AMS to focus on quiet advocacy, marshalling data, producing reports, talking behind the scenes to the Administration or making presentations to the Board of Governors.

On the other hand, sometimes the AMS, being students, just wanted to have fun, to throw a party, to build a slide, to start a brewery even. And sometimes you get tired of your work and want to just up and go on a trip to see the United Nations or take a Boat to Gaza. Embarrassing, it's true. Or sometimes some of your members let loose with hugely inappropriate cheers. Worse than embarrassing.

But for the most part the AMS in this decade positioned itself as a player to be consulted and as the organization that could even change the nature of the conversation: Let's build a new Student Union Building in the centre of campus. That will end the back and forth over University Town versus Academic. And it did (sort of). And entering its second century the AMS moved into its new Nest, re-examined and restructured itself, and tried as always to connect with the students.

2005 TO 2006

The Return of Professionalism: That's how the *Ubyssey* described the presidency of Spencer Keys, who came to power in the wake of the previous year's disruptions and protests. And this was a good thing, according to the *Ubyssey*. Yes, the radical *Ubyssey*, not so radical anymore and noting with what almost sounded like approval the waning of activism.

AMS president Spencer Keys.

But Not So Fast: Taking up the radical position left vacant by the *Ubyssey* was the *Knoll*, a publication sponsored by the Student Resource Groups and taking its name from the grassy knoll beside the SUB, which became a symbol of opposition to the University's development plans.

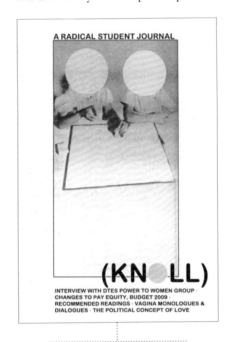

A RADICAL STUDENT JOURNAL

(KN LL)

INTERVIEW WITH DTES POWER TO WOMEN GROUP · CHANGES TO PAY EQUITY, BUDGET 2009 · RECOMMENDED READINGS · VAGINA MONOLOGUES & DIALOGUES · THE POLITICAL CONCEPT OF LOVE

The new radical publication on campus.

What Would Wesbrook Think? Part of the University's plans included a residential development for non-students, which was given the name of the University's first president, thus becoming Wesbrook Village. There was also a Hawthorn Place towards the south of campus, which replaced the old B-lots where students used to park. But the most controversial part of the University's plans concerned University Boulevard, the knoll, and the centre of campus. Here is where University Town was to thrive, after the removal of the knoll and the building of an underground bus loop, along with retail stores and highrise housing.

Oh, and a Drugstore: Suddenly a Shoppers Drug Mart appeared at the corner of University Boulevard and Wesbrook Mall. Wait a minute, some people said, weren't we still discussing this? And do you realize that this is the first thing people will see now when they come to UBC?

Maybe Things Are Getting a Bit Too Commercial: Jess Klug, the AMS VP-external, raised the issue at Council, but some councillors pushed back, saying there was too much kneejerk anti-corporatism and after all the money had to come from somewhere. The AMS itself was going to get money from Molson's for sponsorship of the Welcome Back Barbecue, though it was no longer getting any from . . .

Coca-Cola: The controversial Coke deal was done, sort of. Coke no longer had to pay, but because students hadn't met the challenge (of drinking the amount of Coca-Cola specified in the contract), Coke got two more years of exclusivity on campus without having to pay a cent. Oh, well.

And Maybe We'll Never Let You Back on Campus Again: Or maybe not. Some American campuses were banning Coke because of allegations of bad labour practices and worse, and there was even a full-scale investigation to which the AMS sent a representative. If we don't think they're ethical, we may not do business with them again was the idea. But there were still rumours of a new deal.

More Professionalism: The AMS was getting more and more into hiring part-time student staff to assist the Executive with research and advocacy, and to run the services and the art gallery. For some reason the hiring fell to the VP-academic, who complained about the workload. This led to the creation of even more student staff positions (starting with an associate VP-academic) and to the divvying up of hiring responsibilities. But the point was, this wasn't your grandfather's AMS anymore. It wasn't Council members who were expected to do the main work on AMS campaigns, and it certainly wasn't a Mamooks Club that was tasked with promoting them.

Meanwhile in the Okanagan: AMS president Spencer Keys and VP-Finance Kevin Keystone went to speak to our brothers and sisters at the new, second UBC campus, but found a somewhat chilly welcome. The UBCO students belonged to the radical CFS group, while the AMS from UBC Vancouver was in the more moderate student federation, CASA. But things would eventually improve.

Nobody Here but Us Pigeons: To increase accessibility to the SUB, automatic sliding doors were installed. However, the main result was to prove that pigeons on campus had quite a high IQ: they learned to wait for the doors to open, then sauntered in. So did a lot of wind and rain, because the doors stayed open too long. By the end of the year they had been replaced.

Making way for Irving Barber: knocking down a wing of the Main Library.

And No More Arcade Either: The SUB Arcade, a longtime haunt for videogamers, closed its doors, but the Conversation Pit got an upgrade, and the AMS cookie store, Blue Chip Cookies, got mentioned on a PBS show and in its recipe book.

Elsewhere on campus, the old south wing of the Main Library came down, and the new social space for Science students (the Ladha building) was going up.

And students walked around, headed for class or for food or to study. Like always.

Lobbying: The AMS worked to allow international students to work off campus and serve on the University's Board of Governors. They also got the government to make Health and

Pigeon in the SUB.

Students walking on campus.

Dental fee payments tax deductible and pushed the University to consult students when increasing ancillary fees. Good work, said the *Ubyssey* (is this really the same *Ubyssey*? but it had been becoming friendlier to the AMS and more moderate for a few years now).

The University Strikes Back: After years in which AMS food outlets cut into UBC's business, the University invited Starbucks onto campus, and even into the SUB, prompting one of the few protests of the year.

And in Other News: When asked by the *Ubyssey* what they would change at UBC if they could, students said: (a) the rain (of course), (b) the qual-ity of their professors (uh huh), (c) the never-ending construction, (d) park-ing, and (e) the lack of school spirit.

Wait, Parking? But who's parking anymore? There's a U-Pass, cheap transit, and anyway the B-lots are gone, and the parkades are too expensive. But some diehard driv-ers continued to use their vehicles, driving close to campus, then bus-ing from there. The neighbours were not amused. UBC warned, West Point Grey is not a parking lot.

Student Court: That cheap bus pass, along with the Health and Dental plan, made AMS membership attrac-tive. People wanted to pay AMS fees. We're members, aren't we, said co-op students, along with students in part-time Commerce diploma programs. Council decided to ask Student Court. Who's an AMS mem-ber, exactly? Why, just about anyone, said the Court, even students in con-tinuing education courses. Hmm, said Council, that can't be right. This would lead to trouble.

Travelcuts: In other court news, the decade-long lawsuit over the CFS travel agency ended in a settle-ment, with the AMS and some other non-CFS schools granted minority shareholder rights. But travel agen-cies were on the way out anyway, along with . . .

Flip Phones: Well, nobody knew this yet. They were still the latest thing. One student got disciplined for using one to photograph an exam.

And What's Coming In? Strategic plans. The AMS produced one. YouTube: students put a lipsync video up on it. Committee reform: the AMS was talking about it. Broad Based Admissions. Dance clubs, and more dance clubs: Dance Horizons, a swing dance club, a salsa club, the Dance Team. And skimboarding. And beads and crafts. But unfortu-nately also . . .

Depression: An issue much talked about on campus this year. Anti-depressants were the top-selling pharmaceutical. There were waiting lists for counsellors. There was even a Suicide Awareness Project.

So sad. A student's life is not an easy one.

AMS EXECUTIVE
2005-2006

PRESIDENT *Spencer Keys*

VICE-PRESIDENT ACADEMIC
Gavin Dew

VICE-PRESIDENT FINANCE
Kevin Keystone

VICE-PRESIDENT ADMINISTRATION
Manj Sidhu

VICE-PRESIDENT EXTERNAL *Jess Klug*

UBYSSEY EDITOR *Jesse Marchand*

2006 TO 2007

What's the Plan? So said the University, like a bad teacher with a leading question. Guess what we have in mind. But students didn't have to guess: the University's plan was quite clear, a University Town full of condos and retail stores in the middle of campus. No, said the students, we don't want that. And don't pretend to consult us when you've already decided; give us meaning-

The University asked for input, but the students didn't think they were really listening.

ful consultation. And meanwhile the University was going ahead with its preparations, but running into delays, especially for its underground bus loop (which never happened). And students said, Save the knoll, but the University said, No, no, no, that knoll, it must go.

The grassy knoll that students wanted to keep.

Speaking of Teaching: The University did not do well in a National Survey of Student Engagement (NSSE). The AMS talked of reviving its *Yardstick* of student evaluations and even set up an Academic Quality Committee. There were rumblings of discontent, but no real protests.

And the AMS lobbied successfully for a spot on UBC's Development Permit Board to have a say in all the campus development, but VP-Academic Jeff Friedrich, the moving force behind the lobbying, said that the main problem was that there was no real check on what the University chose to do, no municipal governance. That's not true, said the University, we have to go through the GVRD (the Greater Vancouver Regional District)—but they wouldn't for much longer.

But we have a plan, said the students in Commerce (now called the Sauder School of Business). We'll increase our own student fees by $500 to pay for upgrades to the Henry Angus Building. That will make things better.

No, no, no, said AMS Council, why are the students paying extra for academic improvements? And the province stepped in and said this fee would violate the tuition cap, so it was halted for the moment. But it would be back.

Speaking of student fees, where are all our athletic fees going? We pay huge amounts and then still have high user fees for things like the Bird Coop fitness centre. AMS complaints on this did seem to have an effect, and Bird Coop fees came down.

Meanwhile, The GSS (representing the graduate students) was not happy, but directed their ire not at the administration but at the AMS. We're a distinct society, they said (Quebec, muttered their detractors); we don't get the services we need from the AMS. Pay us more money, or we'll secede. An agreement was worked out, and the grad students stayed.

Internally, the GSS had its own problems, with a mudslinging presidential election involving an older student of longstanding who liked to write letters to the *Ubyssey*. Not Kurt Preinsperg, I hear you say. No, but . . .

261

Kurt 2.0: Patrick Bruskiewich, a grad student in physics, who began publishing in the *Ubyssey* in 1999 on everything from Pope John Paul II to Pierre Trudeau and from abortion to mandatory retirement. But his most controversial comments were about the superiority of Science to Arts, which unsurprisingly produced a strong reaction from Arts students.

Then he ran for GSS president, accusing a rival candidate of conflict of interest, only to be accused in turn of libel. Neither of the two won, and Patrick stormed out of student politics, saying he had been treated with disrespect. He went back to writing opinion pieces for the *Ubyssey*, which a few years before had called him one of the Top 10 reasons to read the paper.

And Don't Forget the Children: The AMS agreed to pay $100,000 a year for ten years to improve child care facilities on campus.

But No More Coca-Cola: At least not exclusively. It was more than rumours now: the University was definitely negotiating a new deal. No, no, no, said AMS Council. Coke is bad. Exclusivity is bad. Corporations are bad (well, sometimes, some corporations). No more exclusivity deals for soft drinks ever again, UBC. And for us too, someone asked? Oh, wait a minute, that's different. You hypocrites, someone said. So AMS Council said neither UBC nor the AMS should ever enter into a cold beverage exclusivity agreement ever again. Ever.

And It Snowed and Rained, and campus closed for a day, and some students bought essays or commented about that (It's so cool, said one; is it illegal?). And the *Ubyssey* said the most important things to read for background for all your courses were Homer, Edward Said's book on orientalism, Frederic Jameson on postmodernism, and *Clash of Civilizations* (about globalization).

With campus closed for the day, one student filled his time by snowboarding at the SUB.

And Students Wore Lululemon for Yoga, and lined up for the latest Harry Potter book, or watched Al Gore's *An Inconvenient Truth,* or *Borat,* or went to *The Vagina Monologues* at Freddy Wood (and ate a chocolate vagina). Or ate at the Naam or Sophie's Cosmic Cafe and worried about putting on the Freshman 15, and there was even some more . . .

Alma Mating: The previous year's VP-external, Jess Klug, married the AMS minischool coordinator and lived happily ever after, even though it was in Ontario.

And the AMS put on FarmAde in support of the UBC Farm, and did composting, and sold only fair trade coffee (now there's some exclusivity it could get behind), and talked of a Lighter Footprint . . . but it's all lip service, said a *Ubyssey* columnist. It's so easy to talk about going green and being environmentally friendly, but we need to *do* something. Look at all the garbage we produce: "The stability of our planet as a whole is on shaky ground."

Hmm: Perhaps the writer needed some of the free hugs some students were giving out. Or they needed to get out more, go to Ecuador or Uganda to help the people there, or to Nunavut or the Downtown Eastside. Students were volunteering and going on exchanges and seeing the world.

Or Would a Little Fasting and Cleansing Have Helped? But stay off those amphetamines. Maybe try the SUB climbing wall. Or if you really need to rant, try the Soundoff video booth the University and the AMS installed. And just think: if you're lining up to book rooms for your club, you won't have to spend the night outside the SUB anymore. And you could always drop in on a Council meeting for the free food or go to the Cold Fusion concert for Science Week or watch Science students do jello wrestling or see the Science student president get dunked, voluntarily, in a dunk tank.

Or Maybe You'd Like to Help Out in a Good Cause: Shining shoes to fight cystic fibrosis (as part of Shinerama): Even the new UBC

Jello wrestling in the SUB.

president, Stephen Toope, pitched in to shine Jeff Friedrich's shoes—well, they weren't really Jeff's shoes, just a pair of high heels someone had lying around. (Don't ask.)

UBC president Toope shines the shoes of VP-Academic Jeff Friedrich for Shinerama Day.

Or Go Watch Some Sports: UBC created a Blue Crew to promote athletics, and this was a very successful period for UBC athletes. The men's and women's swim teams each won their tenth consecutive national title, women's soccer and women's field hockey also won titles, the basketball teams were coming off

Athletic banners on display in the War Memorial Gym.

stellar years (though this one was a bit disappointing), and the *Ubyssey* noted that UBC was second only to U of T in national titles, having garnered sixty-seven in forty years.

And Finally, How About a Little Turbo Democracy? A little what? Later to be known as Voter-Funded Media, Turbo Democracy was an idea of Mark Latham's, an outsider who showed up with $10,000 cash to fund an experiment in increasing voter turnout by having a media contest as part of AMS elections. Sounds crazy, I know, but $10,000 . . . So the AMS tried it. Not their money after all. It didn't increase turnout (nothing increases turnout except a U-Pass question), but people liked it anyway and kept it going.

AMS EXECUTIVE
2006–2007

PRESIDENT *Kevin Keystone*

VICE-PRESIDENT ACADEMIC
Jeff Friedrich

VICE-PRESIDENT FINANCE
Sophia Haque

VICE-PRESIDENT ADMINISTRATION
David Yuen

VICE-PRESIDENT EXTERNAL
Ian Pattillo

UBYSSEY EDITOR *Eric Szeto*

2007 TO 2008

The Battle of Trek Park: On the first day of classes protesters established themselves on the little parking lot next to the Knoll, creating a makeshift park and protest zone in opposition to the University's development plans, especially the underground bus loop. Save the Knoll, they said, in between tending to their do-it-yourself garden and hosting a concert.

The Battle of University Square: On another front, the AMS pushed forward with plans for a referendum to raise money to renovate the SUB or build a new one. And surveys revealed that what students wanted was green space, not condos, and the University even said, well, we realize now that the centre of campus should feel like an academic space and not a street in downtown Vancouver. And when the $80 million proposal from the AMS was floated, the University said, Count us in. And so, Victory: a new Student Union Building would occupy pride of place in the proposed University Square (the term that came to the fore this year, replacing "University Town").

But Skirmishing Continued: Something called the Wreath Underground vandalized two University buildings after the University bulldozed Trek Park. And then a revived Trek Park was the scene of a bonfire, which protesters tried to keep from being put out when firefighters arrived on the scene. The police also arrived, about twenty protesters were arrested, including the newly elected VP-external for 2008–9, Stef Ratjen, and there were charges of police brutality and, on the other hand, criticisms of the VP for being involved in such a thing: Don't you know you represent us?

VP-External Stefanie Ratjen.

Not Just That VP: It was a bad year for newly elected vice-presidents. Alex Lougheed won the election for VP-academic, but then it was discovered that he had tried to cast five (or was it twelve?) separate ballots in the election. Student Court ordered him disqualified. AMS Council overruled Student Court. This delegitimizes Student Court and casts a pall over the Executive, people said.

VP-Academic Alex Lougheed.

Activism: Trek Park marked the beginning of an upsurge. A couple of years before, the *Ubyssey* had said that the only things students wanted to protest was their grades, and there was still a focus on the individual this year, and only a small group got up to confrontation, but there was a conference called Resisting the University, a group tried to channel

Playing and protesting at Trek Park.

the 1960s by calling itself Students for a Democratic Society (SDS, just like the radical group forty years before), and there was a protest against the five-year-old war in Iraq.

Comings and Goings: Pepsi was back, but Arts County Fair was gone, the victim of debt and poor turnouts—but it was replaced by the AMS-sponsored Block Party on MacInnes Field. The Irving K. Barber Learning Centre was finally complete. The *Ubyssey* asked some students what they thought of it. Too noisy, said one, too many people talking, perhaps because there aren't many books. The Engineers' Cheeze got shut down, so they hung a Volkswagen from the Lions Gate Bridge (well, they might have done that anyway). And they were accused of painting the Stanley Park gun red, but denied it.

"Irving": mostly for studying.

Not Coming Back: No *Yardstick* for student evaluations, and no UBC-published evaluations either, perhaps because the Faculty Association objected. Well, said the *Ubyssey*, the thing to do then is to sign up for lots of courses and see how they are in the first couple of weeks, then drop all the ones you don't like. Professors

Commerce students raise awareness.

must have loved that. And don't stop there, said the paper: if you don't like your marks, appeal them; and if you get a library fine, appeal that too. And your housing contract. And the penalty for missing an exam.

Why Are You Here After All? If you think it's to learn, you're out of luck, said the *Ubyssey*. Better to party and join a club. Your degree will mostly be a credential. Ah, well. Wait for grad school.

But Partying Is Hard These Days: Yes, said the paper: the RCMP is cracking down on beer gardens. It's all part of the War on Fun. And all these old people are moving into a retirement home on South Campus. They'll get all upset about any noise you might make. Give UBC back to the students (and the partyers).

And the AMS brought locally grown organic food into its outlets and passed a Lighter Footprint

Strategy, and created a Sustainability Coordinator position and a Sustainability Fund. It also changed its name (slightly), adding the word Vancouver (to distinguish it from the student union in the Okanagan), and it adopted a new logo, replacing the one that had served since 1980.

ams | Enhancing Student Life
ams.ubc.ca

After a quarter of a century, the AMS tries a new logo.

And Commerce Students Staged Five Days for the Homeless: In front of the Bookstore, camping out without food or showers in order to raise money and awareness. "We're not all soulless and evil," one of them said.

More Activism? Meanwhile, at the end of the year, the AMS itself seemed to move towards more advanced positions, creating an Equity Committee and Equity Representatives, and also commissioning a study on systemic barriers within the society. Not enough women on Council, some said. Not enough commuters, said someone else. But the study would focus on women (and visible minorities).

And What Were Ordinary Students Up To? Well, if not appealing grades or fines, they were bringing laptops to class or joining the videogaming club or dressing up like videogame characters ("Cosplay") or attending poetry slams and improv nights or illegally downloading music.

Or They Wrote Graffiti: "My gender psych class makes me want to become a misogynist," wrote one.

Or They Took Part in Varsity Sports: The women's teams did especially well this year (again), winning national titles in volleyball, basketball, and swimming. There was also a successful women's Ultimate team. The men did not do quite as well, but there was talk of joining the American NCAA (more on that next year and later).

And the AMS Got a New General Manager, and American news personality Dan Rather came to campus to work with UBC's journalism students, and UBC lost money in the subprime crash (but the AMS did not), and RCMP officers on campus

Jeff Francis pitching for the Thunderbirds before he made it to the major leagues.

got in trouble for flirting with visiting tourists, and a former UBC athlete got to pitch in the World Series.

And What Happened to the Chancellor Elections? Gone. No more. Replaced by a system in which the Board of Governors appointed someone. Stan Persky, eat your heart out.

AMS EXECUTIVE
2007–2008

PRESIDENT *Jeff Friedrich*

VICE-PRESIDENT ACADEMIC
Brendon Goodmurphy

VICE-PRESIDENT FINANCE
Brittany Tyson

VICE-PRESIDENT ADMINISTRATION
Sarah Naiman

VICE-PRESIDENT EXTERNAL
Matt Naylor

UBYSSEY EDITOR *Champagne Choquer*

2008 TO 2009

So How's the New SUB Coming Along? Not so well, actually. The AMS began consultations with the student body, who talked about something more open and cheerier than the Old SUB, but as far as going forward with actual architects and project managers, there had to be an agreement with the University, and that did not seem to be forthcoming. Tristan Markle, AMS VP-administration, insisted on student control, while Brian Sullivan, the University's VP-students, said the University had to have some say. And so things stood, stalled.

Saving the Farm: The UBC Farm was the issue of the year, a symbol of sustainability and opposition to development. There were discussions and a petition. Metro Vancouver even weighed in, saying to preserve it, and at the end of the year two thousand students and other supporters marched for the

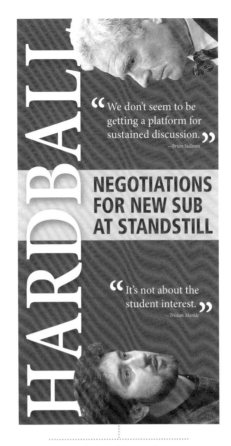

"We don't seem to be getting a platform for sustained discussion."
—*Brian Sullivan*

NEGOTIATIONS FOR NEW SUB AT STANDSTILL

"It's not about the student interest."
—*Tristan Markle*

Going sideways?
The New SUB project hits a roadblock.

cause, eventually convincing the Board of Governors to let it remain a farm and not become a housing development.

The Great Farm Trek.

So Was Activism Back? Well, sort of. Aside from the Farm Trek, there were no big actions (and certainly

no bonfires like last year). Where has the SDS gone, asked the *Ubyssey* nostalgically, and the answer seemed to be that they had moved out of the streets and into the Council chambers. At least, Council seemed inclined this year to adopt various elements of the progressive agenda on topics from equity to the Olympics to Student Court.

Student Court? Yes, the Court, which had survived for decades, but which had run into opposition in recent years, with Council rejecting several of its rulings. However, this year the feeling in the air was that the Court should be strengthened. A consultant recommended this, and Council drafted bylaw changes to do so, subject to a referendum.

And the Olympics? On this topic actually the progressives met some pushback. A report came to Council warning of all the negative impacts the Olympics would bring to Vancouver, but one Councillor said, What about the positive impacts? And the report was sent back to committee, and only returned in modified form. And at the end of the year supporters of the Olympics got Council to hear a pro-Olympics presentation from the University and the Olympic organizing committee.

More Pushback: Elections at the end of the year brought two activists into power on the Executive (though surprisingly, Tristan Markle was defeated in his attempt at re-election). Blake Frederick became president, and Tim

267

Chu VP-external, but they began to discover opposition. When they presented a negative report on CASA, the moderate student federation, some Councillors asked to hear the other side. When Tim asked for $30,000 to support an AMS presence in the provincial election campaign, Council only reluctantly granted it, and when they found out what he'd spent it on, they were even less pleased. And when they saw his "report card" on the parties, which praised the NDP and gave the Liberals an F, there was strong disapproval. A sign of things to come.

Athletic Fees: Earlier in the year one of the biggest successes of the Mike Duncan presidency was the reduction of fees at the Aquatic Centre and the Bird Coop fitness centre as well as for Storm the Wall and the Intramurals program. The University was talking about joining the American NCAA for varsity sports, but Council, led by Duncan, said the emphasis should be on recreation programs for regular students.

President Duncan was known for his pole dancing, jello wrestling, and general light-heartedness, but he had some serious accomplishments, like winning the concessions on recreation fees and helping to organize the Farm Trek.

AMS president Mike Duncan.

War on Fun: The apparent War on Fun perhaps was petering out. The Radical Beer Faction revived and put on No Pants Dances. The two RCMP officers who some thought were behind the War moved on, and UBC president Toope said the University had never been in favour of prohibition.

And the Hipster Phenomenon came to campus, prompting angry debate, though not perhaps as angry as the debate over the . . .

Middle East: Representatives of the Israel Awareness Committee and the Solidarity group for Palestinian Human Rights went at it. Our own private little war. But at least there was no boat.

And smartphones came to campus, and Twitter. And 99 Chairs, the latest replacement for the Bus Stop Cafe, disappeared, to be replaced by a White Spot. And the frats held a male beauty pageant ("Mr. Greek"), the Engineers got caught trying to hang a Volkswagen from the Second Narrows Bridge, and Kyle Warwick astonished his fellow Councillors with a metaphor about pulling nails from a burning fire.

Councillor Kyle Warwick.

And the Chinese Varsity Club got in trouble for making fun of the English skills of members of other Chinese clubs, this on a campus where Chinese students were now the largest group, ahead of Caucasians.

And there were more and more international students, paying much higher fees than domestic students, fees the University hoped would help them deal with their financial reverses.

And more and more graduate students too, with their very own handbook, which this year provoked controversy, and nearly got suppressed, because some Graduate Student Society executives found it too radical. But in the end it was released with a disclaimer.

And the Arts students invented The Great Arts Sendoff (TGAS) as a dinner-dance grad, and listened to a Last Lecture from a guy who turned a paper clip into a house, and Council Speaker Dave Tompkins introduced a snazzy new electronic voting system allowing Councillors to hold roll call votes on everything.

And following in the footsteps of the Commerce students, the students in Architecture and Landscape Architecture voted to raise their own fees to help out their School, prompting one Councillor to shake his head and say students shouldn't pay for what the University should be paying for.

And when the University, in one of its innumerable consultation sessions with Council, sent someone

to talk about how to re-landscape the "public realm" on campus, one Councillor said, "Fix the puddles."

The *Ubyssey* had notions about fixing puddles and all other weather problems, this in a year of big rain and snowstorms: Build a dome. But they were joking.

And they sent one of their under-sized reporters to try out for the UBC football team, resulting in a hilarious article à la George Plimpton.

And the AMS took aim at bottled water and voted money to fix its water fountains. And the 25th Welcome Back Barbecue was a success despite the lack of a big headliner, and Arts failed in bringing back Arts County Fair, but there was still Block Party, and teaching expert and Nobel laureate Carl Wieman expressed surprise that teaching evaluations were still not being made public at UBC.

And people tried to get in the back door of the Pit, and flash mobs were a thing (not just at UBC), and

a Bible class sprung up advertising the Bible as a really famous book, and there was talk of changing the AMS name to something less obscure (but that went nowhere), and Council realized it had to raise wages for AMS employees (who now numbered over 600), and the Ubyssey said it hated old people (but then retracted).

And in the biggest breaking news of the year the *Ubyssey* reported that a psychologist had determined that students tend to procrastinate. It's because of distant deadlines and extra-curricular distractions, he said.

And Imagine Day was extended to all, the Number 33 bus came to campus, it looked like anyone who'd ever got a UBC parking fine might get their money back (but they didn't), a Pass/Fail system was announced for certain courses, Council had to fill three student seats on Senate when only two candidates came forward for the five spots available,

the Condorcet preferential voting system was used for the first time, Blake Frederick was first disqualified but then reinstated when he ran for President, and when asked by the Ubyssey what they were worried about students said student debt and getting lost on campus.

But what worried Council was the budget presentation at the end of the year by the new VP Finance, Tom Dvorak, who warned that the AMS was labouring under a structural deficit and if it didn't address the problem, the whole organization might go up in flames. He even showed an animation of flames consuming the words "Alma Mater Society."

269

AMS EXECUTIVE
2008-2009

PRESIDENT *Mike Duncan*

VICE-PRESIDENT ACADEMIC
Alex Lougheed

VICE-PRESIDENT FINANCE
Chris Diplock

VICE-PRESIDENT ADMINISTRATION
Tristan Markle

VICE-PRESIDENT EXTERNAL
Stefanie Ratjen

UBYSSEY EDITOR *Kellan Higgins*

2009 TO 2010

This Looks Like a Job for the United Nations: AMS president Blake Frederick and VP-External Tim Chu decided that the best way to draw attention to tuition issues at UBC was to lodge a complaint at the United Nations under the relevant International Covenant. That will get people's attention.

Well, It Certainly Did: It's just a stunt, Blake said later, when some complained about the triviality of such a complaint compared to other things the UN had to deal with. Others were appalled that the two executives had done this all in secret, without even informing Council and that it implicitly went against Council's tuition policies.

Council Is Out of Touch with What Students Want: So said the two executives, and a referendum on tuition almost, sort of, agreed with

them. On the other hand, another pair of referendum questions almost removed Blake and Tim from office, so who is to say?

Look, the United Nations has already responded to our complaint! (Two students pretend to be from the UN.)

About that Referendum: Well, about the elections in general. This year the AMS went totally electronic again, and somebody hacked the election, casting 731 fraudulent votes. The hackers didn't alter the Executive results, but did change who one of the elected Senators was and affected the results of the vote on whether the AMS should lobby to reduce tuition fees in such a way that it was impossible to determine whether it had passed or not. So it became the only referendum in AMS history whose result was never known.

But Back to Blake and Tim: The UN complaint wasn't a bolt from the blue, more like "the cherry on the top of the sundae," as the *Ubyssey* put it. Except they'd already awarded that cherry for something Blake had done a month before: issuing a harshly worded press release attacking the University over their plans for an underground bus loop,

a press release that greatly angered UBC president Toope. At that point Council had contemplated censuring their president, but decided to give him one last chance when he said he had heard them "loud and clear." Ah, well.

A President in Name Only: The result was that Council did everything in its power to strip their president of his power. They had wanted to remove him altogether, but found out that the Society Act didn't allow that. So they removed him from his position as chair of the Executive Committee, told him that no more press releases could go out without Council approval, and demanded the submission of timesheets detailing what he did every day. And they voted to have the Annual General Meeting at the earliest point possible, so that Blake's term would end in mid-February before the Olympics.

The Olympic Games: Yes. They came to campus, sort of. There'd been all sorts of expectations of activities and protests, but although a few events took place at the Doug Mitchell Thunderbird Sports Centre, mostly the campus was very quiet—except on Day

UBC gets excited about the Olympics.

LEFT Students cheer for Canada at the Pit.

RIGHT A happy signing ceremony. The AMS president signs the New SUB agreement with UBC's VP-finance.

One, when the Olympic torch passed through. Then thousands gathered in excitement and support (though a couple of hundred protested).

Protested? Yes; while once they were on, the Games were hugely popular, beforehand there'd been objections, especially on campus, especially from the forces of the left, who warned of threats to civil liberties and the waste of money when so many were homeless. Because the AMS president and VP-external were on the side of the protesters, the AMS did little to celebrate the Games—until the transition to the next Executive, which instantly put ads in the paper inviting students to enjoy themselves at the Pit, where they could watch the Canadian hockey team go for gold.

The Left? Yes, the forces that for a brief moment seemed to have been able to shift the AMS in a new direction. But now they suddenly gave way. "The right has risen," said the *Ubyssey*. The AMS Equity program was ended, the Council seat for an international student (created just the year before) was abolished, and the attempt to create a similar seat for students with disabilities was defeated. Tim Chu got the AMS to leave CASA, the moderate student alliance, but his successor as VP-external, Jeremy McElroy, got Council to put the AMS back in. The culture of opposition associated with Blake Frederick was replaced by a spirit of accommodation when the students elected Bijan Ahmadian, who promised to repair relations with the University. Perhaps he's too close to the University, some muttered; perhaps, said the *Ubyssey*, it's not such a great thing to swing from one extreme to the other, but there you go.

The New SUB: And now the New SUB went ahead, with a signing ceremony and a search for architects, and everyone was happy except there were these . . .

Financial Problems: After years of prosperity, the AMS was suddenly falling on hard times. There would have to be cuts. Perhaps even to Safewalk; after all, hardly anyone is using it anymore (this would change within a couple of years, but . . .). Why all the focus on services, one Councillor complained.

And, Oh, Another Election Problem: This time in the Arts Undergraduate Society, where an appeal went all the way to AMS Student Court, which ruled the whole election invalid, only to see AMS Council overturn its ruling. Yes, again, just like in the Lougheed case and several others, and this after pro-Court forces (those forces on the left again) had pushed to increase the Court's powers and not let Council gain the upper hand like this. But Council did, and after this the Court was not heard from again.

In the Meantime: While the civil war between Left and Right raged within the AMS leadership, what were the regular students up to? Well, . . .

Joining Clubs: There were lots and lots of clubs, over three hundred now. Too many, said a *Ubyssey* editorial: "It's weirdly reflective of the fragmented collective student identity." But they seemed to enjoy reporting on the fragments in a way that would have warmed the heart of the AMS Council of years gone by, which used to plead in vain for its newspaper to cover what the clubs were up to. So now there were features on the Science Fiction Society and the Equestrian Team, the Jugglers and the Potters, the Debaters and the Sailors, not to mention the Scuba Divers (in Aquasoc).

And Quirky Professors Too: The *Ubyssey* this year began running features on professors with offbeat interests, like Stanley Coren in psychology, who cared about what dogs think, or the law professor who studied vampires, or the professor who did a documentary on shoe flinging.

But Back to the Students: What else were they interested in this year? Well, if you can believe the *Ubyssey* . . . sex. In fact, they were perhaps . . .

Too Sexy: That was the name of a regular column in the paper, dealing in part with broader relationship issues but mostly focusing on various types of sexual activity and what was or was not taboo. Should I go after my prof? What about my TA? Is it okay to sleep with multiple partners? What if I want something in bed, but my partner doesn't? Oh, and can my cat watch?

What the well-dressed protester is wearing these days.

And Fashion: There was a regular fashion column too, telling students what to wear in the rain (patterns), what was being worn for the Olympics, and even what was being worn to protest the Olympics (bandanas and combat boots).

And Complaints: The *Ubyssey* invited complaints and got them, about leaf blowers and clocks that didn't run right, construction noise, and cyclists.

Cyclists? Yes, some people said they were terrorizing pedestrians. But mostly cycling was celebrated in the paper, with a feature on how to cycle in bad weather and another on how to fix your bike. Not to mention maps of bike routes.

Sexual Assault: The University started its annual Sexual Assault Awareness Month, and the Arts undergraduate paper got in trouble for running a joke article making light

of rape. In response, some spoke of a "culture of rape," though at least one commentator called this an overreaction, indeed called the whole awareness month an overreaction, and wished the Women's Centre (Womyn's Centre?) would decide which vowels it wanted to use.

And What Else? The women's volleyball team won its third straight title, a hospice was going to go up near a student residence but complaints got it to move, a student (Geoff Costeloe) got elected vice-chair of the University Senate, the AMS successfully fought off an attempt by TransLink to charge extra for trips to the airport, and an attempt to bring back election slates failed. The men's hockey team wore pink for breast cancer month, the swine flu came and went (causing much less disruption than feared), there were more places to eat on campus (the Point Grill, Caffe Perugia), meaning more competition for AMS food outlets, and there was . . .

Committee Reform: While most AMS political news focused on the UN and CASA, AMS Council quietly adopted a revamping of its committee structure. Dressed at one point like a character from *Battlestar Galactica*, Councillor Matt Naylor convinced Council to streamline the committee system and put regular councillors instead of executives in charge. There was also an Agenda Committee and a virtual ban on ad hoc committees. But it didn't last.

Matthew Naylor, the moving force behind committee reform.

The President's Fund: Once upon a time a grateful alumnus decided to give something back to his Alma Mater. Did he mean the University or the Alma Mater Society? It was unclear, but the lawyers said probably the latter. So a legacy came to the AMS to be put in a President's Fund.

But oh, the problems it caused. Who should use it? For what? And eventually it all got spent, and people were almost relieved.

Commerce Fee: And the Commerce students ignored warnings from the rest of the AMS and said, yes, yes, we will pay an extra $500 a year to fix the Henry Angus building.

And the Canada Line arrived, but what about a SkyTrain to UBC? And the University argued with Metro Vancouver over who should control zoning, with the AMS eventually siding with the University. And students sent postcards to the provincial government to protest cuts in financial aid, and then went off campus to drink at places like Jeremiah's (previously known

"It's your fault I'm here," said Fred Penner about his gig at the Pit, "because your generation has grown up."

as Jerry's Cove, and later just the Cove). And the University promised more drinking fountains, and the AMS introduced biodegradable cutlery and baby change rooms. And the University finally created an Ombudsoffice, taking on much of what the AMS Ombudsoffice used to do. And there was a Deans Debate (won by the Dean of Applied Science, apparently), and an event to raise money for the victims of the earthquake in Haiti, and Fred Penner, the children's entertainer, came to the Pit of all places, and that went over well, but when the Barenaked Ladies headlined at Block Party, that didn't go well at all.

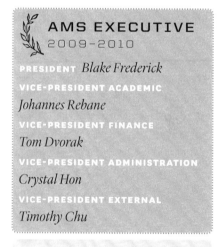

AMS EXECUTIVE
2009-2010

PRESIDENT *Blake Frederick*

VICE-PRESIDENT ACADEMIC
Johannes Rebane

VICE-PRESIDENT FINANCE
Tom Dvorak

VICE-PRESIDENT ADMINISTRATION
Crystal Hon

VICE-PRESIDENT EXTERNAL
Timothy Chu

UBYSSEY EDITOR *Paul Bucci*

2010 TO 2011

A Slow Boat to Gaza: Solidarity for Palestinian Human Rights (SPHR), an AMS club, wanted to make a donation to the Canadian Boat to Gaza, part of a flotilla meant to break the blockade of Gaza by Israel. The AMS Social Justice Centre tried to give them $700 to do this, but AMS VP-finance Elin Tayyar declined to sign off on the transaction without Council approval. So ensued weeks of debate in and out of Council, including a three-hour Council meeting held in the Norm Theatre to accommodate the two hundred guests who wanted to attend.

Student money should not go for something like this, some said. Why not, said others, it's completely within the rules. Which it seemed to be, though it would be a violation of Canadian law, it seemed, to give money to a terrorist group. Was the Canadian Boat a terrorist group? AMS president Bijan Ahmadian said

this would be looked into, provoking much anger and derision, though the AMS's own lawyers had suggested checking on this.

And in the end? The money was approved, but the rules got changed. No more donations to outside groups. Also, the mandatory fee that funded the Social Justice Centre became optional. And there was peace in the Middle East. Well, no, but at least that was the end of conflict at UBC over the Middle East. Well, no, not that either.

YOUR DOLLARS TO GAZA?

S.S. UBC

The *Ubyssey* had some fun with the Gaza boat situation.

President Bijan: For the second year in a row controversy surrounded an AMS president. Whether over Gaza or UBC land use, upgrades to his office, or his involvement in the campaign to choose his successor, Bijan found himself at odds with his fellow executives and Council. At the end of the year Council debated a motion to censure him, and he threatened to sue (the motion failed). He did succeed in getting a UBC's Got Talent show put on in

the Chan Centre and even participated in it, singing a duet with UBC president Toope, and he was later involved in the shooting of a lip-synching Lip Dub video on campus. But overall a divisive figure.

Be Nice! After an incredibly acrimonious election campaign, it was suggested that there be an award for people who ran more civil campaigns, like the one run by Justin Yang for VP-academic. So Council created an award for fair play, named after Evelyn Lett (but it was never awarded).

All You Need Is . . . Money? The AMS was short of it again. We're paying so many more people now, and our businesses aren't what they were, and we had to cut so much from our services last time: we just can't go on like this. So there was a fee referendum to save the Society, and it passed (though just barely), and everyone thought that was the solution, but hard times were not over just yet.

LOOK, MA! WE PASSED!

The *Ubyssey* was not too impressed with the victory in the fee referendum.

Reduce Tuition? Another referendum passed, this one initiated by members of the Social Justice Centre (the last bastion of activism within the AMS, apparently): to have the AMS lobby to reduce tuition. In response, Council amended its tuition policy to call for a tuition reduction when possible, but AMS lobbying in this period was focused more on . . .

Land Use: Gage South was the battleground, the area south of the Gage residences, next to the SUB and MacInnes Field. We can use that for market housing, said the University. No, you shouldn't, said the AMS, so the University agreed to think again.

Also Transit: When news came that a rapid transit line to UBC was at the bottom of Metro Vancouver's priority list, the AMS campaigned to change things. There are still too many pass-ups by crowded buses, they said. There would be more talk about this over the next few years, but still no promise of a UBC SkyTrain.

And the New SUB: Planning was underway. There were workshops and open houses and a Design Cube in the Old SUB, where the architects hung out and listened to suggestions. How about a discreet room for smoking marijuana, suggested the *Ubyssey*? Or a miniature golf course? But these things would not be.

Too Asian? Controversy raged after *Maclean's* magazine published an article quoting students as saying they wouldn't want to go to a university at which "Asian" values like hard work were valued over partying. Racist stereotyping, said some. A realistic report on what some people think, said the *Ubyssey*.

Too Irish? The *Ubyssey* itself got in trouble for reporting on rowdiness surrounding Irish visitors who liked to stay in UBC's frat houses. The frats also won unwanted attention after an assault at one of their parties. The Engineers this year were uncharacteristically subdued and not involved in any of this, causing the *Ubyssey* to lament their quiescence. We're not here for your entertainment, said a past Engineering president. But the Engineers did continue their tradition of celebrating Christmas with a brass band, caroling, and some spiked eggnog.

And day care was still an issue, and plagiarism, and animal research, but mostly it was a time of . . .

Surfing and hiking and fencing and film-going, gaming and wakeboarding and drinking cappuccinos. Or making sure you had a mini-fridge or playing laser tag or Quidditch or going skiing or snowboarding or to a foreign country (on exchange). Or running a student-directed seminar or using your new smartphone (there was even an app from the University) or buying furniture at Ikea (on an AMS-organized excursion) or sledding down the Knoll. But not diving off the high board at the outdoor pool in the middle of the night (because there was a roof over it now).

A Harry Potter–inspired game of Quidditch on MacInnes Field.

And the deans debated what to do about zombies and White Spot gave way to Triple O's (but could anything ever be as good as the old Bus Stop Cafe?). And a UBC student in Japan complained about being forced to go home under the new UBC policy on safety abroad (after the tsunami hit) and the AMS tried Toonie Tuesdays (selling cheap beer until the RCMP put an end to it) and Koerner's Pub in the Graduate Student Centre was closed, then opened, then closed again.

And the *Ubyssey* declared Facebook old hat, and the Arts Undergraduate Society had four presidents (not at the same time), and students bought food at the UBC Farm Market or Sprouts, and the AMS introduced water filling stations to encourage students to fill up water bottles instead of buying bottled water. And Condorcet preferential voting was on, then off, then on again in the AMS elections. And there was an early sighting of Unecorn (the odd abbreviation for the University and External Relations Committee).

275

AMS EXECUTIVE
2010–2011

PRESIDENT *Bijan Ahmadian*

VICE-PRESIDENT ACADEMIC
Ben Cappellacci

VICE-PRESIDENT FINANCE *Elin Tayyar*

VICE-PRESIDENT ADMINISTRATION
Ekaterina Dovjenko / Mike Silley

VICE-PRESIDENT EXTERNAL
Jeremy McElroy

UBYSSEY EDITOR *Justin McElroy*

2011 TO 2012

Gage South is Ours! A victory for the students. The University gave in after a petition campaign spearheaded by Neal Yonson, blogger, researcher, perpetual thorn in the University's side.

Blogger? Yes, this was the thing, in part encouraged by the AMS Voter Media contest. Neal blogged for *UBC Insiders*. There was also *AMS Confidential*, run by Taylor Loren, a different sort of thing altogether. The previous year, when UBC president Stephen Toope came to Council, Neal quizzed him about Gage South, and Taylor asked if he preferred unicorns or rainbows (Answer: Unicorns).

Neal Yonson, making a point.

But Back to Gage South (the Central Campus Area Near the SUB): The University agreed to zone it as "Academic," perhaps with housing, but student housing, not more condos.

Condos, Condos Everywhere: Maybe not in the centre of campus, but around the edges. And who will rule over them? Two years before, the province had stepped in to, in effect, give control to the University, taking it away from Metro Vancouver. A supposedly temporary step, but . . .

The *Ubyssey* hammered away at what they saw as a lack of democracy: we're a town without a municipal government. Even the condo residents weren't happy; they had a University Neighbourhoods Association (UNA) to represent them, but that didn't stop that hospice, the one the students didn't want next to a student residence, ending up near a condo building. And then the University proposed to increase the density of Wesbrook Village. No, no, no, said the residents, but what could they do?

And What Was Student Government Up To? Well, first of all, we're not so much a government as a non-profit society running businesses and offering services, said President Jeremy McElroy. And it was an introspective year for the AMS, as he put it, with the focus on internal restructuring. A consultant came (former AMS executive Glenn Wong) and told AMS Council to change things around: add more senior managers, introduce incentive programs and strategic planning and goals and metrics. Oh, and keep your hands off your businesses. Follow the motto . . .

Nose In, Hands Off: And VP-Finance Elin Tayyar especially pursued this, proposing to split off the businesses into a separate corporation, or when that didn't prove feasible, into a semi-autonomous entity governed by a special business board. Still answerable to Council, but allowed to act more independently to focus on making the money needed to fund the services. The businesses were still flagging, and this might pep them up.

Elin Tayyar, AMS VP-finance.

Pep: That's what the campus needs, said the *Ubyssey*. There's the giant pep rally on Imagine Day, but after that, nothing. Well, UBC is so immense, said AMS VP-administration Mike Silley: close to 48,000 students now. You have to find community in "small pockets," said VP-Academic Matt Parson. And if things get too stressful, said VP-External Katherine Tyson, then study.

But No, No, No, Said the *Ubyssey*: Where's the outrageousness, the eccentrics, the students planning to start their own businesses? (Wait, what?) And where's the Left? Gone except for the Animal Research protesters, who did succeed in getting UBC to release information on the number of experiments going on.

And We Even Lost Some Eccentric Touches: Brian Sullivan (the University's VP-students) moved on with his bowtie and Dave Tompkins (the longtime Speaker of Council) with his plaid shirt, and more sadly, Travis, the homeless man who'd hung out in the SUB for years, died this year, prompting students to leave flowers at his empty chair.

Travis, "the Old Man in the SUB," in his usual seat.

Disturbances in the Force: Minor ones mostly this year. Three UBC students got arrested for their part in the Vancouver hockey riot of 2011. Bike thefts were up, prompting the introduction of additional bike lockers and security measures. Bike sharing was talked of (something more than the purple and yellow communal bikes offered by the Bike Kitchen), but what arrived instead was car sharing.

And there was . . .

Separation, or Talk of Separation: The graduate students again, and this year also the Engineers, unhappy at the role the AMS played in negotiations over the new Engineering student centre. And the AMS itself went ahead and separated for real from CASA, the federal student lobbying group, despite the objections of AMS president McElroy: this after years of dropping down to associate status, deciding to leave, deciding to come back to associate status, and finally . . . gone. More money for provincial lobbying, some said, and there was talk of creating a provincial lobbying group, but it wasn't here quite yet.

A Year without Scandal? Well, perhaps a sort of scandal over Council's decision to raise the pay of the executives in the middle of the year. There were petitions and angry words. One member of the AMS Budget Committee resigned in protest. But it was all smoothed over, and the real long-lasting result was not so much the raise itself, but the way it was structured. Picking up on the notion of incentives, Council made part of the salary a bonus, or no, a restriction, a . . .

Performance Accountability Restriction (PAR), later to be renamed a Performance Accountability Incentive (PAI). Either way the idea was to exert Council control over the Executive by threatening to withhold this bonus/incentive/restriction if the Executive did wrong. People remembered the UN fiasco and the president who threatened to sue his own Council, and thought, This will stop that. And perhaps it did, but it led to other problems and eventually was done away with.

And Ground Was Broken for the New SUB: And there was talk of putting a giant slide in it (that never happened) and a brewery, or a brew pub (that was still being talked about some years later). Another consultant came and said, Change all the names of your food outlets: No more Pie R Squared or Honour Roll. Switch to Boom! Pizza and Peko Peko. Some cringed, but the new names seemed set to go ahead, at least for the moment.

AMS VP-administration Mike Silley digs in while other AMS executives and UBC officials look on at the ceremonial groundbreaking for the New SUB.

277

Rebranding and Other Changes: Speaking of new names, the UBC Bookstore tried to change its name to UBC Central, but after much pushback changed its mind. And the AMS was changing its logo again. And the Pendulum food outlet disappeared, because of the first stages of construction of the New SUB (though its menu went in part to the Gallery Lounge). And the University decided not to join the American NCAA athletic league, but SFU did, which meant . . .

No More Shrum Bowl. And to make matters worse for UBC football, they had to forfeit all their wins this year for using a technically ineligible player. But the women's volleyball team continued its winning ways, capturing another national title, and the *Ubyssey* was now reporting that UBC sports teams had won the most national titles of any university in the country.

And Japanese-Canadian students from 1942 who had been forced to give up their studies because of internment were granted honorary degrees after much discussion. And the University also created the CSI (Centre for Student Involvement) and advisors called ESPs (Enrolment Services Professionals). And because skateboarding was so popular there was talk of building a skatepark, and because there were still so many

commuter students the University introduced lounges ("collegia") for them, though took flak for not making them free. And there was a course called Sustainability 101, and solar-powered garbage cans (but the biodegradable cutlery from two years before turned out not to be biodegradable).

Where's Buchanan A? And students posted a video that went viral about things UBC says (like, "Is this Buchanan A?"). And they used electronic iClickers to participate in class, and played Angry Birds on their smartphones, and made fun of the music video called "Friday," and did spinning classes and an Undie Run, or took part in the Mr. Arts beauty pageant, or tried out apps for dating and for ordering food at AMS outlets.

Disturbances in the Force, Part II: There were problems with getting U-Passes for students on exchange from UBCO, the Sexual Assault Support Centre kept losing coordinators, and the editor of the *Ubyssey* had trouble doing his job because his cousin was president of the AMS: it was a very McElroy year. (Justin McElroy was the editor and Jeremy McElroy was the president.)

Selling the Lodge? And Art? The AMS went to referendum to sell Whistler Lodge, which had fallen on hard times and was becoming a drain on its finances. But the students said no (this time). But they said yes to selling off some of the AMS art collection because some pieces were expensive to insure and protect (but the sale did not happen).

And What Is the Quintessential UBC Experience? The *Ubyssey* did a survey in the form of a March Madness basketball bracket form sheet, asking students to pick their favourite—and beating out Block Party, construction, and giant puddles was Storm the Wall. Sleeping in class was in the mix too, and Pit Night, Imagine Day, Wreck Beach, and B-line bus pass-ups, but Storm the Wall, the thirty-year-old Intramurals competition, carried the day (though the editors noted this could have been influenced by the fact that Storm the Wall was going on during the survey; still . . .).

Charles Kadota, one of eleven surviving Japanese-Canadian students who were prevented from completing their degrees in 1942, receives an honorary degree from UBC president Toope.

2012 TO 2013

Construction as far as the eye can see: even the Goddess of Democracy had to move.

The Year of Ripping Everything Up: Construction to the right of us, construction to the left of us: how were people even to get around the campus? And the noise. And by the way, the disruption is keeping people from the Old SUB and hurting business there. There was a giant hole in the ground where the New SUB would go, and other construction projects were underway too, or about to start: upgrades to Main Mall and University Boulevard. A new alumni building.

And soon there would be a new Aquatic Centre where MacInnes Field used to be, and without a field where will Block Party go? And Welcome Back Barbecue? And we're losing trees and green space. This is not just the periphery; it's the very core of campus, said the *Ubyssey*. But it did concede that when the Martha Piper Fountain on Main Mall was finally done, it looked sort of nice.

The Year of Quiet Diplomacy: Not a year of protests. No shouting and marching: well, some students paraded outside the premier's office to protest pipelines, and there was a campus demonstration as part of the countrywide Idle No More campaign for Indigenous rights, and another to save the Music Library, but mostly the campus was quiet.

Which didn't mean the student leadership was idle; it was busy presenting reports and objections to the administration about everything from housing to creating an online exam database to lowering the tuition for the new Bachelor of International Economics degree. A lot of this work came from the office of AMS VP-academic Kiran Mahal, whom the *Ubyssey* described as "scarily competent."

They still didn't think she'd get the University to change its mind on anything, but they were wrong.

Kiran and her associate vice-president, Sean Cregten, also produced the first Academic Experience Survey of the students, confirming that students do indeed feel stress about money, course overload, and housing.

Kiran Mahal: "scarily competent."

Lifestyle Advice: Perhaps thinking to relieve the stress, the *Ubyssey* throughout the year ran helpful hints for their readers: save money by buying secondhand clothes at Value Village (and don't wear TOMS shoes). Don't waste time on New Year's resolutions: you're never going to eat better or start going to bed earlier ("No one does this"). Save money by living with your parents—or no, move out and learn to be independent.

Social Media: And the *Ubyssey* liked to talk about social media. Ban lap-

tops in the classroom so we don't get distracted and miss what the lecturer is saying, said one columnist. And it's so easy to get distracted: I'll just take a minute to see what's happening on Facebook and . . . uh oh.

But Don't Worry, the World Is Ending Anyway: The Mayan Calendar said so. Or we're going to have a zombie apocalypse. Even Margaret Atwood came to campus to talk about the zombie apocalypse. And there were zombie walks and that television show called *The Walking Dead*, prompting students around North America to organize "Walking Debt" demonstrations. The AMS planned one for Halloween.

Rapid Transit: The AMS External Office also worked on transit issues this year, helping create a Get On Board coalition to support increased funding for new SkyTrain lines, not even necessarily to UBC: the idea was, let's get funding increased generally by road tolls or bridge tolls or general taxation. But by the end of the year there was more and more agreement (from the City of Vancouver, for instance) that a line

to UBC would be a good thing. Only problem: who will pay for it?

Groups: Besides Get On Board, there was a group called Where's the Funding (cheekily abbreviated as WTF), which grew into a more general student group called the Alliance of BC Students (ABCS). Could this be the provincial lobbying organization the AMS was looking for?

Guess Who's Coming to UBC? Students with averages below 90%, now that the University had decided that broad-based admissions were the way to go: marks aren't everything. And students from non-traditional international locations and school systems, to go into a new special program called Vantage College.

And there was intercultural education and a plan to review athletics, and the AMS created the Business and Administration Governance Board (BAGB) to oversee its businesses, which unfortunately were still struggling. And it changed the Performance Accountability system for its executives from a restriction to an incentive, at least in name, try-

ing to switch to the carrot from the stick, but it was all a bit vague, and if the aim was to fulfill your goals, won't the executives stop setting ambitious goals?

And the students listened to Gangnam music and went to hear Bassnectar and dubstep at the Arena or Down with Webster at the Pit. Or they followed Shindig, CiTR's annual battle of the bands, or read CiTR's offbeat publication, the *Discorder*, which was celebrating its thirtieth anniversary. Or they used the new Vine app on their phones or countless other apps, some created by UBC students: there was even an app to shut down your other apps.

Or they did more athletic things, like Day of the Longboat (while listening to Gangnam music) or Zumba exercises (while listening to Latin music) or salsa dancing (also while listening to Latin music). Or they joined the wrestling team, which really wanted to be a Varsity sport but wasn't allowed to be; or they joined the Sailing Club or played Ultimate Frisbee (two other athletic endeavours not included in the UBC Varsity program).

Or they actually did take part in Varsity sports, which had quite a successful year. The women's volleyball team won their sixth straight title, and national titles also went to the women's field hockey team and the men's soccer team. The women's ice hockey team astonished everyone by making it to the national finals after finishing last the year before. And various student athletes took part in the London Olympics, including Inaki Gomez, a former AMS staff member, who competed in the 20k race walk.

And the Arts students voted for a new social space, and the Engineers came to an agreement with the University on who would run their social space, and the Commerce students wanted to invest in a University endowment fund (but AMS Council said wait a minute), and the talk now was that the proposed new brew pub would be a full-sized brewery and go not in the New SUB but in a new complex being built on the UBC Farm.

And the AMS started a panel discussion series called Bar Talk (pet project of President Matt Parson), and UBC president Toope announced his resignation, and the joint Food for Fines program continued, under which students could pay off their library fines by donat-

The annual Food for Fines campaign.

ing food to the AMS Food Bank—but why would there be any fines? Was anyone still borrowing books? (The libraries were increasingly moving their books into storage and opening up space for students to work in groups and use their laptops.)

And a UBC lecturer (Robert Gateman) got perhaps too involved in the AMS, sending his economics students off to find projects to work on, such as modifying the AMS fee for Athletics and Intramurals. It made AMS VP-finance Tristan Miller shake his head. And people kept pulling the fire alarm during Pit Night and passed their colds along by putting their germ-laden hands on bus poles (the buses should carry hand sanitizers, said someone in the *Ubyssey*). And Sprouts, the organic food store in the SUB, opened a branch in the Graduate Student Centre: Seedlings. And finally what about . . .

Spirit: There was the obligatory article in the *Ubyssey* lamenting the lack of student spirit, but this year one of the regular columnists (Gordon Katic) responded by saying he hated spirit: all that rah-rah groupthink

The new look of libraries at UBC: the Chapman Learning Commons in the Irving K. Barber Centre.

stuff. Screaming U-B-C as loud as you can: that's not spirit, he said.

Another columnist, in dealing with the Question—you know the Question, the What Are You Planning to Do question, asked by students' grandmothers and their parents' friends, to every student's great consternation . . . To answer that question he said, well, it sounds cheesy, but follow your inner voice.

AMS EXECUTIVE
2012-2013

PRESIDENT *Matt Parson*

VICE-PRESIDENT ACADEMIC
Kiran Mahal

VICE-PRESIDENT FINANCE
Tristan Miller

VICE-PRESIDENT ADMINISTRATION
Caroline Wong

VICE-PRESIDENT EXTERNAL
Kyle Warwick

UBYSSEY EDITOR *Jonny Wakefield*

2013 TO 2014

Uh Oh: The Commerce students got in trouble for a lewd chant at their Frosh event. As long as we did it in private, they said, we thought it was okay. Heads rolled. Two executives resigned from their positions. Pressured by the dean, some said. The dean also asked the Commerce Undergraduate Society to come up with $250,000 to hire a counsellor who might deal with the trauma of sexual violence, which in a way was prescient because this year also saw a string of . . .

Sexual Assaults: Half a Dozen of Them. The police stepped up their presence. The University pledged to improve lighting, trim foliage, and repair its emergency Blue Phone system. Safewalk, whose usage had been in decline, saw an exponential increase in demands for walks—or rides, as the service began a shift to using vehicles. The campus made the news, but for all the wrong reasons.

The Engineers of all people tried to lighten the mood by pulling off one of their let's-hang-a-Volkswagen-on-the-Clock-Tower stunts, but a pall hung over the campus, and some warned against an overreaction that could lead to the administration exerting too much control over student organizations.

Intersectionality: There was talk of rape culture, and when it emerged that there had been a second chant at the Commerce Frosh about Pocahontas, something seen as demeaning to Indigenous people, there was talk of needing to make systemic changes to address both gendered violence and Indigenous stereotypes.

Truth and Reconciliation: All this took place against the backdrop of the countrywide Truth and Reconciliation movement concerning the Indian Residential Schools. The University cancelled classes to encourage students to attend Truth and Reconciliation events, and the AMS lent its endorsement. But the mood was sombre or panicky.

And There Were Other Troubles: The New SUB was delayed and over budget. The University stirred up controversy with a review of its athletics program. They're going to cut football, some said. Or hockey. Or . . . But in the end it was only skiing and softball that got shifted to a new category of competitive sports club, and the University later backtracked on softball.

And someone fell off the partially built New SUB, and the AMS cut out free food at its Council meetings to save money, but actually its revenues did better than expected, and when a referendum to reorganize its fees passed, people thought maybe it will be all right. AMS businesses did not suffer as much as feared from construction around the SUB, but it turned out that this was because the largest construction project (building a new Aquatic Centre) was delayed till the following year, and when it finally began, uh oh.

TOP New SUB construction: someone fell down here.

BOTTOM The half-built New SUB.

But Wait Till We Get into the New Building: The New SUB will save us, AMS people said, though AMS VP-finance Joaquin Acevedo warned against thinking of it as the "holy grail."

And What Are We Going to Call This New Building? Isn't New SUB good enough? No, no, said the student staff, Brock Hall had a name, and so shall we. They conducted a naming process which led to two final candidates, neither of which stirred much enthusiasm at Student Council, but eventually, by a narrow margin, Council agreed to call their new home the AMS Student Nest (rejecting AMS Student Hub).

And Those Slides? No, no slides in the Nest. Insurance issues. Safety. Liability. And no brewery either, at least not in the Nest, but maybe at the Farm? But Council thought it was too risky and said no, so the brewery's supporters forced a referendum and the students said yes. So in principle there would be a brewery if there could be agreements and proper financial planning and . . . well, we would see.

And Whistler Lodge? Gone too, or almost. Council debated and decided it didn't want to continue subsidizing the money-losing operation. But it's a tradition, said some. Just a luxury sport, said others. Sad to see it go, said Phaidra Ruck, Councillor of the Year, but sometimes it's what you have to do. So it went, at least to referendum, and the students said okay, sell it, and it went up on the market.

And Mini School and the AMS Internship Program and the Outdoor Pool: It was time to say goodbye to those too. But perhaps the saddest goodbye, at least for regulars at AMS Council, was to . . .

Raj Mathur: For twenty years Raj, a former councillor, had attended Council meetings, every one, sitting in a corner, helping out by taking attendance. And then one day he stopped attending, and it turned out he had passed away. RIP, Raj.

Raj Mathur in his days as the Music representative on AMS Council.

But Koerner's Pub came back, and there was a food truck on campus, the first of many started up by the University, which wasn't necessarily a good thing for the AMS and its food outlets. And the University also opened a new Italian restaurant, Mercante, in the new Ponderosa Commons (a mix of housing, retail, and study space).

More Goodbyes: Two AMS executives (Kiran Mahal and Derek Moore) left in the middle of their terms, something almost unheard of in recent decades, and the name Boom! Pizza also made a premature departure, though in this case most people were happy. Let's stick to calling our pizza place Pie R Squared, said Council members and others; it's our persona.

Bottled Water and Fossil Fuels: Some people wanted to say goodbye to them. There was even a referendum calling on the AMS to urge

The Hungry Nomad: the first UBC food truck. But not the last.

UBC to divest from fossil fuels. There was also another referendum calling on the AMS to lobby for lower tuition fees. So a few sparks of activism, though the *Ubyssey* kept saying that the Left was gone and apathy ruled. Is there a culture of apathy? No, no, said a student from SFU (SFU?), it's just a culture of talking about apathy.

And on a Lighter Note: The AMS Hempology Club decided to put words into action and introduce a marijuana vaporizer into the SUB. They were supposed to just be about awareness, said AMS president Caroline Wong. Oh, well.

AMS EXECUTIVE
2013-2014

PRESIDENT *Caroline Wong*

VICE-PRESIDENT ACADEMIC
Kiran Mahal/Mona Maleki/Anne Kessler

VICE-PRESIDENT FINANCE
Joaquin Acevedo

VICE-PRESIDENT ADMINISTRATION
Derek Moore/Barnabas Caro/Ava Nasiri

VICE-PRESIDENT EXTERNAL
Tanner Bokor

UBYSSEY EDITOR *Geoff Lister*

2014 TO 2015

The Nest! The Nest! Finally, after years of planning and negotiating, delays in construction, and the appearance of Gus the Seagull as mascot, the New SUB, aka the AMS Student Nest, opened. The AMS moved from the suddenly shabby looking Old SUB to the spectacular new building next door, which quite dwarfed the Old SUB and everything else in the area.

The New SUB, dwarfing the Old, the edge of which can be seen on the right.

Protest! Maybe activism wasn't dead after all. First, some UBC students demonstrated in support of the Hong Kong pro-democracy protesters. But that was nothing compared to the furor that erupted when the University announced increases in tuition and residence fees. A new group was formed: I Am a Student. They sported red squares, emulating protesters in Quebec, and organized opposition. There was a teach-in. There was quorum at an AMS Annual General Meeting for the first time in nearly 40 years, and motions were passed opposing the increases and calling on the AMS to continue protesting until the increases were reversed. (But the increases went through and the protests faded away.)

TOP Supporters of the "umbrella protest" in Hong Kong decorated the Goddess of Democracy.

BOTTOM Students gather to talk about the proposed tuition and residence fee hikes.

More Furor: This time over the Middle East. A petition was circulated, forcing a referendum on boycotting Israeli products and divesting from Israeli companies, all as part of the worldwide BDS (Boycott, Divest, Sanction) campaign against Israel. The campus was divided. Council held a long and heated meeting. In the end, the referendum went forward, Council recommended that students vote no or abstain, and the question failed to reach quorum.

Even More Furor: Arvind Gupta was UBC president, then he wasn't. Rumours flew. What had happened? A professor speculated. The chair of the University's Board of Governors told her not to. The professor complained, then the Board chair resigned too. What is going on? AMS Council met and called for . . . stability. Stability? What would Stan Persky think?

Happier times: UBC president Arvind Gupta takes the ice bucket challenge with AMS president Tanner Bokor, in support of research on ALS. Imagine Day 2014.

And a Little Bit More Protest: UBCC350, the group behind the fossil fuel divestment referendum the year before, this year got the Faculty Association to sign on too, and convinced AMS Council to commit to lobbying the Board of Governors to get rid of its fossil fuel holdings.

Transit: The AMS endorsed the provincial referendum on raising taxes to improve transit, but it failed. Students continued to get passed up. Some people fraudulently sold their U-Pass cards (don't do that, said the AMS), but it became impos-

sible anyway with the arrival of the new Compass card system. The *Ubyssey* helpfully advised students to move to the back of the (crowded) buses: and please don't blast your loud Katy Perry music through your headphones.

Speaking of music, where were Block Party and the Welcome Back Barbecue to go now that their former home, MacInnes Field, was just a big hole in the ground? The AMS made do with a reduced Back Yard Barbecue near the Old SUB, then used a parking lot in the Health Sciences part of campus. People still had fun, but . . .

The last Block Party at the old MacInnes Field.

How About if We Make a Really Tall Building Out of Wood? The University decided to do this, setting a record for the tallest wooden building in the world (eighteen storeys). It was meant to create more student housing on campus, which would be useful because the total student population was almost at fifty thousand and there were students being put up temporarily in residence lounges: it's 2001 all over again.

UBC's tall wood building.

Whistler Lodge was sold for over a million dollars, and AMS Council got more serious about relations with the Musqueam, listening to a talk on the history of the Musqueam presence in what was now the campus, and deciding to begin every Council meeting with an acknowledgement that it was taking place on unceded Musqueam territory. And when a student showed up at Block Party wearing a native headdress, the AMS issued a press release saying not to do that. No more cultural appropriation.

And When Not Protesting, What Were Students Up To? Playing eSports like DOTA and League of Legends, joining a club about the hit television show *Game of Thrones*, brewing their own beer in the brewing club (BrUBC) and hoping the brewery would come to campus.

Also posting complaints and self-deprecating comments on the *UBC Confessions* Facebook page, talking to the professor in residence at Totem Park, or attending Frosh events that were all renamed to take away the memory of the unpleasant events at the Commerce Frosh the year before.

And some of them (or were these outsiders?) got lost and drove their cars down campus steps, and some raced the Dean of Applied Science in a 2k "Turkey Trot" to raise money for charity, and others made friends with the UBC coyote.

But what a lot of them weren't doing was using the campus recycling bins properly. Are they intimidated by all the options, a *Ubyssey* writer wondered? Just lazy? Confused? Some seem to approach the bins shamefacedly as they dumped all their scraps into the not-for-recycling bin, so it's not as if they didn't know about sustainability. Maybe they were just tired of multiple choice questions.

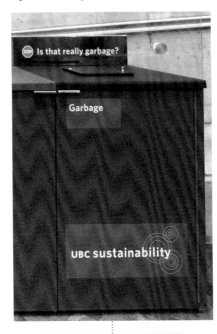

Why are we getting a pop quiz when we're not even in class? This is so confusing.

Carter, the campus coyote.

POSTSCRIPT AFTER 100

Looking Ahead: And so they moved into their new building and a new century, with a new logo, but tried something very old: reviving school spirit, though perhaps with more success than usual. Hanging football banners in the Nest and talking of sending Council members out to classrooms to talk about the AMS.

AMS president Aaron Bailey and VP-Administration Ava Nasiri cut the ribbon for the official opening of the Nest while UBC president Martha Piper *(far left)* and other dignitaries look on. Also present: Dialog architect Joost Bakker *(second from left)*, UBC VP-students Louise Cowin *(second from right)*, and John Metras, managing director of UBC Infrastructure Development *(far right)*.

A new brand for a new century.

Construction Will Always Be with You: The big hole where MacInnes Field used to be was gradually filled with the new Aquatic Centre, and a new housing development for faculty and staff went up across from the Shoppers Drug Mart, with surprisingly little protest, but this was perhaps still a non-protesting era.

And the Alumni Got Their Very Own Building: Their Brock Hall if you like, though they named it after Robert H. Lee, a former UBC chancellor. And they became neighbours to the AMS Nest.

Lest We Forget: The Old SUB was still there, largely handed over to the University, but with some parts of it still reserved for the AMS.

What Else? There were tuition increases and AMS objections, some of which the University even listened to. And the University promised to improve fitness facilities and upgrade the War Memorial Gym, or would that old building have to go? The General Services Administration Building went, as had the old law school a few years before: removing some of the evidence of the brutalist period in UBC architecture.

Growth: And the student body exceeded fifty thousand, and there were more than four hundred clubs, and the AMS kept coming up with new services, like Vice to deal with addictions, and eHub to encourage

The Alumni Centre *(right)* and the Nest *(left)*: The former students and the current ones were now right next door to each other.

entrepreneurship. And there was talk of a service to transport people with disabilities around campus (in golf carts?), and there was already an umbrella sharing service (why hadn't anyone thought of that before?), and a dog therapy service: come pet a dog and ease your stress.

Faculty Cup: An old inter-faculty competition from decades before was revived, and there were other revivals and resurrections, such as . . .

The Gallery Lounge: Bring back the Gal, students said when it disappeared along with the Old SUB. And when the Perch, the high-end dining establishment at the top of the Nest, didn't work out, the AMS replaced it with Gallery 2.0.

Martha Piper: Yes, she was back too, temporarily, until the University could find a new permanent president: Santa Ono.

The Honour Roll: This came back too, as the old/new name for the AMS sushi place, replacing Peko Peko. And beside it a new AMS bubble tea establishment named Ph Tea, reviving the AMS tradition of intellectual puns.

The GSS: The graduate students were talking about separating from the AMS again, and the Engineers' new building opened. The students in Kinesiology almost followed in the footsteps of the Commerce students by voting to pay for what would largely have been a University building, but then the building didn't go ahead.

Agora: That was going to be the name of the central space in the Nest, but the Agora Cafe run by the students in Land and Food said, That will be a problem, so the Nest Agora became the Atrium.

Block Party and the Welcome Back Barbecue were still looking for permanent homes. They tried Thunderbird Stadium, but that didn't really work out. Perhaps when the new MacInnes Field comes back . . .

Restructuring: Yes, the AMS was at it still, largely reversing the restructuring of previous years. Executives went back to chairing committees, the Oversight Committee and the Performance Accountability Incentive were retired, to no one's dismay. Ditto for the Agenda Committee, but there was some regret over the loss of Unecorn (the University and External Relations Committee, replaced by a new body called the Advocacy Committee). And after forty years SAC was gone too.

ABBA: Musical whimsy in part led to the renaming of the Business and Administration Governance Board (BAGB), but the name ABBA (the Advisory Board for Business and Administration) did not look set to survive long either. And the division of the AMS into business and student sides was at least partially reversed, and there were shake-ups and reshufflings.

And there were apps and more apps, and software programs, some of which worked and some which, oh, well . . .

And there was talk of a Fall Reading break, and more and more students were taking five years to finish their four-year degrees. And there were bike raves and slacklines and Asian night markets; and bike thefts were down (perhaps because people were being more careful locking their bikes) and students wore hoodies,

That four-year degree might take you longer.

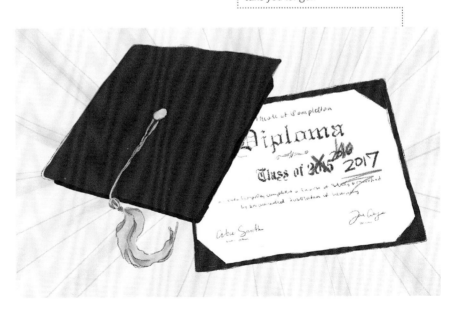

caught colds, and ate sushi. And studied and partied and worried and had fun.

In fact, the second century of students at UBC looked to be much like the first, except of course where it was completely different: For instance, the students decided that . . .

A Cairn Shall Lead Them: In the election of 2017, people found the presidential candidates on offer to be rather lacklustre, so much so that a movement arose in the middle of the voting to have one of the joke candidates, the Engineers' Cairn, become a serious candidate. There was a real person behind the Cairn, of course, just as there'd been a real person behind the Fire Hydrant years before.

And this time the real person, Alan Ehrenholz, emerged from behind his inanimate object and actually won the election, perhaps because he was in fact a respected veteran of AMS politics, having served on AMS Council and been president of the Engineering Undergraduate Society.

Alan Ehrenholz, aka the Engineers' Cairn.

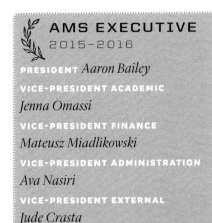

AMS EXECUTIVE
2015–2016

PRESIDENT *Aaron Bailey*

VICE-PRESIDENT ACADEMIC
Jenna Omassi

VICE-PRESIDENT FINANCE
Mateusz Miadlikowski

VICE-PRESIDENT ADMINISTRATION
Ava Nasiri

VICE-PRESIDENT EXTERNAL
Jude Crasta

UBYSSEY EDITOR *Will McDonald*

AMS EXECUTIVE
2016–2017

PRESIDENT *Ava Nasiri*

VICE-PRESIDENT ACADEMIC
Samantha So

VICE-PRESIDENT FINANCE *Louis Retief*

VICE-PRESIDENT ADMINISTRATION
Chris Scott

VICE-PRESIDENT EXTERNAL
Kathleen Simpson

UBYSSEY EDITOR *Jack Hauen*

AMS EXECUTIVE
2017–2018

PRESIDENT *Alan Ehrenholz*

VICE-PRESIDENT ACADEMIC
Daniel Lam/Jakob Gattinger/ Max Holmes

VICE-PRESIDENT FINANCE
Alim Lakhiyalov

VICE-PRESIDENT ADMINISTRATION
Pooja Bhatti

VICE-PRESIDENT EXTERNAL *Sally Lin*

UBYSSEY EDITOR *Jack Hauen*

AFTERWORD

In the introduction to this book I suggested that though many things have changed over the course of the University's first century, many things have remained the same. This is true, but with a qualification. As I also say in the introduction, there was a big watershed moment during the hundred years, happening oddly enough right at the halfway mark.

It's true that the students were always concerned about tuition fees and rent increases, and were always pitching in to provide new facilities and services. But something essential did change at the halfway point. The sixties happened, and with them a culture change (a counter-cultural change, if you will) and a change in the political dynamic of the University.

Before 1965, the students prided themselves on their self-government, or autonomy, but it was a somewhat limited autonomy. Especially in the very early years, the Senate and the Faculty Council could veto decisions made by the AMS. Moreover, the autonomy often seemed to mean only that the University let the AMS decide how to carry out directions from on high. There's too much noise in the library, the University would say, leaving it to AMS Council to pass motions telling students to keep quiet. It was something like a junior partner situation, with the AMS as willing lieutenant.

Of course, there was sometimes disagreement, but on the whole, for its first half century the AMS was rather like Canada in relation to Great Britain circa 1920: with internal autonomy, but subject to British oversight and deferring to the mother country on issues like foreign policy.

But then 1965 happened. The students rose up, and won not just a more complete autonomy for the AMS within its own jurisdiction, but a say in running the whole University: seats on Senate and the Board of Governors, on faculty and departmental committees, and so on. It's as if Canada had won the right to elect members of the British House of Commons.

The University after 1965 became a different sort of place, and the AMS became a more powerful, self-confident organization, even branching into business, and offering an array of services unheard of in earlier years. So although there were continuities, something fundamental did change fifty years on. Student concerns remained similar in some ways (tuition, residence fees, etc.), but student power expanded. Never enough to satisfy the radicals, but enough to say that though it is possible to succumb to a shock of recognition when looking at events from a century ago, on the whole a student transported from the University in 1915 to the University a hundred years later would suffer more from the shock of the new.

At least a student leader would. Perhaps a regular student would find less difference. Dress was more casual, there was less public mischief, musical tastes had changed, and everyone would be carrying strange mobile devices, but it was still study, study, study, play, play, play. The surface was changed, the very buildings were changed, the student body was larger and more diverse, but in essence the student experience was perhaps as it had always been.

And yet even for the ordinary student the atmosphere had changed: religion had faded, and other ideologies such as feminism had gained ground. Sustainability was the watchword, and there was respect for Indigenous culture rather than appropriation of it. One might say there was a more liberal ethos on campus, as in Canadian society more generally.

And though most students in 2015 did not bother with such things, it would not have seemed strange to them to know that there were student representatives on the University's governing bodies, and they took for granted the idea that their views were to be taken into account on teaching evaluation forms. The student role was not quite what it had been a hundred years before; 2015 was not 1915; and perhaps that was largely because of what had started in 1965.

The most telling example of this, perhaps, was at the very end of 2014–15 when in the midst of the uproar over the resignation of the UBC president, with the Faculty Association calling for the resignation of the chair of the Board of Governors, AMS Council, the body representing the students, called for stability. Yes, the heirs of the student radicals of the sixties were not talking liberation; they were calling for things to settle down. Amusing, one might say. A complete reversal of the sixties—and yet not really. For without the sixties and the change in the student role at the University, would Council have even have thought to comment?

So there you have it: student life at UBC from 1915 to 2015 (and beyond), and after student life, well, of course . . .

ACKNOWLEDGEMENTS

In 2011, then AMS president Jeremy McElroy proposed the idea of writing a history book to mark the one hundredth anniversary of the AMS (the student society at the University of British Columbia Vancouver). It seemed like a daunting idea at first, but a later AMS president, Caroline Wong, came up with an excellent suggestion for how to organize a century's material: do it year by year. And so now we have this year-by-year account.

Helping with the account were the assistants who scoured the pages of the *Ubyssey* newspaper looking for material: Emily Booth, Heather Muckart, Roxanne Kalenborn, Nicole Satchell, Alan Woo, Farah Tarannum, and Momoko Hirano.

Other assistants (Victoria Gomez, Melissa Enns, and Yu Su) kept the Archives running while the archivist was writing, and still others (Fraser Sutherland, Lindsay Peloquin, and Melissa Martin) provided yeoman service scanning photographs to accompany the text. Lindsay and Melissa also assisted greatly in tracking down photographers and cartoonists for permissions, as did Viktorie van Deursen in the UBC Development and Alumni Engagement Office.

Also providing invaluable assistance in scanning photographs was Candice Bjur of the University's Archives, which provided a great many of the photographs found in this book. My thanks to the University archivist, Chris Hives, for his assistance in facilitating this.

Thanks as well to past and present staff in the AMS Communications department, including Lori McNulty, Kris Anderson, Anthony Incardona, Abby Blinch, and Jollean Willington (who came up with the line "More peepers than streakers" to describe the streaking episode in the 1970s). Also to Daniel Levangie, the former AMS executive director, who made the suggestion to divide the book into decades; to Ken Yih, the AMS senior human resources manager; and to Keith Hester, the AMS managing director. And to last year's AMS president, Ava Nasiri, who lit sparklers to mark the book deal with Heritage House, and to this year's president, Alan Ehrenholz, for all his enthusiastic support. Also to Lara Kordić and Leslie Kenny of Heritage House, who have seen the book through the press.

Herbert Rosengarten and Eric Damer, the authors of the University's own centennial history, were generous with advice about managing such a project, and their book provided much useful background material.

Vanessa Clarke very enthusiastically printed excerpts from the book in *Trek*, the UBC alumni magazine, and Alumni UBC provided research assistance and funding. A special thanks to Alumni UBC's Fred Lee for his help in promoting the book, and thanks as well to the UBC Centennial Fund for its generous grant.

The *Ubyssey*'s Will McDonald, Fernie Pereira, Jack Hauen, Gerald Deo, and Geoff Lister kindly helped out with photographs, as did the Ubyssey Alumni Association, and I'd like to specially thank Tom Hawthorn, Saturn Seven Beynon, and Berton Woodward for helping locate photographers and cartoonists. Thanks should also certainly go to the *Ubyssey* itself, the main source for much of the story in this book.

Patrick Meehan provided a copy of *The Chuck Davis History of Metropolitan Vancouver*, which provided a useful model for a year-by-year history.

My girlfriend, Roberta Haas, read various parts of the manuscript along the way, offering suggestions and encouragement, as did several others: Hilary Reid, Patrick McDonagh, Sebastien de Castell, Donna Hilton, Morgan Pendleton, and of course my mother and sisters, Marilyn Goldfarb, Beverly Goldfarb, and Sylvia Goldfarb. Thanks also to the Vancouver Writers Social Group for their support during the process of writing.

Finally, to all the staff at the AMS who helped in the course of this unexpectedly long journey, to the AMS Council members who appreciated snippets when shared with them at Council meetings, and to all the students past and present whose story this is, thank you and enjoy.

SHELDON GOLDFARB
October 2017

IMAGE CREDITS

BACK COVER

Students occupy the unfinished science building, 1922, Ab Richards Photograph Album, UBC Archives Photograph Collection [UBC 156.1/149]

FRONT COVER, CLOCKWISE FROM TOP LEFT

Smoking cigars, 1922–23, Albert E. Richards fonds [UBC 158.1/021]; Protestors at Wreck Beach, 1973–74, Information Services fonds, UBC Archives [UBC 41.1/54-1]; Freshmen, 1938–39, UBC Historical Photograph Collection, UBC Archives [UBC 1.1/12149]; Apec protestors, Richard Lam, *The Ubyssey*, 1997; Goddess of Democracy, Cherihan Hassun, *The Ubyssey*, 2014/10/6; Soldiers-in-training, *The Totem*, 1942; Protesting the Olympics, 2010, Michael Thibault, 2010/3/8

AMS ANNUAL

15 (top right), 1916; **18 (bottom)**, 1921; **18 (top)**, 1918

AMS ARCHIVES

17; **19**, DI: 8644; **28**, DI: 1073; **32**, S.J. Rowman, DI: 8651; **33 (left)**, S.J. Rowman, DI: 8651; **34**, DI: 392; **40 (bottom right)**, Bridgman Studio, DI: 8654; **40 (top right)**, Bridgman Studio, DI: 8654; **43 (left)**; **43 (right)**, Bridgman Studio, DI: 8655; **48 (top right)**, DI: 3990; **50 (left)**, "Song Book"; **52 (top)**, DI: 8658; **54 (bottom right)**; **54 (top)**, DI: 8662; **57 (far right)**, John Tyrell, DI: 5452; **57 (middle)**; **58**, DI: 366; **64 (bottom)**, DI: 5480; **64 (top)**, DI: 5497; **76 (bottom)**, J.C. Walberer, DI: 8673; **83 (top)**, J.C. Walberer, DI: 8673; **84**, DI: 8675; **85**, J.C. Walberer, DI: 8674; **86 (top)**, DI: 1818; **87 (top)**, DI: 100; **88 (right)**, DI: 203; **89 (bottom)**, Krass Studio, DI: 8676; **92 (bottom left)**; **92 (top)**, DI: 8677; **94 (bottom)**, DI: 974; **95 (bottom)**, Campbell Studios, DI: 8678; **95 (top)**, Campbell Studios, DI: 8678; **96**, Polyfoto, DI: 8679; **97 (bottom)**, Polyfoto, DI: 8679; **101 (bottom)**, DI: 354; **101 (top)**, DI: 354; **103**, Campbell Studios, DI: 8681; **104**, "Report on the Results of Competition for a Student Union Building at UBC" (1964 Architectural Competition); **111 (top left)**, Campbell Studios, DI: 8683; **112 (top)**, Campbell Studios, DI: 8684; **121 (bottom)**, Campbell Studios, DI: 8688; **121 (top)**, Artona Group, DI: 8687; **125 (bottom)**, DI: 678; **131 (bottom)**, DI: 3663; **131 (top)**, DI: 6314; **135 (top right)**, DI: 8691; **136**; **141 (bottom left)**, Campbell Studios, DI: 8692; **141 (top left)**, Campbell Studios; **147 (top right)**, DI: 516; **148 (bottom)**, D.H.H. Visser, DI: 1883; **150 (bottom left)**, DI: 6318; **150 (top left)**, DI: 4309; **153 (bottom)**; 159 (bottom right), DI: 606; **163**

(right), DI: 5270; **164 (top)**, DI: 5950; **168**, DI: 5659; **176 (bottom)**, DI: 192; **179 (bottom right)**, Jim Banham, DI: 304; **179 (middle)**, DI: 4; **180 (top right)**, DI: 1750; **181**, Peter Menyasz, DI: 963; **183 (bottom)**; **183 (top)**, DI: 3306; **184 (top left)**, DI: 1604; **185 (bottom left)**, Rory Allen, DI: 1331; **186 (bottom)**, Steve Chan, DI: 1799; **186 (middle)**, Peter Menyasz, DI: 205; **187 (bottom right)**, DI: 1705; **188 (left)**, DI: 5679; **189 (right)**, DI: 5669; **193**, Neil Lucente, DI: 1710; **194 (top)**, DI: 5689; **196 (top)**, DI: 4306; **200 (bottom)**, DI: 2192; **202 (middle far right)**, DI: 89; **202 (top left)**, DI: 1875; **202 (top right)**, DI: 62; **203 (top)**, Neil Lucente, DI: 1731; **204 (bottom right)**, DI: 1265; **204 (top left)**, DI: 1226; **205 (top)**, DI: 1826; **206 (bottom)**, DI: 1567; **206 (top left)**, Steve Chan, DI: 3291; **207**, Jennifer Lyall (?), DI: 741; **208**, Pat Nakamura, DI: 1808; **209 (middle)**, DI: 3353; **212**, David Loh, DI: 3395; **214 (bottom)**, Artona Group, DI: 8701; **214 (top)**, Artona Group, DI: 8701; **215 (middle)**, Artona Group, DI: 8701; **215 (right)**, DI: 603; **216 (left)**, Don Mah, DI: 1698; **216 (top)**, DI: 967; **220**, DI: 5331; **222 (top)**, DI: 4471; **225 (top)**, DI: 3315; **226 (bottom)**, Artona Group, DI: 2895; **233 (bottom left)**, DI: 987; **233 (right)**, Chris Nuttall-Smith, DI: 1015; **233 (top)**, DI: 623; **234 (left)**, DI: 5302; **234 (right)**; **238 (bottom left)**, DI: 3018; **238 (top left)**, DI: 3016; **239 (bottom right)**, Artona Group, DI: 8706; **239 (bottom left)**, Artona Group, DI: 9707; **240 (right)**, Artona Group, DI: 2451; **243 (bottom right)**, DI: 5698; **244 (bottom)**, DI: 3965; **244 (top)**, DI: 4520; **246 (top right)**, Artona Group, DI: 8713; **248 (top)**, Artona Group, DI: 8713; **250 (top)**, Artona Group, DI: 7845; **251 (bottom)**; **252 (bottom right)**, DI: 4171; **252 (left)**; **252 (top)**, Artona Group, DI: 7854; **253 (bottom)**, Kellan Higgins [DSC4885, insider2006]; **258 (left)**, Artona Group, DI: 7920; **258 (top left)**; **259 (bottom)**, Kellan Higgins [insider2006, 6769]; **261 (top)**, DI: 5277; **264 (middle)**, DI: 7439; **264 (top)**, Artona Group, DI: 8038; **265 (bottom right)**; **267 (bottom)**, Gerald Deo; **268 (left)**, DI: 6837; **268 (right)**, Artona Group, DI: 8085; **271 (right)**; **276 (right)**, Artona Group, DI: 8131; **279 (bottom)**, Artona Group, DI: 8466; **282 (bottom)**; **283 (middle)**, Artona Group, DI: 2706; **287 (top)**; **289**

CAMPUS TIMES

222 (middle), Reid, 1993/2; **219 (bottom left)**, 1992/9/8; **228 (left)**, 1994/11/2

INDIVIDUALS

11, Ema Peter; **217**, Paul Joseph; **239 (top left)**, Daniel Lins; **253 (top)**, Kellan Higgins; **256**, Ema Peter; **264 (bottom)**, David Zhang; **269**, Josh Beharry; **281 (top)**, Paul Joseph; **282 (top)**, Michael Kingsmill; **283 (top)**, Paul Joseph; **284 (left)**, Ema Peter; **285 (middle)**, Gerald Deo; **285 (top)**, Paul Joseph; **286 (bottom)**, Justin Lee; **286 (top)**, Paul Joseph; **287 (bottom)**, Paul Joseph; **287 (left)**, Geoff Lister; **291**, Goh Iromoto, Trevor Melanson

MCGILL ANUUAL

16 (top left), Walter John, 1912–13

MISCELLANEOUS

20 (bottom right), Napoleon Sarony, WC; **83 (middle)**, WC; **112 (bottom)**, NASA, WC; **142 (top, left to right)**: Cédric Thévenet, WC/ Postal drop box, Montreal, 1971, Harryzilber, WC/Red Guard, source unknown/Joan Baez, Hamburg Germany, 1973, Heinrich Klaffs, WC/The Fabs, 1964, US Library of Congress, Prints and Photographs division, DI: cph.3c11094/Maharishi Mahesh Yogi, MUM, Iowa, 1979, WC/Kerensky vs Lenin, source unknown/Timothy Leary, 1969, Roy Kerwood, WC; **163 (left)**, Archives New Zealand, WC; **173**, source unknown; **225**, WC

THE TOTEM

15 (top middle), 1966; **36 (top)**, 1927; **46 (bottom)**, 1950; **47 (bottom left)**, 1931; **53 (right)**, 1933; **67 (bottom)**, Pierre Berton, 1940; **69 (left)**, 1941; **69 (right)**, 1941; **71**, 1942; **114 (bottom)**, 1959; **120 (right)**, Dean Gregory, 1961; **129 (left)**, 1963; **135 (bottom right)**

THE UBICEE

22 (top)

THE UBYSSEY

20 (bottom left), 1918/10/17; 25 (bottom right), 1922/2/9; 29 (bottom), 1922/11/09; 37 (left), 1926/01/15; 44 (top), 1929/03/08; 47 (bottom right), 1930/10/03; 48 (top left), 1930/11/07; 50 (right), W. Tavender, 1932/02/05; 56 (bottom left), J. Davidson, 1934/11/20; 56 (bottom right), 1934/10/09; 57 (top middle), 1935/01/25; 67 (right), 1940/01/26; 68 (bottom), 1941/03/28; 70 (bottom left), 1952/02/11; 75 (left), 1943/12/03; 87 (bottom), Gordon Dowding, 1948/10/13; 115 (bottom), 1959/020/19; 118 (bottom), 1959/10/27; 118 (top left), 1959/10/23; 118 (top right), 1959/09/29; 119 (top), 1959/11/5; 120 (left), 1960/2/26; 125 (top), 1962/2/20; 129 (right), 1962/10/2; 132, 1964/1/17; 135 (left), Jeff Wall, 1964/10/29; 138, 1967/2/10; 141 (middle), 1966/1/27; 142 (middle), Arn Saba, 1965/9/24; 144, 1967/1/26; 145 (top), Arn Saba, 1968/2/13; 146 (bottom left), 1966/10/14; 146 (bottom right), Rae Moster, 1967/10/19; 147 (top left), 1968/2/29; 152 (bottom left), 1969/10/1; 152 (right), John Kula, 1970/1/27; 152 (top), 1969/11/14; 153 (top), 1970/1/27; 155 (top left), 1970/9/29; 162 (bottom left), 1974/3/26; 162 (bottom right), 1973/9/18; 165, 1975/2/20; 170 (right), 1975/12/2; 170 (top), Dave Wilkinson, 1976/2/13; 171 (bottom right), John Kula, 1975/9/5; 171 (left); 171 (top right), John Kula, 1975/9/5; 174 (bottom), Dave Hancock,

1977/2/24; 174 (top left), Bob Krieger, 1976/9/23; 175 (top right), Bob Krieger, 1976/9/17; 177 (middle), Verne McDonald, 1978/3/16; 177 (top left), 1977/9/13; 177 (top right), Verne McDonald, 1978/1/31; 178 (bottom left), 1978/2/17; 178 (top left), 1979/2/13; 178 (top right), 1980/9/16; 179 (bottom left), 1979/3/6; 179 (top right), 1979/1/23; 185 (bottom right), Mulhall, 1980/11/18; 185 (top), Ron Deiss, 1980/9/11; 187 (middle left), Verne McDonald, 1981/9/24; 190 (middle), Robby Robertson, 1982/10/1; 190 (top), Robby Robertson, 1982/10/26; 191 (bottom), 1983/2/22; 191 (middle), Victor Wong, 1983/1/11; 191 (top), Victor Wong, 1982/11/12; 192, Saidock, 1983/11/25; 194 (bottom), 1992/2/25; 194 (middle), Yaku, 1985/3/8; 195 (bottom left), 1985/4/3; 195 (bottom right), Dave Hancock, 1985/9/10; 195 (top), 1984/10/10; 196 (bottom), 1984/9/14; 198, 1989/9/6; 200 (top), Kelly Smith; 201 (bottom), 1986/3/11; 201 (middle right), 1985/11/22; 201 (top left), 1986/10/28; 201 (top right), 1985/11/22; 202 (middle left), 1986/1/28; 202 (middle bottom), 1985/11/5; 204 (bottom left), 1986/9/9; 205 (bottom), 1987/2/6; 209 (left), 1988/9/7; 210, 1988/11/4; 215 (left), 1991/1/29; 218, 1991/11/29; 219 (bottom right), 1991/10/22; 219 (top left), 1992/3/6; 219 (top right), 1992/1/7; 224, 1993/11/26; 230, Jeremy Beaulne, 1999/11/23; 232 (left), 1996/1/12; 237 (top), Richard

Lam, 1997; 239 (middle right), Jeremy Beaulne, 1999/1/15; 240 (left), Jeremy Beaulne, 1999/1/29; 242 (left), Tara Westover Wren, 1999/11/26; 243 (bottom left), Jeremy Beaulne, 1999/9/28; 243 (far right), 1999/11/23; 243 (top), Jeremy Beaulne, 1999/10/5; 246 (bottom), 2001/8/15; 246 (top left), 2001/9/14; 248 (bottom), 2003/9/14; 250 (bottom), 2003/11/5; 261 (left), courtesy of UBC Campus and Community Planning, 2006/10/17; 262, Kellan Higgins; 263 (bottom), Kellan Higgins, 2006/9/12; 263 (right), 2006/11/28; 263 (top), Kellan Higgins; 265 (bottom left), Kellan Higgins; 265 (top), courtesy of Sauder School of Business, 2008/3/18; 267 (top), 2009/1/30; 270 (bottom), Gerald Deo, 2010/2/15; 270 (top), Gerald Deo, 2009/11/30; 271 (left), Gerald Deo, 2010/3/1; 272, Michael Thibault, 2010/3/8; 273 (left), Gerald Deo, 2010/1/7; 273 (right), Geoff Lister, 2010/3/8; 274 (left), Indiana Joel, 2010/11/22; 274 (right), Virginie Ménard, 2011/3/14; 275 (bottom), Geoff Lister, 2011/10/27; 276 (left), Geoff Lister; 277 (left), 2012/2/13; 277 (right), Geoff Lister, 2012/2/13; 279 (top), Yara van Kessel, 2012/5/13; 280, Carter Brundage, 2012/10/3; 281 (bottom), 2012/10/29; 284 (middle), Will McDonald, 2014/10/14; 284 (top), Cherihan Hassun, 2014/10/6; 285 (left), Mackenzie Walker, 2014/9/2; 288, Aiken Lao, 2015/8/26; 202 (middle top), 1985/10/4

UBC ARCHIVES

ii, Dominion Photo Co., UBC Historical Photograph Collection [UBC 1.1/862]; iv, Leonard Cox, Leonard Cox fonds [UBC 72.1//11]; **10 (top)**, UBC Historical Photograph Collection [UBC 1.1/1375]; **12**, UBC Historical Photograph Collection [UBC 1.1/1314]; **14 (left)**, UBC Calendar 1915–16; **14 (right)**, Blythe Eagles fonds [UBC 11.1/10-3]; **15 (bottom left)**, UBC Historical Photograph Collection [UBC 1.1/5739-3]; **15 (bottom)**, UBC Historical Photograph Collection [UBC 1.1/1373]; **16 (bottom)**, Albert E. Richards fonds [UBC 158.1/098]; **16 (top right)**, UBC Historical Photograph Collection [UBC 1.1/2295]; **21 (bottom)**, Blythe Eagles fonds [UBC 11.1/9-5]; **21 (top)**, Arthur Evan Boss fonds [UBC 156.1/013]; **22 (bottom left)**, Alumni Association fonds [UBC 93.1/571]; **22 (bottom right)**, Arthur Evan Boss fonds [UBC 156.1/016]; **23 (bottom)**, Regan and McMillan, UBC Historical Photograph Collection [UBC 1.1/15825-8]; **23 (top)**, Arthur Evan Boss fonds [UBC 156.1/197]; **24 (bottom)**, Bridgman Studio, UBC Historical Photograph Collection [UBC 1.1/16074]; **24 (middle)**, Blythe Eagles fonds [UBC 11.1/9-2]; **24 (top)**, Arthur Evan Boss fonds [UBC 156.1/081]; **25 (bottom left)**, Geo T. Wadds photography, UBC Historical Photograph Collection [UBC 1.1/9741]; **26 (bottom right)**, Albert E. Richards fonds [UBC 158.1/036]; **26 (left)**, Regan and McMillan, UBC Historical Photograph Collection [UBC 1.1/9741]; **26 (middle right)**, Albert E. Richards fonds [UBC 158.1/021]; **26 (top right)**, Albert E. Richards fonds [UBC 158.1/030]; **27 (bottom left)**, Albert E, Richards fonds [UBC 158.1/057]; **27 (bottom right)**, Albert E. Richards fonds [UBC 158.1/055]; **27 (top)**, Albert E. Richards fonds [UBC 158.1/047]; **29 (middle left)**, Ab Richards Photograph Album, UBC Archives Photograph Collection [UBC 156.1/149]; **29 (middle right)**, Dominion Photo Co., UBC Historical Photograph Collection [UBC 1.1/862]; **29 (top)**, Arthur Evan Boss fonds [UBC 156.1/149]; **30 (bottom left)**, National Film Board of Canada, Norman Mackenzie fonds [UBC 23.1/532]; **30 (bottom right)**, Alumni Association fonds [UBC 93.1/188]; **30 (top)**, UBC Historical Photograph Collection [UBC 1.1/4916-1]; **31 (bottom left)**, Regan and McMillan, UBC Historical Photograph Collection [UBC 1.1/15825-6]; **31 (bottom right)**, UBC Historical Photograph Collection [UBC 1.1/519]; **31 (middle right)**, Alumni Association fonds [UBC 93.1/576]; **31 (top left)**, Albert E. Richards fonds [UBC 158.1/086]; **31 (top right)**, Albert E. Richards fonds [UBC 158.1/076]; **33 (bottom right)**, UBC Historical Photograph Collection [UBC 1.1/2305]; **33 (middle right)**, UBC Historical Photograph Collection [UBC 1/7368]; **33 (top right)**, Blythe Eagles fonds [UBC 11.1/9-1]; **36 (bottom)**, donated by Jason Vanderhill [UBC 178.1/1]; **37 (bottom right)**, Stuart Thomson, UBC Historical Photograph Collection [UBC 1.1/1245]; **37 (top right)**, John Owen fonds, [UBC 103.1/3]; **38**, Leonard Frank, UBC Historical Photograph Collection [UBC 1.1/1216]; **39 (bottom)**, Stuart Thomson [UBC 1.1/1059]; **39 (top)**, John Owen fonds [UBC 103.1/73]; **40 (top left)**, Alfred Young fonds [UBC 78.1/1]; **41 (right)**, Leonard Frank, UBC Historical Photograph Collection [UBC 1.1/167]; **41 (left)**, Bridgman Studios, UBC Historical Photograph Collection [UBC 1.1/16079]; **42**, John Owen fonds [UBC 103.1/68]; **44 (bottom)**, Leonard Frank, UBC Historical Photograph Collection [UBC 1.1/1264]; **45**, Frank Buck fonds [UBC 29.1/172]; **46 (top)**, Frank Bucks fonds [UBC 29.1/163]; **47 (top)**, Alumni Association fonds [UBC 93.1/842]; **48 (bottom)**, UBC Historical Photograph Collection [UBC 1.1/1329]; **49**, Leonard Frank, UBC Historical Photograph Collection [UBC 1.1/60]; **51 (bottom)**, Alfred Young fonds [UBC 78.1/19]; **51 (top)**, Stuart Thomson, UBC Historical Photograph Collection [UBC 1.1/1435]; **53 (bottom)**, Frank Buck fonds [UBC 29.1/12]; **54 (bottom left)**; **55 (left)**, Alumni Association fonds [UBC 93.1/25]; **55 (right)**, School of Nursing fonds [UBC 56.1/063]; **56**, J.M, Turnbull, UBC Historical Photograph Collection

[UBC 1.1/1044]; **57 (bottom)**, UBC Historical Photograph Collection [UBC 1.1/1701]; **57 (top left)**, UBC Historical Photograph Collection [UBC 1.1/5149]; **60 (bottom right)**, Garnett Sedgewick fonds [UBC 25.1/80]; **60 (left)**, Historical Photograph Collection [UBC 1.1/2289]; **60 (top right)**, UBC Historical Photograph Collection [UBC 1.1/1243]; **61 (bottom)**, Leonard Frank, UBC Historical Photograph Collection [UBC 1.1/381]; **61 (top)**, Leonard Frank, UBC Historical Photograph Collection [UBC 1.1/699]; **62**, UBC Historical Photograph Collection [UBC 1.1/910]; **63**, Leonard Frank, UBC Historical Photograph Collection [UBC 1.1/834]; **65**, UBC Historical Photograph Collection [UBC 1.1/12149]; **66**, UBC Historical Photograph Collection [UBC 1.1/3822]; **67 (top left)**, UBC Historical Photograph Collection [UBC 1.1/346]; **68 (top)**, UBC Historical Photograph Collection [UBC 1.1/16140]; **70 (left)**, UBC Historical Photograph Collection [UBC 1.1/3779]; **70 (top)**, Margaret Sage fonds [UBC 39.1/50]; **72**, John Owen fonds [UBC 103.1/87]; **73**, John Owen fonds [UBC 103.1/88]; **74 (bottom)**, John Owen fonds [UBC 103.1/80]; **74 (middle)**, John Owen fonds [UBC 103.1/79]; **74 (top)**, John Owen fonds [UBC 103.1/78]; **75 (right)**, Leonard Cox, Leonard Cox fonds [UBC 72.1//11]; **76 (top)**, UBC Historical Photograph Collection [UBC 1.1/15827]; **77 (bottom)**, Norman MacKenzie fonds [UBC 23.1/299-8a]; **77 (top)**, UBC Historical Photograph Collection [UBC 1.1/5852-2]; **78**, UBC Historical Photograph Collection [UBC 1.1/11507-2]; **80 (bottom)**, UBC Historical Photograph Collection [UBC 1.1/12260-4]; **80 (top)**, UBC Historical Photograph Collection [UBC 1.1/2277]; **81**, UBC Historical Photograph Collection [UBC 1.1/13081-1]; **82**, Patrick McGeer fonds [UBC 12.1/1-2]; **83 (bottom)**, UBC Historical Photograph Collection [UBC 1.1/15568]; **86 (bottom)**, Information Services fonds [UBC 41.1/2205]; **86 (middle)**, Audio Visual Services fonds [UBC 5.2/9-7]; **88 (left)**, UBC Historical Photograph Collection [UBC 1.1/2656]; **89 (top)**, UBC Historical Photograph Collection [UBC 1.1/10594-9]; **90 (bottom)**, UBC Historical Photograph Collection [UBC 1.1/16101-1]; **90 (top)**, UBC Historical Photograph Collection [UBC 1.1/1338]; **91 (bottom)**, UBC Historical Photograph Collection [UBC 1.1/16575]; **91 (middle)**, Extension Department fonds [UBC 301/372-2]; **91 (top)**, Extension Department fonds [UBC 3.1/372-1]; **92 (bottom right)**, Information Services fonds [UBC 41.1/2294]; **93 (bottom)**, Extension Department fonds [UBC 3.1/1026-3]; **93 (top)**, Extension Department fonds [UBC 3.1/295-2]; **94 (middle)**, UBC Historical Photograph Collection [UBC 1.1/6596]; **94 (top)**, Extension Department fonds [UBC 3.1/1033]; **95 (middle)**, UBC Historical Photograph Collection, [UBC 1.1/16211]; **97 (top)**, Norman Mackenzie fonds [UBC 23.1/299a-57a]; **98 (left)**, Alumni Association fonds [UBC 1.1/15889]; **99**, School of Nursing fonds [UBC 56.1/027]; **100**, Joe Quan, UBC Historical Photograph Collection [UBC 1.1/826]; **102**, UBC Historical Photograph Collection [UBC 1.1/15974]; **106 (bottom)**, UBC Historical Photograph Collection [UBC 1.1/1219]; **106 (top)**, Extension Department fonds [UBC 3.1/406-1]; **107 (left)**, Extension Department fonds [UBC 3.1/1029-2]; **107 (middle)**, Extension Department fonds [UBC 3.1/360]; **107 (top)**, Extension Department fonds [UBC 3.1/845-1]; **108 (bottom left)**, UBC Historical Photograph Collection [UBC 1.1/6319-6]; **108 (top left)**, Robert Osborne fonds [UBC 110.1/20]; **109 (bottom)**, Information Services fonds [UBC 41.1/2358]; **109 (top)**, UBC Historical Photograph Collection [UBC 1.1/16141-1]; **110**, UBC Historical Photograph Collection [UBC 1.1/802-8]; **111 (bottom)**, George Lenko, UBC Historical Photograph Collection [UBC 1.1/15936]; **113 (bottom)**, UBC Historical Photograph Collection [UBC 1.1/11094]; **113 (top)**, UBC Historical Photograph Collection [UBC 1.1/2279]; **114 (middle)**, Basil Stuart Stubbs, Extension Department fonds [UBC 3.1/1466-2]; **114 (top)**,

Extension Department fonds [UBC 3.1/1061-2]; **115 (top)**, UBC Historical Photograph Collection [UBC 1.1/13093]; **117**, UBC Historical Photograph Collection [UBC 1.1/13171]; **119 (bottom)**, Bill Cunningham, UBC Historical Photograph Collection [UBC 1.1/13425]; **122**, UBC Historical Photograph Collection [UBC 1.1/13266]; **124**, Extension Department fonds [UBC 3.1/1283-1]; **126**, UBC Historical Photograph Collection [UBC 1.1/1566]; **127 (bottom)**, UBC Historical Photograph Collection [UBC 1.1/986]; **127 (top)**, UBC Historical Photograph Collection [UBC 1.1/15701]; **128 (bottom)**, Alumni Association fonds [UBC 93.1/718]; **128 (top)**, Al Baronas, Alumni Association fonds [UBC 93.1/724]; **130**, Extension Department fonds [UBC 3.1/1063]; **133**, Extension Department fonds [UBC 3.1/738-2]; **134 (bottom)**, UBC Historical Photograph Collection [UBC 1.1/4144-1]; **134 (top)**, Audio Visual Services fonds [UBC 5.1/90]; **140 (left)**, Extension Department fonds [UBC 3.1/705-1]; **140 (right)**, Extension Department fonds [UBC 3.1/1015-4]; **141 (top right)**, Audio Visual Services fonds [UBC 5.2/55-2]; **142 (bottom)**, Extension Department fonds [UBC 3.1/1077-4]; **143 (bottom)**, Guy Palmer, Guy Palmer fonds [UBC 107.1/49.2]; **143 (top)**, Information Services fonds [UBC 41.1/2420]; **145 (bottom)**, Audio Visual Services fonds [UBC 5.1/2435]; **146 (top)**, School of Architecture fonds [UBC 57.1/8]; **147 (bottom)**, W.J. McCormick, Information Services fonds [UBC 41.1/2685-2]; **148 (top)**, Information Services fonds [UBC 41.1/2340-4]; **149 (bottom)**, Information Services fonds [UBC 41.1/2222]; **149 (middle)**, B.C. Jennings, UBC Historical Photograph Collection [UBC 1.1/15709]; **149 (top)**, Meredith L. Smith, UBC Historical Photograph Collection [UBC 1.1/12643-5]; **150 (right)**, Audio Visual Services fonds [UBC 5.1/2974]; **154**, Information Services fonds [UBC 41.1/2070]; **155 (bottom left)**, David Margerison, UBC Historical Photograph Collection [UBC 1.1/13021-1]; **155 (bottom right)**, UBC Historical Photograph Collection [UBC 1.1/12699-1]; 155 (top right), David Margerison, UBC Historical Photograph Collection [UBC 1.1/13021-3]; **156**, Audio Visual Services fonds [UBC 5.2/357-3]; **157**, Audio Visual Services fonds [UBC 5.2/402-1]; **158 (bottom)**, UBC Historical Photograph Collection [UBC 1.1/15764]; **158 (top)**, Carol Gordon, UBC Historical Photograph Collection [UBC 1.1/15761]; **159 (bottom left)**, Jim Banham, UBC Historical Photograph Collection [UBC 1.1/12770]; **159 (top)**, Public Affairs fonds [UBC 44.1/42-3]; z, Deni England, UBC Historical Photograph Collection [UBC 1.1/13071]; **161**, Information Services fonds [UBC 41.1/54-1]; **162 (top)**, Jim Banham, UBC Historical Photograph Collection [UBC 1.1/12886]; **164 (bottom)**, Information Services fonds [UBC 41.1/559-5]; **170 (bottom)**, Jim Banham, UBC Historical Photograph Collection [UBC 41.1/168-2]; **172**, Information Services fonds [UBC 41.1/2476-1]; **174 (top right)**, Facilities Planning fonds [UBC 105.1/65]; **175 (bottom)**, Information Services fonds [UBC 41.1/256-2]; **175 (top left)**, Jim Banham, Information Services fonds [UBC 41.1/358-3]; **176 (top)**, Jim Banham, Information Services fonds [UBC 41.1/757-1]; **177 (bottom)**, Jim Banham, Information Services fonds [UBC 41.1/513]; **178 (bottom right)**, John Morris, Information Services fonds [UBC 41.1/2305]; **179 (top left)**, UBC Historical Photograph Collection [UBC 1.1/12315]; **180 (bottom)**, UBC Historical Photograph Collection [UBC 1.1/16133]; **180 (top left)**, Information Services fonds [UBC 41.1/2712-2]; **182 (bottom)**, Jim Banham, Information Services fonds [UBC 41.1/705-1]; **182 (top)**, Jim Banham, Information Services fonds [UBC 41.1/751-1]; **183 (middle)**, Jim Banham, Information Services fonds [UBC 41.1/391]; **184 (bottom left)**, Information Services fonds [UBC 41.1/2711-1]; **184 (middle left)**, Information Services fonds [UBC 41.1/738-3]; **184 (right)**, Information Services fonds [UBC 41.1/256-5]; **186 (top)**, Alumni Association fonds [UBC 93.1/489]; **187 (middle right)**, Alumni Association fonds [UBC 93.1/648]; **187 (top right)**, Information

Services fonds [UBC 41.1/1547]; **189 (left)**, Alumni Association fonds [UBC 93.1/838]; **203 (bottom)**, Public Affairs fonds [UBC 44.1/606-1]; **204 (top right)**, Jim Banham, Information Services fonds [UBC 41.1/845-2]; **210 (right)**, Martin Dee, Public Affairs fonds [UBC 44.1/385-1]; **211 (bottom)**, Media Services, Public Affairs fonds [UBC 44.1/509-3]; **211 (top)**, Martin Dee, Public Affairs fonds [UBC 44.1/514]; **213**, UBC Historical Photograph Collection [UBC 1.1/242-4]; **216 (middle)**, Judy McLarty, Public Affairs fonds [UBC 44.1/2541]; **219 (middle)**, Charles Ker, Public Affairs fonds [UBC 44.1/1203]; **221**, Warren Schmidt, Public Affairs fonds [UBC 44.1/2620]; **222 (bottom)**, UBC Historical Photograph Collection [UBC 1.1/16147-1]; **223 (bottom)**, Public Affairs fonds [UBC 44.1/2390b]; **223 (top)**, Public Affairs fonds [UBC 44.1/2314]; **226 (bottom left)**, Public Affairs fonds [UBC 44.1/2312]; **226 (top)**, Media Services, Public Affairs fonds [UBC 44.1/2453a]; **227 (left)**, Gavin Wilson, Public Affairs fonds [UBC 44.1/690]; **227 (right)**, Gavin Wilson, Public Affairs fonds [UBC 44.1/1173]; **228 (right)**, Gavin Wilson, Public Affairs fonds [UBC 44.1/1434]; **229**, Gavin Wilson, Public Affairs fonds [UBC 44.1/1443]; **232 (right)**, Public Affairs fonds [UBC 44.1/3078-1]; **233 (top left)**, Martin Dee, Public Affairs fonds [UBC 44.1/670]; **235 (top right)**, Gavin Wilson [UBC 44.1/752]; **235 (bottom right)**, Dianne Longson, UBC Campus Photograph fonds [UBC 175.1/56b]; **235 (left)**, Public Affairs fonds [UBC 44.1/3037-1]; **236**, Gavin Wilson, Public Affairs fonds [UBC 44.1/779]; **237 (bottom)**, Martin Dee, Martin Dee fonds [UBC 128.1/82]; **242 (right)**, Dianne Longson, UBC Campus Photograph fonds [UBC 175.1/56d]; **245**, Dianne Longson, UBC Campus Photograph fonds [UBC 175.1/67b]; **247**, Dianne Longson, UBC Campus Photograph fonds [UBC 175.1/25d]; **249**, Michelle Cook, Public Affairs fonds [UBC 44.1/2123]; **251 (top)**, Public Affairs fonds [UBC 44.1/1802]; **259 (top)**, Jill Pittendrigh, Library fonds [UBC 76.1/089]; **260**, Bayne Stanley, Public Affairs fonds [UBC 44.1/1813]; **266**, Public Affairs fonds [UBC 44.1/2240]; **278**, Don Erhardt, Ceremonies Office fonds [UBC 35.1/982]

UBC REPORTS
151, 1968/10